MANIPULATING MASCULINITY

PREVIOUS PUBLICATIONS

This Isn't a Picture I'm Holding: Kuan Yin. With Photographs by Joseph Singer. Honolulu: U of Hawai'i P, 2004.

Virginia Woolf against Empire. Knoxville: U of Tennessee P, 1994.

Dying Gods in Twentieth-Century Fiction. Lewisburg, Pa.: Bucknell UP, 1990.

"Between the Third Sex and the Third Reich: Brecht's Early Works." *Literature and Homosexuality.* Ed. Michael Meyer. Amsterdam: Rodopi, 2000. 71–92.

"One of Those Aliens: Empire and Homosexuality in Melville's Billy Budd." *Strategies: Journal of Theory, Culture and Politics* 13 (Nov. 2000): 163–74.

"Jane Harrison and Modernism." *Journal of Modern Literature* 17.4 (Spring 1991): 465–76.

"Exorcising Faustus from Africa: Wole Soyinka's *The Road.*" *Comparative Literature Studies* 27.2 (1990): 140–57.

Books are to be returned on or before
the last date below.

**7 – DAY
LOAN**

LIBREX–

Manipulating Masculinity

War and Gender in Modern British and American Literature

Kathy J. Phillips

MANIPULATING MASCULINITY: WAR AND GENDER IN MODERN BRITISH AND AMERICAN
LITERATURE

First published in 2006 by
PALGRAVE MACMILLAN™
175 Fifth Avenue, New York, N.Y. 10010 and
Houndmills, Basingstoke, Hampshire, England RG21 6XS
Companies and representatives throughout the world.

PALGRAVE MACMILLAN is the global academic imprint of the Palgrave
Macmillan division of St. Martin's Press, LLC and of Palgrave Macmillan Ltd.
Macmillan® is a registered trademark in the United States, United Kingdom
and other countries. Palgrave is a registered trademark in the European
Union and other countries.

ISBN-13: 978–1–4039–7195–1
ISBN-10: 1–4039–7195–1

Library of Congress Cataloging-in-Publication Data is available from the
Library of Congress.

A catalogue record for this book is available from the British Library.

Design by Newgen Imaging Systems (P) Ltd., Chennai, India.

First edition: June 2006

10 9 8 7 6 5 4 3 2 1

Printed in the United States of America.

Contents

Credits   vi

Introduction   1

Chapter 1
Background: Sexuality and War   19

Chapter 2
World War I: No Half-Men at the Front   41

Chapter 3
World War II: No Lace on His Drawers   85

Chapter 4
The Vietnam War: Out from Under Momma's Apron   131

Conclusion   175

Epilogue
The Wars against Iraq: Red Alert on Girly Men   191

Notes   203

Works Cited   211

Index   225

Credits

Gwendolyn Brooks, excerpt from "the white troops had their orders but the Negroes looked like men," reprinted by consent of Brooks Permissions.

Keith Douglas, excerpts from "How To Kill" and "Mersa," from *The Complete Poems*, 3rd ed. Reprinted by permission of Faber and Faber Ltd for world rights and Farrar, Straus & Giroux for Faber USA.

Yusef Komunyakaa, excerpts from "Dui Boi, Dust of Life" and "Tu Do Street," from *Dien Cai Dau* ©1988 by Yusef Komunyakaa and reprinted by permission of Wesleyan University Press.

Wilfred Owen, from *The Collected Poems of Wilfred Owen*, copyright ©1963 by Chatto & Windus, Ltd. Reprinted by permission of New Directions Publishing Corp.

Cover: Combat Artist Reuben Kadish's World War II painting *Three Dead Chinese Soldiers*, Courtesy of the National Museum of the U.S. Army, Army Art Collection. With additional thanks for help to the Reuben Kadish Art Foundation.

Introduction

It was a bloody century. Nine million soldiers died in World War I, seventeen million in World War II. To take just one of the innumerable, smaller wars of the twentieth century, America's war in Vietnam left 58,000 Americans and three million Vietnamese dead, including two million civilians (Turner 8). In the world wars, some sixty million civilians died (Hynes, *Soldiers' Tale* xii). The mind shuts down. In fact, opposing sides have a remarkable capacity not to see war as death and suffering, blocking that view before, during, and after hostilities with a more palatable vision of noble and always defensive manliness.

Many ordinary citizens all over Europe, Allied and Central Powers alike, actually welcomed World War I (Eksteins 174; Stromberg 198). In England, people expected the war to unify a fragmented population, at a time when street demonstrations over three issues had been exposing profound divisions. In these protests, the Irish were contesting English colonization, workers were threatening a general strike, and women were agitating for the vote and a different view of gender (Macaulay 6). Germans too hoped to stitch over their own domestic schisms by making the war a common cause.[1] On the whole, both sides seemed to prefer waging real battles to facing these "internal wars," as the newspapers had dubbed them (Hynes, *War Imagined* 7). The antagonists found it more comforting to rally against a foreign power than to address questioners at home, easier to confront the guns than to think and change.

The first two protests in England, concerning colonies and incomes, point to some of the underlying causes of twentieth-century wars. Yet if such prizes lure governments and businesses, why do citizens agree to war, when they have small prospect of making much money and a clear prospect of losing everything most valuable: life, limb, and loved ones? For one thing, people might hesitate to object when they face jail time for evading the draft, the firing squad for deserting, and police action for protesting.[2] Despite these Repressive

State Apparatuses (in Louis Althusser's term), some Britons and Americans did oppose World Wars I and II.[3] America's war in Vietnam provoked large demonstrations, by protesters of all ages and backgrounds, who poured into the streets a half-million or more at a time (Franklin 70–75; Moser 3; Dickerson). Nevertheless, even for the Vietnam War, more Americans enlisted than were drafted (Baritz 284).[4] Why were millions in all three wars so ready to fight?

Manipulating Masculinity addresses not the causes of World War I, World War II, and the Vietnam War but the consent to them. The theorist Antonio Gramsci explains "consent" as a "collective pressure," exerted though "an evolution of customs, ways of thinking and acting, morality," in such a way as to make "necessity and coercion" seem like "freedom" (242). Althusser similarly suggests that societies control people not only through Repressive but also through Ideological State Apparatuses (such as media, schools, religions); he defines ideology as the "imaginary relationship of individuals to their real conditions of existence" (143, 162). One major clue to consent to modern war can be found in the third of the British street protests conveniently hushed up by World War I: the women's movement, which was jostling contemporary ideologies of gender. While changing views of women may appear tangential to war, the polarization of gender (the construction of masculine and feminine as if they have little in common), along with the positioning of women as lesser, powerfully enabled the wars of the twentieth century. My thesis is that societies which arbitrarily label a number of purely human traits "feminine" possess a tactic useful to war-making, for men are bound to detect some of these human traits in themselves—and then worry that they have strayed into a feminine, inferior realm. Placed in a constantly renewed insecurity about their status, men must scramble to amass "proofs" of masculinity. If a society also convinces its citizens that men love to fight and women hate to fight (or cannot fight), then that society can manipulate men to go to war, simply to verify that they are not women.

But would a man go to war just to prove a point in a gender debate? Surely soldiers wish to sacrifice themselves for the greater good. However, servicemen from World War I, World War II, and the Vietnam War seldom mention any grand cause for which they are supposedly fighting (Hynes, *Soldiers' Tale* 11). Even if some idealistic recruits resolve to make the world better, governments on both sides of a war can often assuage the need to fight on the side of "right" with a tag of "patriotism" that has little to do with a country's real aims. Even indisputably good causes, such as stopping Nazi extermination of Jews, may be recognized only in retrospect. Apparently, only five percent of

American GIs during World War II knew anything about fascism (Adams, *Best War* 88), and governments were slow to respond to the persecution of the Jews (Shalom 113–17). As Samuel Hynes looks over the memoirs and letters from the wars of the twentieth century, he finds that "*Why* is not a soldier's question" (*Soldiers' Tale* 11).

Instead of asking about bigger purposes, men at the time of their wars predominantly pursue smaller, more personal aims. A man who seeks out or accepts a soldier's life may lack employment or feel bored in a tedious job. He may flee parents, escape a soured domestic relationship, or tire of a conventional life. If frustrated and angry enough at the limitations of his present society, he may dream an apocalyptic overthrow of everything—including his own street; at the turn of the century, popular future-war stories treated England to the savory spectacle of the familiar swept away (Keep 8). And, as Virginia Woolf points out, if stifling conditions for women persist, a soldier's sisters may similarly welcome a cataclysm, as they too savagely endorse "our splendid Empire, our splendid war" (39).

According to Hynes, dullness plus lack of economic opportunity sent soldiers searching for adventure in World Wars I and II and the Vietnam War. However, instead of probing the economic and social factors that keep work at home so unfulfilling, Hynes indulgently backs the quest for excitement through wars. No doubt many veterans fondly look back on a cherished chance to travel or establish their closest friendships. Nevertheless, Hynes has to admit that beyond adventure and glory, "the strongest and commonest motive for enlisting," in all the wars of the twentieth century, is simply, "I hated being thought a funk" (qtd. in *Soldiers' Tale* 49). Caught up in the tide of what everybody is doing, a man doesn't want to be thought a coward. But why is that particular reputation so central? Although Hynes does not say so, the subtext for the label "funk" or "coward" is the socially induced, gendered assumption about who is a "sissy" and who is not.

A surprising number of British and American men in the twentieth century went to war to prove they were not "sissies," that is, to assert they were not "sisters," as the etymological root of the taunt suggests. Looking back at World War I in her memoir *Testament of Youth* (1933), Vera Brittain recalls that early in the mobilization, her fiancé, Roland, who "neither hated the Germans nor loved the Belgians," fretted because "effeminate" Englishmen, whom he "despised," had already gone to France (129, 126). Some of these men, Roland noticed, were even starting to return with wounds (that automatic badge of courage), whereas he had yet to embark. Brittain is astounded to have to conclude that Roland hurried from Oxford

University to the trenches not for specific community causes but to pass a manliness test of "heroism in the abstract" (129).

The British middle and upper classes at Roland's Oxford did not monopolize this need to project a manly image. The working-class soldier Weeper Smart in Frederic Manning's novel *The Middle Parts of Fortune* (1929) also felt peer pressure pushing him to sign up: "When a [I] saw all them as didn' [*sic*] know any better'n we did joinin' up, an' a went walkin' out wi' me girl on Sundays, as usual, a just felt ashamed . . . . But a tell thee, now, that if a were once out o' these togs an' in civvies again, a wouldn't mind all the shame in the world" (150–51). It wasn't his girl's presence in private—kissing behind the barn, say—that decided Weeper to enlist, but rather walking with his girl in public. Something about being seen by other men, vis-à-vis women, determined his military service. However, now that he experiences war for himself, he is learning not to care if others consider him manly or not.

World War II veterans also recall motives centered on a desire to verify masculinity. An infantry rifleman tells interviewer Studs Terkel, "I was going to gain my manhood then. I would forever be liberated from the sense of inferiority that I wasn't rugged. I would prove that I had the guts and the manhood to stand up to these things" (37). Similarly, Paul Fussell, trained as an officer, looks back on his company plodding through Alsace in 1944: "Some few may have been following the higher morality and offering their lives and limbs for the Allied cause and the Four Freedoms, but 90 percent of us were engaged in something much less romantic and heroic. We were maintaining our self-respect, protecting our manly image from the contempt of our fellows" (*Doing Battle* 124). The ringing rhetoric of Freedom from "want and fear" or Freedom for "speech and religion" (Adams, *Best War* 136) lost out to an inner clamor to meet an elusive standard of masculinity.

By the time of America's war in Vietnam, the cause of manliness was still drowning out all other motives. A high school teacher advised John Ketwig to enlist because the war would "make you a man . . . get you out from under mommas's apron" (18). African American Stephen Howard remembers that his mother, drilled in racial and gender stereotypes, lectured him "to work hard to strive to be as good as" whites; indoctrinated that war would produce that transformation, she greeted her son's draft notice with satisfaction: "You'll be back a man" (W. Terry 123). However, when Howard's deeds do match his white companions', he can only grieve: "And the lie was you ain't have no business bein' there in the first place . . . . And you don't fight a civilized war. It's nothing civilized about—about war" (W. Terry 133). Similarly altered, paratrooper Gene Woodley performed whatever it took to achieve "combat-type manhood," but he realizes that the "man" in him was nowhere in sight: "Before I reached my nineteenth birthday, I was a animal" (W. Terry 243, 251).

To study connections between gender expectations and war, I follow Michel Foucault in focusing on "discursive events": scrutinizing what actually gets said, why only certain utterances can occur at given times and places, and, especially, what experiences those discursive events create (*Archaeology* 27–28). Foucault treats discourses not as "signs" referring to already existing "contents," but as "practices that systematically form the objects of which they speak" (*Archaeology* 49). Applied to writings on war, this focus exposes that when speakers do occasionally stray into vocabulary considered feminine, other words considered ultramasculine surge up on the same page, as if to neutralize the transgressive womanliness. An investigator must then question to what degree these language games dictate and require the masculine experiences that the discourse claims to discover already formed by biology.

Most of my examples of war discourse derive from novels, stories, poems, and plays about World War I, World War II, and the Vietnam War (with some references to the Korean War), written either at the time of hostilities or long afterward.[5] I am not claiming that literary works about war, even those produced by veterans, can uncover how all soldiers felt but only how consent or resistance is imagined. However, when I compare literature to memoirs, letters, newspapers, and essays (such as Freud's), I take as axiomatic that this "nonfiction" also participates in elaborating and perpetuating artificial social constructs. As the practitioners of "new cultural history" contend, "systems of representation bear directly on historical change by establishing habits of thought crucial to rationalizing particular actions. In this way, culture and social practices are inextricably linked" (Gullace, "Blood" 10). To the extent that literature is read (and surely *All Quiet on the Western Front, Catch-22*, and *The Things They Carried*, for example, have attracted millions of readers), literature ferries many socially assumed connections between gender definitions and war.

In more specific terms, I highlight imaginative literature for several reasons. First, the emotion generated draws readers' attention to social problems and renders these problems real and urgent. Raymond Williams makes this point in an example from nineteenth-century Britain. Whereas early Victorian ideology was blaming the effects of poverty, debt, and illegitimacy on personal failure, novels by Charles

Dickens and Emily Brontë shifted the view of private catastrophe to a "general condition," which may befall anyone, not just "deviants" (*Marxism and Literature* 134). Only later did an explicit, alternative ideology develop, blaming economic systems rather than personal deficiency; yet the new formulation about social causes would not have been possible, Williams implies, without the novelists' prior promotion of emotional involvement, which helped dislodge the explanation for suffering away from personal flaws.

The force of fictional emotion will be familiar to anyone who has ever winced through Wilfred Owen's controlled but seething poems about World War I, endured Alexander Baron's alternately tender and despairing World War II novel *From the City, From the Plough*, or stood aghast, horrified and pitying, at the revelations in Emily Mann's implacable Vietnam play *Still Life*. For those who engage such literature, the impetus to question why these wars were fought and how they may have been prevented is, I believe, much greater than for those noncombatants aware of war either through popular media (TV, movies, pulp novels, children's toys, video games, or news bites without analysis) or through the scholarly offerings under military history, which overwhelmingly dwell on tactics and immediate causes, rather than on effects on people and long-term, underlying social causes of wars. Literature may also enable combatants to distance themselves from a need to justify their wars, allowing veterans to assess larger causes, since the fictions typically provide a cushioning of sympathy for individual soldiers.

A further reason for highlighting literature among possible discourses on war is that imaginative works expose the contradictions in ideologies particularly well. Perhaps because novelists or playwrights or poets do not need to keep to a thesis or set out consistent arguments, these authors can (sometimes consciously, often inadvertently) usefully mirror and crack open the inconsistencies in social constructions of gender and in war rationales. The questions I pose for the discourses of war follow Foucault's prompting to look for the "rules of [discursive] formation," including "correlations," "functionings," and "transformations" (*Archaeology* 38). Does calling a man a "sissy" insult him more in some decades than in others? Does the content of womanliness remain constant or change? What factors influence any changes? How do nations forge links between gender fears and other motivations driving men to war?

The taunt of womanliness to goad a man to war is not, of course, new. Even the god Krishna, in the ancient Hindu classic *The Bhagavad Gita*, reminds the reluctant warrior Arjuna that if he fails to fight, people will dishonor him for "unmanliness" and "cowardice" (Purohit 15, 18). Ironically, Krishna's needling contradicts some of the god's other arguments, for he has already told Arjuna that he can fight only if he ignores the personal "fruit" of the action (Purohit 21). This prohibited personal fruit may offer either the lure of reputation and possessions, or the threat of danger and trouble. Such private ego involvements must not determine a war, Krishna warns, only beneficial effects (which he assumes but nowhere specifies) for the larger community. However, when Krishna then stoops to conjure up possible disgrace, he contradictorily does feed Arjuna's ego, encouraging him to worry about glory or disrepute. Could a little snickering rattle a soul at peace with itself?

Arjuna knuckles under and fights. Mainly, he succumbs to Krishna's insistence on caste duty and the god's reassurance that the souls of the enemy (whose bodies Arjuna pities) will survive to reincarnate in other bodies. Nevertheless, Krishna's jibe about unmanliness at least reinforces his other arguments in favor of war. Does the fact that this name-calling continues to prod men, whether Arjuna or Vera Brittain's fiancé, mean that we're dealing with something universal? Not at all.

For one thing, the taunt "womanly" only works to send men to war in cultures that strongly polarize the sexes and count women as lesser. This hierarchy of men over women does organize gender formations (in different ways and to varying degrees) in third-century India, 1914 Britain, and America in the years of the Vietnam War. Without such polarization, a man called "sissy" might rejoice, "Oh, do you think so? I've been trying to live up to the example of that great sister of mine. Thank you!" Furthermore, a number of factors converged by the end of the nineteenth century to make the label "sissy" not just peripheral but central as a manipulator to war, and these factors stayed active throughout the twentieth century. The risk of perceived unmanliness is likely to compel modern European and American men even more than Arjuna because of (1) the inheritance from nineteenth-century imperialism, (2) the particular way sexologists defined homosexuality as effeminacy, and (3) backlashes against the women's movement and its renewals. These three forces render the appeal to manliness in the twentieth century both specific and formidable.

In Europe and America, the nineteenth century bolstered the link of manhood to bellicosity (a connection learned in part from the Greek and Roman classics), because it was useful to empires. In *Tom Brown's School Days* (1857), long popular in England, Thomas Hughes circulates the message of his imperial culture by urging young readers, "what would life be without fighting, I should like to know? From the cradle to the grave, fighting, rightly understood, is the business, the real, highest, honestest business of every son of man" (280). Sports prepare the boys for their inevitable, belligerent future. On a personal level, competitiveness sinks in so deeply because it has been linked to proof of manliness, more than acquisitiveness or even righteousness: "I am as sorry as any man to see folk fighting the wrong people and the wrong things, but I'd a deal sooner see them doing that, than that they should have no fight in them" (Hughes 281).

In America, the same goals of national conquest in an imperial era pushed boys to fight and girls to wait. Although nominally bestowing on women the high charge of guiding men toward spirituality, this ideology, in reality, devalued girls. In one of the autobiographical "Camera Eye" sections of the novel *The 42nd Parallel* (1930), John Dos Passos recalls that, in the years leading up to World War I, comparing a boy to a girl slurs him beyond any other mockery. The sole proof that a boy carries no taint of girlhood resides in the fight: "you've got to fight the Kid" (104). Interestingly, none of the principal contenders in Dos Passos's scene want to scrap at all, but the crowd is able to egg them on with the worst epithet in the world: "Gotta fight him . . . if not you're a girlboy" (104). Mark Moss reports that in Ontario of the same time period, increased nervousness about manliness after losses in the Boer War pressured boys to fight rather than laugh off a taunt of "sissy" (17). All these North American boys schooled to fear supposed girlishness would mature just in time for Great War butchery.

The examples under "sissy" in *The Oxford English Dictionary* (*OED*) for the usage newly applied to men in the late nineteenth century make it clear that the most accepted way to certify manhood was the fight. A fragment cited from the *New Orleans Lantern* in 1887 links fighting and manhood through a description of men who "Look and walk too much like sissies to do much fightin'," and the *British Weekly* in 1926 tries to promote someone's merits by boasting, "There was nothing 'sissy' about him. He was a born fighter" (1989 ed.). Interestingly, the *OED* does not mention that "sissy" ever insinuated anything about sexual orientation. By contrast, *Webster's New World Dictionary of the American Language* explicitly gives as its second definition for "sissy" "a homosexual" (1953, 1974). The section in chapter 1 on early-twentieth-century sexologists discusses the complex process by which societies construe homosexuality in men to mean effeminacy, and the effects of this arbitrary social construction in increasing the need for men, both homosexual and heterosexual, to validate manhood through war.

The confidence with which mudslingers affixed the labels "sissy" (sister-like) or "effeminate" to men implies, of course, an equal complacency in defining "feminine" traits for women. Charles Darwin, for example, asserted in *The Descent of Man*, "the average standard of mental power in man must be above that of woman"; once he had excluded her from the arenas of intellect, Darwin elbowed her away from most other endeavors too (everything except "tenderness"), declaring wildly that "man" surpasses her in any task requiring "deep thought, reason, or imagination, or merely the use of the senses and hands" (2: 311–12). Even supporters who thought that they were praising women and working for their causes strictly separated and ranked the sexes. Ralph Waldo Emerson separated womanly "sentiment" from manly "logic" and believed that women monopolized the "affections," whereas men cornered "will" (338–39). As assigned "civilizers," women might restrain combatants, but more often the civilizing task left wives to decorate drawing rooms, in "that ornamental life in which they best appear" (340–41).

To upset the assumptions of women's deep handicaps in logic and action, feminists in the nineteenth and twentieth centuries tried two tactics. One group accepted the divisions laid down by many patriarchies and just reversed the evaluation of them. If women were naturally more loving, unselfish, and peaceable than men, as Darwin (2: 311) and Emerson (339) thought, then all the more reason that women should participate in government and business (Higonnet et al. 7).[6] A second group of feminists, instead of arguing that women occupy a superior position by automatically opposing war, have claimed that women could engage in "patriotic" war equally with men. To prove their worth, women may attempt to enlist or, if thwarted there, may undertake war-related tasks that require the same manliness.[7]

Helen Zenna Smith's novel *Not So Quiet* (1930), for example, depicts the pressures on women in World War I to be as good as men, in exactly the same terms: endure hardships stoically, suffer pain and perhaps death, never flinch, and never ask why. The narrator, Nellie, does keep bravely driving her ambulance at the front, despite roads icing over and bombs falling, and she watches the bloody deaths of companions impassively, convincing all of her heroism. Eventually, however, she dissects this heroism as at base a numbness, more and more difficult to thaw once the immediate danger has passed (239). In her most profound insight, she devalues the "masculine" bravery that she does muster and rejects her much-praised "professional calm," because the two together lend an aura of legitimacy to the "futility" and immorality of further carnage: "I may be helping to alleviate the sufferings of wretched men, but commonsense [*sic*] rises up and insists that the necessity should never have arisen . . . . In twenty years it will repeat itself" (90). She implies that now both men and women need wars, simply to go on painting their own manly or as-good-as-manly image of stoicism.

Usefully summing up these two main routes that feminism has taken, Sheila Rowbotham in *A Century of Women* points to "the continuing tug among feminists" whether to attempt a "strategy of equality with men in the world as it was," or to argue that "women were indeed different from men," including women's supposedly greater cooperativeness and peacefulness (514, 575). However, a third position insists that if women do differ from men, they have done so only situationally, not essentially, and that the social "world as it is" needs to change for both women and men. Among feminists who have deconstructed gender and war to call for changes for both sexes are Helena Swanwick in *Women and War* (1915); Cynthia Enloe in *Bananas, Beaches and Bases* (1989); Susan Jeffords in *The Remasculinization of America* (1989); Miriam Cooke and Angela Woollacott (eds.) in *Gendering War Talk* (1993) (especially the excellent essays by Lynda Boose, Carol Cohn, and Stanley Rosenberg); and Lois Ann Lorentzen and Jennifer Turpin (eds.) in *The Women and War Reader* (1998). Yet as Joshua Goldstein warns in *War and Gender* (2001), "Feminist literatures about war and peace of the last 15 years have made little impact" in the fields of political science, military history, or international relations (34). He finds that most books in these areas index nothing at all under "gender"; a "recent and comprehensive survey of scholarship on war and peace" does list six items but "devotes only about one-tenth of one percent of its space to gender" (35). Moreover, any of the rare "gender references concern women; men still do not have gender" (35).[8]

These authors and others have taught me several theoretical assumptions about masculinity: (1) it's a social construct; (2) in a given society, requirements for masculinity shift over time; (3) at any one time, masculinity is multiple, providing for masculinities; and (4) masculinities are contradictory, not just over time and in different domains, but at any moment in the same domain.

Masculinity is a social construct. Gayle Rubin, in her influential essay "The Traffic in Women," draws from anthropological studies to explain how made-up "sex/gender systems" can smooth economies, enforce reproduction, and give a false impression of inherent gender differences. She looks at the work of Claude Lévi-Strauss, who finds that while most societies fashion some kind of division of labor by sex, the exact roles vary widely (i.e., in some, women farm and carry heavy burdens; in some, men care for children). Lévi-Strauss concludes that these gender assignments cannot therefore derive from biology but from a need "to insure the union of men and women by making the smallest viable economic unit contain at least one man and one woman" (Rubin 178). As Rubin provocatively points out, Lévi-Strauss "comes dangerously close to saying that heterosexuality is an instituted process. If biological and hormonal imperatives were as overwhelming as popular mythology would have them, it would hardly be necessary to ensure heterosexual unions by means of economic interdependency" (180).

This social division of labor by sex then produces the illusion that the sexes must differ inherently and radically. However, Rubin cautions, "Far from being an expression of natural differences, exclusive gender identity is the suppression of natural similarities. It requires repression: in men, of whatever is the local version of 'feminine' traits; in women, of the local definition of 'masculine' traits . . . . The same social system which oppresses women in its relations of exchange, oppresses everyone in its insistence upon a rigid division of personality" (180). Contrary to the view commonly promoted by popular media, feminism is not women "talking stink" about men, but women and men talking about social systems that hurt both women and men. The clearest way that gender polarization oppresses men is to designate them expendable, in war.

Masculinity shifts over time. Although some notions of gender stay depressingly the same, such as women's supposed lack of rationality, other stereotypes may gyrate 180 degrees. One requirement for manliness that seems to have changed most radically from the nineteenth to the twentieth centuries is the reversal (at least at first sight) from an ideal of sexual restraint to an ideal of sexual license. Using a medical language crossed by economic concepts, nineteenth-century European and American doctors schooled the middle classes that each man possessed a limited amount of sperm and overall bodily energy; release of sexual energy would "deplete the supply available for other purposes and would thus lead to enervation and lethargy, if not more dire consequences [such as madness]. Ejaculation was described as 'spending' the semen, a metaphor that would have made sense to those who had been taught that 'a penny saved is a penny earned' " (Greenberg 362). This medical language, decreeing health and illness, plus an economic idiom delineating thrift and waste, joined the long-standing religious discourse of good and evil, which had already pushed the body into the inferior camp as "fallen nature." These languages reinforce each other, to blame masturbation, homosexuality, heterosex outside marriage, or birth control within marriage, all as an equal waste of capital.

In the twentieth century, by contrast, the dominant masculine ideal moved from "saving" semen to spending it—in some quarters, to spending profligately. In Richard Currey's novel of the Vietnam War, *Fatal Light* (1988), the soldier Perelli cannot wait to boast to the narrator, "I was meaning to tell you. Scored me some maximum slope trim night before last. Prime cut" (142). As in the nineteenth century, the language for sex combines discourses from several other contexts. Perelli's slang mixes the sports arena ("scored") and the butcher shop ("prime cut"). Sex plays out a competitive game, where winners triumph over losers: over other soldiers, for example, who haven't scored so often. The losers also include, one suspects, the woman herself, who falls behind by both race and gender. The racist term "slope" (a version of "slanty eyed") diminishes her, and the butcher shop terms reduce all women to dead meat. He's the privileged consumer; she's the inanimate consumed.

The values taught to the twentieth-century man have not only shifted from retaining semen to multiplying it, but from tacitness to talk. If Victorian men did not always live up to the ideal of restraint and slipped off to flourishing brothels, they at least hushed up the event in their primary circle of family and business associates. Currey's Perelli, by contrast, cannot wait to advertise: "I was meaning to tell you" (142). He brags in a short, quick, esoteric jargon, packing a punch of density, which enables him to feel superior to outsiders, who don't know his code.

Nevertheless, despite these two changes in the definition of masculinity, toward indulging sex and telling about it, in other ways the new license does not after all mark much of a departure from the nineteenth-century devaluation of the body. From the 1860s to the 1960s, the governing metaphors remain economic. If the Victorian manly man saved bodily fluids, he could invest better elsewhere, putting his energy into tying up business deals, or putting semen into making legitimate sons who could inherit his riches. Perelli also sets economic markers. He doesn't consume ordinary meat but a "prime cut," a "trim" piece. He's eating high on the hog, and he is anxious to let others know that he can afford the best, in a world where money and status count.

Of course, this economic aspect of Perelli's transaction does not stay at the level of metaphor. When the narrator cautions, "Be sure you pay her," Perelli grumbles, "I paid her, asshole. Fucking bleeding heart" (142). Although the narrator, unlike Perelli, seems to have some inkling of the economic need driving this woman to accept paying customers, neither man registers the huge change in mores and economics brought about in Vietnam by America's participation in the war. With 25 million acres of farmland destroyed, 12 million acres of forest wiped out, and 1.5 million farm animals killed in the South alone, income for Vietnamese peasants diminished radically. As a result, the bodies of women—some 200,000 new prostitutes—became a primary source of subsistence for their families (Young 301–02). To Perelli, the quirky detail that his Asian whore has dyed her pubic hair blonde simply enhances storytelling ("Know what? . . . You'll love this"), whereas the narrator uneasily glimpses that a saleswoman desperately needs a gimmick, "Something to bring you back for next time," for the next dollar (142).

If Perelli's whore approaches sex for survival, not pleasure, it may appear that Perelli hoards all the fun. Actually, neither partner escapes the nineteenth-century denigration of sex. For Perelli's society is enjoining him not to seek and give joy but to get power. Moreover, a large part of the nineteenth-century need for manly self-control is still locked into place.[9] Though physically unbuckled, Perelli must not get too emotionally involved—he can't be a "bleeding heart"—for emotion might make him womanly (142). Emotion might also render him vulnerable, and a twentieth-century man is still trained to fear vulnerability as something that might bleed him to death; he is not taught to attempt the courage that would open him to the rigors and rewards of love and compassion.

Although Perelli's military sex code is an extreme case, his license duplicates an only apparent relaxation of sexual mores in American society as a whole. For the culture often uses increased sexual activity to further its values of command, not pleasure, and display, not emotion—whether that emotion be love for the long term or simple considerateness in a brief encounter. For a man, partnered heterosex exhibits a manly image, consisting of status, power, control, and armored detachment. These requirements for image still eclipse the pure pleasures of the body, let alone the more difficult gifts of emotional attachments.

In fact, an important secondary thesis throughout this book is that, in addition to the role played by the polarization of gender definitions, a continuing devaluation of the pleasures of sex also contributes to war. To claim that twentieth- and twenty-first-century America and Great Britain disdain pleasure may look preposterous, but a condemnation of the body still persists. Chapters 2 through 4 (on World War I, World War II, and the Vietnam War) highlight ways in which societies, while patently fearing sexuality, also use sex to further war. Although militaries co-opt sex most obviously by providing prostitution as a lure

(Enloe, "It Takes More Than Two"), I argue that a culture can further exploit sex to fuel wars in three ways: by encouraging the displacement of sexuality into violence; by fostering titillation in combination with guilt and its accompanying need for self-punishment (which war abundantly supplies); and by defining sexual orientations so as to provoke self-doubt and manipulability in everyone.

Few books link consent to war either with gender issues or with attitudes about sexuality. For example, Eric Leed's otherwise excellent study *No Man's Land* looks at the stories people tell themselves about war and shrewdly traces these stories to their conventional and social determinants, yet when he discusses imagery making conquered land feminine, he falls back on the oedipal complex as a biological given rather than another story in need of explanation (162). Leo Braudy offers to illuminate *War and the Changing Nature of Masculinity*, yet he never seriously questions his underlying assumption that men *must* fight, biologically. Much more promising, Cynthia Enloe's books and articles, Eva Isaksson's *Women and the Military System*, and Miriam Cooke and Angela Woollacott's *Gendering War Talk* open up exciting new questions about the connections of gender and war. Joshua Goldstein's *War and Gender* is important in arguing that war is not so much an *effect* of gender difference as a *cause* of the present constructions of gender in the West. Studies about the way sexual beliefs contribute to war are even more rare: see Wilhelm Reich's *The Mass Psychology of Fascism*, George Mosse's *Nationalism and Sexuality*, and Liz Kelly's "Wars against Women." *Manipulating Masculinity* fills a gap by tying together the ideologies of sex, gender, and war.

Masculinity is multiple. As Raymond Williams explains the struggles and accommodations of competing ideologies, old concepts may remain "residual" under present "dominant" versions, while new "alternative" or "oppositional" ideologies may be emerging ("Base" 41). At any given time, those ideologies defining masculinity may incorporate residual masculinities or jostle against alternatives. For example, within social expectations about the relation of sexuality and war, one widespread assumption asserts that heterosexual "aggression" promises well for the fight and makes a man masculine. I call this assumption the Apollo Syndrome, after Ovid's classical tale of Apollo and Daphne. The Apollo Syndrome does have a long history in the West and dominates in the modern world. However, a contradictory view persists: a very active heterosexuality instead feminizes (i.e., weakens) a man and disables him from (still masculine) fighting. I call this residual notion the Antony Syndrome, from Shakespeare's play *Antony and Cleopatra.* Such an assumption clashes, of course, not only with the competing Apollo Syndrome but also with the sexologists' emerging, late-nineteenth-century premise that homosexuality, not heterosexuality, feminizes a man. The one constant in these jumbled, often simultaneously held beliefs is that a man must not exhibit too many traits labeled "feminine," although just what constitutes such traits can shift to fit varying social needs for manipulating men as well as women. (See chapter 1 for a discussion of the Apollo and Antony Syndromes.)

Trained in the study of International Relations, Charlotte Hooper emphasizes that dominant or "hegemonic" masculinities display considerable fluidity, gliding easily between popular culture and professions, while borrowing from subordinate masculinities and even former femininities: for example, appropriating the keyboards of "women's work" for "power" computing (61, 225). She cautions that analysts cannot automatically associate a hegemonic masculinity with "phallocentric imagery." A society negates that centrality of the body for men when it relegates women to "nature" and makes men uphold "culture" (60), or, in the example I gave of Perelli's predecessors, when the nineteenth-century middle class made sexual restraint, not phallic prowess, the ideal for middle-class men.

Masculinities also multiply according to class, race, region, or occupation. In fact, intersecting categories of class, race, and gender only "come into existence in and through relation to each other" (McClintock 5). Darwin, for example, defined white masculinity against a backdrop of black masculinity, both mediated by a social construction of femininities. Darwin insisted that white women, like both sexes among the "lower races," must rely on their greater "powers of intuition," whereas all men (but especially white ones) are more "courageous, pugnacious, and energetic" (2: 311, 301). Although pugnacity as part of white masculinity may look like a flaw, Darwin rehabilitates the aggression necessary for imperial conquest by buffering it between positive courage and energy and by providing a backdrop of a "lower" race and sex.

This profusion of masculinities at any given time may occur even within one occupation. David Morgan cautions that military life itself offers a range of masculinities, from combatant to bureaucrat (175). Self-concepts differ for the members of particular military branches (all referred to as "soldiers" in my book) and for career servicemen, enlisted soldiers, or draftees (169). Among enlisted soldiers, "in societies with high rates of unemployment and with marked class or ethnic divisions, the degree to which a man may be said to have chosen military service may be open to question," so that differences in class, race, and background further separate military identities (176). Lower echelons may survive by mocking higher ones, and a soldier may establish an ironic distance from his own role. While "room for maneuver and negotiation" within military expectations for manliness may simply lead to compartmentalizing one's life (Morgan 178), such room may also open up space for rebellion and reform.

Masculinity is contradictory. Separate chapters on World War I, World War II, and the Vietnam War divide into the same four rubrics, indicating four aspects of the dominant gender ideology that drove British and American men to war throughout the twentieth century:

(a) I fight to prove I'm not my sister (but I suspect I am).
(b) I fight to prove I'm not attracted to men (but I do want to see male bodies).
(c) I fight to prove I'm not emotional (but I do love my comrades).
(d) I fight to protect my sister (but I hate my sister—so as not to be her).

Section (a) posits the gender motive for war in the most general terms, whereas sections (b), (c), and (d) investigate more specific versions of that motive. Section (b) shows that societies push men to hide homo-eroticism and to use soldiering as a supposed guarantee of heterosexuality precisely by constructing homosexuality as effeminate. In section (c), militarized societies try to dampen men's compassion by assigning the so-called softer emotions to women. However, sections (b) and (c) do not divide neatly into bodily versus emotional ties, as homosexual and heterosexual behaviors constantly overlap in the literature of war. As a consequence, references to homoeroticism recur in all sections, as I examine how societies label, appropriate, and rechannel the possibilities for men's interaction by continual reference to stereotypes for women.

The four rubrics structuring chapters 2 through 4 name, then, the gender ideologies that have either stagnated or worsened from World War I to World War II to the Vietnam War. At the same time, however, the rubrics express (within a set of parentheses) flagrant contradictions in the ideologies. Even as these logical flaws confuse and frustrate individuals, they also provide hope for change. For if analysis can bring to consciousness the tensions that the literature of war exposes, the contradictions can then reveal that ideologies, far from the naturalness projected, are artificial and imaginary. And if human beings have made this hurly-burly of gender constructs promoting war, perhaps we can remake them.

Although this book focuses on the twentieth century, the need for such remaking is just as urgent in the twenty-first. "Sissy," the taunt demoting a man to his "sister," has mutated into new forms. The derisive word "wimp" combines "woman" with "limp," still incorporating both misogyny and the manipulation of men, in part by using the familiar, inaccurate blurring of sexuality with gender. The slur "wuss" or "wussy" similarly derives from "woman" and "pussy" ("Bush" 6). These taunts all depend on men's detecting within themselves their basic human similarity to women and yet interpreting such commonality as a failure. The fear of showing this inevitably failed masculinity still feeds into war by requiring a perpetual fight as the only proof of a never-finished manhood. If enough men and women believe in this artificial construct of manhood as conquest-in-and-of-itself, they remain available as tools for wars offering profit in money or masculine image.

Chapter 1

Background: Sexuality and War

The supposed connections between sexuality and war, which twentieth-century British and American societies often took for granted, rest on a number of contradictions and paradoxes. This chapter isolates three such clusters that have proved especially useful to war-making and locates them as they circulated in influential discourses, starting at the turn of the century: science (the new sexology and psychology), religion (which marks other discourses, from the popular press to judicial investigations), and education (as seen through key canonical texts).

To exemplify the discourse of science, we will look at Havelock Ellis's *Sexual Inversion* (1896), nowadays useful for what it reveals about the contradictoriness in contemporary constructions of manliness.[1] Next, we will see how a continuing religious discourse of "fallen nature" led a contingent of the British press to welcome the Great War for its "inevitable" power to promote purity and abstinence. Yet after the war, when costs were evident, insistent voices paradoxically blamed losses on war's "inevitable" sexual license. This same oscillation repeated itself, in Britain and America, for World War II and the Vietnam War. Finally, education, grounded in canonical authors such as Ovid and Shakespeare, helped perpetuate a third contradictory cluster of ideas about sex and war, which I call the Apollo Syndrome and the Antony Syndrome. Building on these three sections, later chapters argue that the religious denigration of the body contributes to war by making men tolerate battle as an escape into austerity or a guilty chance for indulgence—with war then providing its own expiating punishment. At the same time, when a society links fears of gender transgression with the threat of sexual failure, then that society can more likely manipulate its doubly insecure subjects to accept war, touted as the guarantor of both masculinity and potency.

Sexologists, Half-Men, and Female Germs

Turn-of-the-century sex reformers such as Havelock Ellis and John Addington Symonds argued that homosexuality derived from natural, inborn desire, not punishable, immoral choice. Yet even as sexologists were bravely trying to create respect for homosexuality, they depended heavily on a socially constructed sex/gender system already in place. Although the sexologists' work promised welcome reform in the law, their language illustrates the way a dominant culture may overtake and "incorporate" alternative ways of seeing and acting (Williams, "Base" 41–42). Soaked in the stereotypes and hierarchies of "masculine" and "feminine" so useful to the British Empire, the newly sketched sexualities diluted their potential to disrupt the status quo and instead inadvertently served the dominant militarism. These reinforced gender ideologies made it more likely that all men, no matter how they aligned themselves with the emerging labels homosexual or heterosexual, would respond to the call to arms in 1914.

The first edition of Ellis's *Sexual Inversion* (1896) included Symonds's essay "A Problem in Greek Ethics," and though these two writers were supposedly working in tandem, their ideas actually strain in opposite directions. Ellis believes that male homosexuals "approach the feminine type, either in psychic disposition or physical constitution" and that lesbians are masculine (119). His term "inversion" betters "perversion" but still echoes it; when "feminine" men or "masculine" women turn expectations upside down, the hint of an inverted fraction puts women on top or men on the bottom, where they do not "belong." By contrast, Symonds, himself homosexual, clearly resents both the residual aspersion of abnormality and the demeaning label feminine. He therefore insists that male pairs are *more* manly than other men, yet when he does so, he locates this masculinity precisely where his peers found it, in the warrior model.[2] The disagreements between Ellis and Symonds neatly sum up and focus larger cultural tensions within the dominant, imperial push for war.

Ellis draws on the theories of Carl Heinrich Ulrichs, who wrote that homosexual men possess "a female soul . . . united with a male body" (qtd. in Ellis 27). At first Ellis appears to scorn Ulrichs's notion that male homosexuals mix masculine and feminine, but actually he objects only to Ulrichs's word "soul." Eliminating the term to claim scientific status, Ellis salvages the idea by substituting for "female soul" the new phrase "female germs" (133). Although "germs" means "seeds," the developing usage "microbes" may have lent an additional negative tinge to the already negative marker "female." To illustrate how such "female germs" can exist in a man, Ellis draws an analogy with nipples in male mammals. Similarly, he remarks, female mammals possess a clitoris, comparable to the penis but only "rudimentary," implying that women too carry a useless, merely ornamental organ like male nipples (132). This ignorance of the source of female pleasure does not promise well for the "scientific" basis of the rest of his theory.

Sure enough, Ellis treats his whole list of feminine traits as inborn, and he offers as evidence only patently trained behavior. For example, one of his "cases" of male inverts stands revealed as "feminine by nature" because he is "neat and orderly in his habits, and fond of housework," as if all women innately love this job (54). When the man under study "helps his mother in washing," doing the laundry becomes a suspect activity, not a kindness, or an acceptance of equal responsibility, or a pleasure in cooperative labor (54). Building muscles through some practical task such as lifting water-logged sheets does not qualify him for masculinity, as lifting barbells for a scorecard would. Furthermore, Ellis seems to have relegated "helping" to a realm of women and womanly men; manly men presumably disdain the helper's role because they assign it to a secondary creature.

Ellis zeroes in on competitive sports as an essential masculine sign, as if British boys spring from the womb flexing their biceps and planning to win, whereas timid girls never move a muscle. He seems surprised when a number of his male inverts excel at athletics, but there's always a *but* at the end of the game: "He is fond of boating and walking, but of no other active pursuits. He is musical" (52) or "His habits are masculine, he has always enjoyed field sports, can swim, ride, drive, and skate. At the same time, he is devoted to music, can draw and paint, and is an ardent admirer of male statuary" (65). One would not suspect that the all-male orchestras and life-drawing classes of Ellis's time had let musical and painterly talent slip entirely into the feminine camp (Woolf 38). Ellis, however, once committed to his *a priori* hypothesis that male inverts are womanly, must construe some traits as unfortunate effeminacies.

Along with artistic sense, other nineteenth-century staples for "feminine," such as "sensitive" and "intuitive," now define "effeminate" too (54, 120). If "feminine by nature" means "gentle," masculine men must, by nature, be harsh (54). All too willing to tar heterosexual men with an inevitable touch of cruelty, Ellis allots to women and womanly men the capacity to be "affectionate" (54). Affection leads to "self-sacrifice," which Ellis also leaves to effeminacy—though one would think male soldiers, undoubtedly manly in his scheme, made sacrifices too (108). Interestingly, Ellis connects self-sacrifice with masochism, but when he finds one male invert who wishes "to experience physical pain and rough treatment at the sexual climax," Ellis is not surprised, because masochism "is by some regarded as almost normal in women" (66). Although he seems to be noticing the discouragement that some women and homosexuals might feel because of social denigration, Ellis interprets any dejection as congenital abjectness and self-hurting.

Despite this supposed propensity of women toward self-hatred, Ellis also thinks women are drawn toward self-love. He calls "vanity, irritability and petty preoccupations" inherently womanly and, thus, effeminizing in men (76). Here he implicitly stamps as "petty" the education of small children, the usual "preoccupation" of women of his time, mothers themselves or nannies; if women don't occupy themselves with more serious matters—such as his university attendance and research?—it must be inborn "irritability" that prevents those women from buckling down to an education, not closed gates and quota systems (Woolf 154). Ellis further assigns "love of scents, ornaments and fine things," assumed to be womanly, to a "vain" invert (76). Ignoring beribboned generals and all the pomp of an imperial durbar (Woolf 150), Ellis can recall no heterosexual men who adorn themselves (though they are presumably present to some degree in the military and civil services), and he apparently knows of none who are "fond of admiration," since that thirst too signals inversion (76).

One of Ellis's most bizarre markers for homosexuality in men is an inability to whistle, mentioned several times: "He cannot whistle. He thinks he ought to have been a woman" or "He never succeeded in his attempts to whistle" (64, 62). Why doe Ellis magnify this statistically irrelevant detail into a portentous failure? He needs masculine traits by which to exclude the invert, so he plucks one out of his intensely gendered late-nineteenth-century world. Perhaps Ellis conjures up a whistling boy, going fishing with a carefree and impudent air. Girls do not show such independence—and when they do, folk sayings blame them: "Whistling girls and crowing hens / Always come to some bad ends."[3] If women sound bold and not meek, Ellis condemns them as a monstrous "sport" of nature (133). Moreover, a second figure seems to stand behind Ellis's favored whistling boy: the man who wolf-whistles his admiration and thereby summons (he hopes) a woman to his bed. Men are supposed to be the ones commanding and choosing, not the ones chosen.

To counter such categorization, however, Symonds does not take apart the binary labels themselves. Instead, he proves that homosexual men are masculine in Ellis's own terms. And those terms culminate, as they did for Symonds's classical Greek sources so many centuries before, in one final role: soldier. Over and over he dredges up examples of pairs of warriors from the ancient world (Symonds, "Greek" 189ff.). Without sifting just and unjust causes, he searches for evidence of "Fire and valour," to blot out any imputation of "tenderness or tears" (174). Sometimes his warriors win their battles; other times 300 perish (but go down fighting), so that Philip of Macedon praises them and weeps at their loss (189). (Apparently, history may now and then condone men's tears, if the loss is bloody enough.) Even when Symonds ventures to suggest that ancient men valued poetry and philosophy, he is careful to combine those interests with the gymnasium and the battlefield (244). He implies that both partners in the ancient warrior pair are masculine, "tolerating no sort of softness," whereas Ellis, diametrically opposed, argues that both men are feminine (186, 119). Although the two writers are equally trying to bring about positive legal gains for homosexuals in British society, each puts a limitation on male pairs by imagining them either as born needle workers or as born soldiers.[4]

Imbued with the militaristic psychology of imperialism, which requires a victor capable of first overcoming, then "civilizing" his conquest, Symonds is also furiously engaged in "othering" not only women but also another group whom he, like the Greeks, calls "barbarians" (226). He puts off onto Asians, supposedly less civilized, the very enjoyment of sexuality that he too would like to claim but cannot, because of the low repute in which his Christian ethos has placed bodily pleasures. Symonds therefore insists that the bonds between his model warrior pairs "cannot be confounded with any merely Asiatic form of luxury" (171). Like many of his peers, Symonds projects "sensuality" onto both Asians and women, to draw off puritan attacks on the same sensuality that he finds in himself (or potentially in any human) (173). However, he then defines Greek "paiderastia," or "boy-love," as "partly martial, partly luxurious" (169, 185). He slips the luxury of sensuality into his definition of male bonds by linking it to European adulation for the classical age, meanwhile diverting any opprobrium to the Asian Other. A Greek man wrestles and hunts and "dares to court his friend in daylight," whereas a sensual barbarian must be "haunting the dusk, lurking in desert places and secret dens" (qtd. in Symonds 172). Here Symonds contrasts "us" with "them," noble with effeminate, and spiritual with sensual, yet when he even sets day against night, he hints at a home-grown cause for all this dichotomizing. Perhaps the only distinction between his "good" and "bad" male couples is not Greek versus Asian but approval versus scorn—the very scorn that promotes furtiveness in the first place. In late-nineteenth-century England, it took enormous courage for Symonds to announce his "Greekness" and to claim openly the right to be homosexual, refusing to "lurk" in secret.

As Symonds poignantly struggles to bring his sexual orientation into the light of day, he clinches what he hopes will become the new acceptability of homosexuality by means of one adjective, "martial" (185). Why should this magical word again be Symonds's most available recourse to prove masculinity, as it was for his classical Greek models? Historically, both imperial Athens and the British Empire were developing ideologies to sustain territorial expansion, which called for valorizing a bellicose version of masculinity. As John MacKenzie argues, the last three decades of the nineteenth century in England were characterized by "renewed militarism, a devotion to royalty, an identification and worship of national heroes, together with a contemporary cult of personality, and racial ideas associated with Social Darwinism" (2). Imperial propaganda agencies helped disseminate militarism widely, into "the educational system, the armed forces, uniformed youth movements, the Churches and missionary societies, and forms of public entertainment like the music hall and exhibitions" (MacKenzie 3). These cultural formations, plus literature, in turn mutually reinforced each other in consolidating a belligerent version of masculinity. The militarism, misogyny, racism, and orientalism so helpful to empire-building multiplied virulently enough in these decades to infect Symonds's personally important defense and Ellis's "scientific" exploration of sexual orientation.

The new theories of sex, in turn, inadvertently fed militarism. For Ellis sketched the markers for inversion so broadly that *most* men must have worried that the sexologist might be fingering *them*. Virtually everyone, like Ellis's hypothetical invert, must have helped a mother, grown bored at dunking the ball, flubbed whistling, savored music, or, perhaps, at least for a moment or two, felt attracted to another man. Yet any of these signs, in Ellis's view, pointed to effeminacy and inversion. As Eve Sedgwick argues, dominant interest groups find ways to use local conceptions of homosexuality and a "carefully blurred, always-already-crossed line" between homosocial and homosexual to gain leverage over all men (88–89). Certainly the interest group made up of twentieth-century military authorities might benefit from such a blurry line. Because Ellis's and Symonds's contemporaries regarded "feminine" as weak and cowardly and "masculine" as fighterly and fearless, a new tactic emerged for manipulating consent to war. For if a man of any sexual orientation objected *for any reason* to fighting in 1914, he left himself open to a public label of homosexuality: still "sinful" to some, now "sissy" to others.

Popular literature by soldiers helped circulate the sexologists' language and suggests that the new, enhanced taunt of "womanly" contributed to anxiety about any appearance of antimilitarism. In Richard Aldington's novel *Death of a Hero* (1929), the main character, George Winterbourne, hates army life and judges the war futile, yet he still finds some value at the front: "These men were men . . . They had been where no woman and no half-man had ever been, could endure to be" (263). "Half-man" echoes Ellis's notion that male inverts contain "female germs" (133), or the similar, contemporary vocabulary of an "intermediate" sex, half man and half woman (Rowbotham and Weeks 110–11). Showing that Aldington has ingested both the gender prescriptions and the sexual categories of Havelock Ellis, who is mentioned by name in the novel, the narrator goes out of his way to dissociate soldiers' brotherhood from inversion: "Let me at once disabuse the eager-eyed Sodomites among my readers by stating emphatically once and for all that there was nothing sodomitical in these friendships" (23, 17). When Winterbourne praises the "masculine" men who have seen combat, he adds, "I don't care a damn what your cause is—it's almost certainly a foully rotten one. But I do know you're the first real men I've looked upon. I swear you're better than the women and the half-men, and by God, I swear I'll die with you rather than live in a world without you" (264).[5] Chillingly, the character endorses even unjust wars, as long as they keep anyone from accusing him of effeminacy.

Like Aldington's Winterbourne, the idolized soldier-poet Rupert Brooke also signs up to distance himself from "half-men," as he says in his famous sonnet "Peace" (49). He ostentatiously scorns their "dirty songs and dreary," as if to escape a sullying, sexual lure at home (40). Brooke is relieved that the western front will ensure nothing "lost but breath," no more "shame," in a place where "the worst friend and enemy is but Death" (40). All these phrases hint that he has left a dangerous "friend and enemy" in England, who could have lost him something more valuable than life: his ticket to heaven? his reputation as a man? Brooke is known to have experimented briefly with homosexuality (Adams, *Great Adventure* 96), a common experience of future officers during their years in the segregated British public schools (Graves, *Good-bye* 19, 40). The important point is that whatever the nature of a man's private sexual practices, his public persona needs military service in a war as proof that he is not an invert. The acceptable syllogism reads: there are no half-men at the front; I am at the front; therefore, I am not a half-man.

If the dominant ideology proclaimed homosexuals incapable of the fight, another, opposite stereotype slurred all German soldiers as homosexual and *therefore* more capable of ruthless fighting. A British Sunday newspaper from 1915 ranted, "When we hear of German brutality in Belgium, of their employment of chlorine, of the *Lusitania* and the bombardment of open towns, there should be no matter of surprise. For years the Germans have cultivated a wholesome brutality as part of the military training, and latterly this brutality has found natural vent in sexual perversion. Such things do not make men gentle, humane or noble" (qtd. in Hynes, *War Imagined* 223). Actually, British as well as German commanders in World War I advised the bombing of civilians in towns (Griffin 255), and Allied chemists were racing to develop poison gas, with no qualms about adopting such "brutality" as soon as they could (Graves, *Good-bye* 145–46). Whereas cruelty or same-sex practices can occur on all sides, propaganda links them and then makes them exclusive to one side. The two contradictory notions—that homosexuals are more gentle than other men or, no, less gentle—alternate with each other not according to facts but according to usefulness for war.

War as Cure for Decadence

In a lecture of 1865 to young soldiers at the Royal Military Academy at Woolwich, British art critic John Ruskin claimed that war maintained a "proper level of manly nature" and that peace was "death" (132–33). Papering over the selfishness of imperial wars, he disdained peace not only for its imputed, immoral "selfishness," but also for its "sensuality," a "corruption" that war would suppress (133). This religious discourse denigrating the body as corrupt, "fallen nature" continued to circulate in the twentieth century in both sacred and secular language. In the decades leading up to World War I, Christian "purity" campaigners were again damning all but procreative sex, and scientists were thundering their own jeremiads. The German neurologist Richard von Krafft-Ebing warned that masturbation would turn men "cowardly" and foment "effeminacy, sensuality, and luxury" (qtd. in Mosse 34). American advice books at the turn of the century agreed that masturbation by men would cause "feminization" (Kimmel, *Manhood* 129): an odd characterization, considering that respectable women of the time were often assumed to have no sexuality. In this murky atmosphere, a surprising number of Europeans and Americans welcomed World War I as a bizarre antidote to sensuality, especially sexual indulgence.

For example, a vicar in a 1918 patriotic British novel by Horace Annesley Vachell rejoices that young soldiers undergoing arduous military maneuvers can escape sensual temptation, and he reassures the boys that it is "good even to die, if the supreme sacrifice were demanded, clean of limb and mind, leaping joyously upward, unfettered by disease or vice" (124). Historian Michael Adams dryly comments that the vicar "believes it is better to be machine-gunned than masturbate" (*The Great Adventure* 117). Not satirizing this character and his sublimated leapings, Vachell apparently endorses the notion that a soldier is fortunate to die young, before fully exploring the joys of the flesh, which must inevitably sully him.

If solitary sexual "vice" excited the patriotic censor, so did shared sex. A British court banned D. H. Lawrence's novel *The Rainbow*, which celebrates sex, in 1915: "A thing like 'The Rainbow' has no right to exist in the wind of war. It is a greater menace to our public health than any of the epidemic diseases" (qtd. in Hynes, *War Imagined* 61–62). Other doomsayers singled out homosexuality as the worst sign of decadence, which they expected war to root out. This group revived the memory of the court cases against Oscar Wilde in 1895 to epitomize what they called the terrible "Condition of England before the War" (Hynes, *War Imagined* 17). One critic predicted the salutary effects of the war on all sexual morals and literature: "Cynicism, self-advertisement, sexuality, perverse eccentricity—there will be no room for some time to come for violences of this kind" (qtd. in Hynes, *War Imagined* 60). Such doublespeak calls sex between consenting adults "violence" and damns private pleasure as self-"abuse." Meanwhile, the twentieth century, like the nineteenth, doggedly mislabels violent war as health and peace as death.

One irony, however, of expecting war to end the "violence" of sexual enjoyment is that in some ways mobilization increased the opportunities for sex and the need for solace. VD rates increased (Hynes, *War Imagined* 371), as servicemen found prostitutes or others who heeded pleas for a last comfort. The female ambulance driver in Helen Zenna Smith's novel *Not So Quiet* (1930) foresees "in the years to come old men in their easy chairs . . . accusing us of barnyard morals when we use love as a drug for forgetfulness because we have acquired the habit of taking what we can from life while we are alive to take" (166). Equally ironic is the hope that the war would stop men from noticing the bodies of other men, when military life throws soldiers together intimately day and night.

If World War I provided more opportunities for all kinds of sex, at the same time literary works register a backlash, against both hetero- and homosexuality, as if some sexualized "other" had caused all a soldier's vulnerabilities. The first backlash—men against women—can be seen in two British stories about traumatized veterans, Richard Aldington's "The Case of Lieutenant Hall" (1930) and Mary Butts's "Speed the Plough" (1923). In Aldington's tale, Lieutenant Hall experiences many symptoms of shell-shock, including obsessive memories, insomnia, and self-loathing. Within a "sort of agony of contrition over the whole war," he hates himself for one particular incident, when he killed four Germans who had already surrendered (86). However, he evades his self-disgust by turning it outward, into a virulent hatred of women. He especially abhors the naked bodies of the "red lamp" women, because they remind him of the exposed flesh of the soldiers he saw mangled on the western front (85). Dissociating himself from his own physical fragility by projecting it onto women, he deals similarly with emotional pain, berating himself for "crying like a silly girl" (85). Instead of recognizing that both men and women might justly cry at the vistas of human folly that the war displayed, he is angry with girls, as if they have contaminated him with "their" tears.[6]

In Mary Butts's "Speed the Plough," a lamed and lethargic World War I soldier is sent to a farm to recuperate, but, like Lieutenant Hall, he now recoils from any evidence of female flesh, whether in brawny, booted squire's daughters or even in cows. The messiness of lactation and the rapid perishability of milk remind him of a terrifying mutability, which he knows all too well from the decay of human bodies in the trenches. However, unlike Hall, who shuns women altogether, this convalescent begins to adore women—as long as he can shift his regard from real people to an artificial feminine ideal, found in fashion magazines. He dotes on the pictures of celebrities, whose lush names, "Georgette" and "Delysia," echo those of their robes, "crêpe georgette," "crêpe velours," and "organdie" (45–46). The fabrics might appear to be flimsy, but an organdie gown still lasts longer than many teens at the front. The names seem to him beautiful, not ugly like the war, and "that faint windy stuff aerophane" comfortingly contrasts with the unforgivingly hard "aeroplanes," which tracked him in a steady row "like a travelling eye of God" (45–46). He implies that he must have deserved to be punished in war, but for what crime?

Although the convalescent does not expatiate on his failures, he seems to have sinned just in being born, for birth launched him toward growth and decay, toward sexual feelings and natural death. Like most of his culture, officially focused on transcendence, the convalescent cannot accept these natural changes, so he distances himself from real life. Just as on the farm he prefers a white Lyons jug to the perishable milk inside it, in the city he prefers to handle the textiles that wrap his rich customers, rather than discover the women themselves. Prizing things "for show" rather than "for use" (49), the convalescent seems to be reviving a late-nineteenth-century dictum of art-for-art's sake and refashioning it into a modernist ideal of beautiful patterning. Yet Butts's story reveals that one impulse behind that ideal (which turns out to be very useful after all) is to hide the dirt and torn flesh of bodies at war. Better that patterns refer reflexively to themselves than to the memory, now hushed up, of putrefying corpses.

The longing by Butts's character for mellifluent words and pliant textures may seem to express an obvious pleasure-ethic. However, the veteran has actually banished any substantial joy from his life. By staying always on sleek surfaces, he avoids both emotional and sexual involvement. Butts's story shows that at least some of the apparent approbation of pleasure in modernism hides an old fear of sexuality and life (which includes natural death), because these intense experiences have been confused with and blamed for the very different death-by-violence in war.

While Aldington's and Butts's veterans typify a revulsion against heterosexuality, which showed up in literature following World War I, at the same time England witnessed a backlash against homosexuality, in the form of scapegoating. When actress Maude Allan decided to sue Member of Parliament Pemberton Billing for "libeling" her as lesbian, he gladly took the opportunity to read out names in court from "The First 47,000," a circulated list specifying "perverts" whom the Germans were supposedly recruiting as spies, in exchange for silence about their sex lives (Hynes, *War Imagined* 226). When Pat Barker depicts this sensational trial of 1918 in her fictional trilogy, her soldiers bitterly complain that civilians riveted by news of the court case were trying to deny the tragedy of the war by distracting themselves through farce (*Eye* 221). Britons could also blame war losses on an imagined betrayal of state secrets by infiltrated enemies. Repeating a long-standing ploy of representing homegrown sodomy as a "foreign" vice (Norton 124), Billing's wildly irrational pamphlets claimed that 47,000 men and women, English though they were, had somehow picked up sexual practices so "vile" that "only German minds" could think them up (qtd. in Barker, *Eye* 152).

This double movement—war conditions offering more opportunities for sexual contacts, then war losses provoking a backlash against sexual scapegoats—repeated itself in World War II. In *Virtue under Fire*, John Costello studies a loosening of heterosexual mores in Britain and America during the war, including earlier consummation of relationships with sweethearts or unpaid strangers, as well as an increase in prostitution. Costello cites men's deep need for comfort under war's extreme threat as one cause for the changes. Yet when women also actively sought sexual experience, along with higher paying jobs previously reserved for men, their initiative fueled resentment. In addition to the well-known post–World War II reaction that pushed "Rosie the Riveter" back to the kitchen (Enloe, *Khaki* 174), some fiction writers depict another scramble to find culprits for the war, one that singled out women's sexuality.

For example, Jean Rhys's short story "I Spy a Stranger" (1966) chillingly imagines an English village in the 1940s fastening on Laura, a Czech refugee, to pile all its wartime troubles on her. Instantly labeling her "that witch of Prague," the villagers draw on a long-standing misogyny, yet the traditional "nasty spirit" of baiting women has grown "worse now, much worse" with the war, according to Mrs. Hudson, the cousin who takes Laura in and narrates the story to her sister, Mrs. Trant (114, 124). Although Mrs. Hudson feels sorry enough for Laura to convey Rhys's sympathies, the two sisters have internalized the low status of women to the extent that they complicitly allow the scapegoating of Laura, in a misplaced revenge for their own unhappiness.

Just as Aldington's Lieutenant Hall evades guilt over his role in the atrocities of World War I by projecting responsibility onto women, Rhys's villagers escape examining their own contributions to World War II by expelling Laura. Calling *her* crazy, they insanely incarcerate her in a sanatorium at the end of the story, punishing her for the crime of voicing unpalatable "cracky ideas" about a fascistic mindset that inhabits England as well as Germany (117). Here Rhys echoes Virginia Woolf's *Three Guineas* (1938), which took the unpopular route of advising the English to root out the "Fascist or the Nazi" in their own hearts and "crush him in our own country" (53, 142). Laura, like Woolf, keeps a notebook of newspaper clippings to document intolerance and, to clinch the allusion to Woolf, pays her cousin precisely "three guineas" a week in rent (123). The elements of English fascism that both Woolf and Rhys skewer include misogyny, xenophobia, militarism, anti-intellectualism, surveillance, and coercion; as one of Rhys's characters points out, their "free country" doesn't offer much "free nowadays except a third-class ticket to Kingdom Come" (115). Moreover, when the villagers finally imprison the outspoken Laura behind locked gates, they eerily resemble the Nazis who put away "undesirables" in concentration camps.

Instead of learning from the ideas generated by Laura's sharp mind, the villagers target her body and sexuality. Anonymous hate-mail sent to her at Mrs. Hudson's threatens an ambiguous "Gun for the Old Girls," with an explanatory obscene drawing (115). Offended by Laura as an unmarried woman, under no man's control, the scribbler would rape her and her half-hearted protector to punish independence. Yet the town's hecklers indict the refugee for contradictory sins: for not making herself sexually available to men, but, at the same time, for making herself too sexually alluring. When Laura fails to come downstairs in an air raid, Ricky Hudson complains nastily, "I expect the zip in her ruddy siren suit's got stuck" (124). Slipping from the siren of the air raid to the dangerous enticers of the *Odyssey* or the red-light district, Ricky both demands and resents that a woman might unzip her body for him and lead him astray; if Laura is too old to enchant him any more, she will further pay for that new unavailability. In fact, the sexual focus (and contradictions) of the villagers' harassment as they heap wartime losses on Laura is paralleled by a widespread hounding of women labeled whores after the war (see section (d), chapter 3).

The oscillation that plagued heterosexuals in World War II, from liberalizing sex to reimposing taboos, jostled the rules for homosexuals too. Britisher Quentin Crisp was surprised to find, thanks to American soldiers in "deliciously tight kit," that "as soon as the bombs started to fall, London became like a paved double-bed" (Horwell 24). After the war, though, a backlash again set in. As in the Pemberton Billing trial in England at the end of World War I, the scapegoating of homosexuals recurred in America after World War II, when Senator Joseph McCarthy hysterically equated "queers" and "commies" and blacklisted them in theatrical, governmental inquisitions. Under the threat of the atomic bomb, it was easier to load troubles on fellow workers, who could be expelled, than defuse Cold War competition with other countries. It also proved more convenient to label "deviants" than examine one's own desires (Edelman, "Tearooms" 569).

Like World Wars I and II, the American war in Vietnam unleashed both sexual license and sexual scapegoating. This war complicated the license by dividing it between soldiers, who followed some of their fathers and grandfathers to use war as a cover for carousing, and war protesters, who proposed sexual liberation as part of an alternative to the "military–industrial complex."[7] Male protesters during the war may have invited women into more beds but not always into more leadership roles; Stokely Carmichael of the Student Non-Violent Coordinating Committee summed up the view of many men when he airily rebuffed the objections of coworkers who wanted to undo sexism along with racism: "The only position for women in SNCC is prone" (qtd. in Rowbotham 375). Such opinions fueled the Women's

Movement, modeled in part on the Civil Rights Movement and benefited by the organizing skills of antiwar activism. When demands for social change touching gender and race provoked a back-lash, resentments often targeted sexual scapegoats. Feminists were portrayed as sex-starved spinsters; black men were depicted as stalkers, more likely to rape than other men; lesbians were construed as monsters; and gay men were imagined as oversexed predators *and* (contradictorily) as undersexed, feminine weaklings.

These sexual phobias often combined with a renewed glorification of war, whether emanating from the government or private militias. Linda Kintz's study of contemporary right-wing America, *Between Jesus and the Market* (1997), finds a pervasive military language in both religious and secular conservatism. For example, one branch of the men's movement, the Promise Keepers, gives study groups names such as " 'Battle Weary'—The Destroyer Group" and " 'Refreshed, Refueled, Refocused'—The Carrier Group" (112). Kintz traces this discourse of battle to leaders who served in Vietnam or grew up in military families, to an apocalyptic frame from the biblical Book of Revelation, and to American frontier mythology, reinforced in 1960s Westerns on television (115–19, 147). Such militarism responds less to real security needs and more to trained associations, of the type we have been discussing, among sex, gender, and fighting. One writer for the Promise Keepers rejects a famous picture of Christ with long hair as too "feminine" and scorns "that pale, limp-wristed Galilean," offering instead a version of Jesus based on the memory of a handsome, virile Israeli soldier (qtd. in Kintz 122). This passage encodes as limp "wrists" a fear of supposedly impotent gays, a notion that bases homosexuality in womanliness, womanliness in asexuality, and masculinity in the fight. These linkages are perhaps more crudely stated but still related to Ellis's and Symonds's imperial inheritance. Moreover, ferreting out supposed sexual offenders and touting war distract from other worries in times of economic and social change.

This strategy for diverting attention from political problems by condemning sex goes far back in Western culture. In the Old Testament, when Assyrian troops invaded Israel, the prophets responded not by sympathizing with slashed villages, or by criticizing the attackers, but by blaming the victims. Once the prophets had placed Israel in the wrong, they personified the territory as "she," the bride of Yahweh who must have betrayed him by "whoring" after other gods (Hos. 2.10–13). Many of the proscribed Canaanite religions, which still competed with Judaism, represented sex as a sacralized part of worship. This older view of sex as good, even holy, as well as the inclusion of female deities, horrified the patriarchal Hebrews (Lerner 10, 196).

Not only the Jewish prophets but also the early Christian fathers epitomized all faults of the enemy, new Rome or old Babylon, in the great Whore (Rev. 17). Allusions to this Whore of Babylon still occur in the literature of World War II and the Vietnam War (see section (d) of chapters 3 and 4). Both the Old and New Testaments, then, bequeath to the twentieth century this pattern of avoiding the real problems causing wars and upheaval by reaffirming traditional sexual customs and gender attitudes and denouncing supposed transgressors. As a consequence, the twentieth-century oscillation during and after wars of seeking sex and then scapegoating sex repeats itself because of two separate inheritances: both antipleasure and misogyny.

The Apollo and Antony Syndromes

Religious discourse contended with a classical inheritance to make up the two main strands of Western education. Canonical educational texts included such staples as Ovid's Latin *Metamorphoses* and Shakespeare's plays, themselves a product of classical, Christian, and other influences. Although Ovid's story of Apollo and Daphne and Shakespeare's *Antony and Cleopatra* did not create what I call the Apollo Syndrome and the Antony Syndrome, these two texts do consolidate in memorable figures conceptions of war and gender that circulated in their own times and have continued to do so down to our present day.

In *Virtue under Fire*, John Costello confidently asserts, "the notion that a sexually aggressive man makes the best fighter has been universal throughout history and in all cultures" (76). Actually, such a link between copulating and killing is neither obvious nor universal. Costello's assumption that sexual "aggression" promises well for the fight and that both activities prove a man masculine makes up the Apollo Syndrome, which does indeed have a long history in the West and dominates in the contemporary world. However, an opposing Antony Syndrome, the view that copulating with women feminizes a man and hence interferes with his (still masculine) ability to fight, also has a long history and remains strongly residual into the present.

The first notion, that a man's heterosexual activity enhances his ability to fight, is epitomized in Ovid's first-century C.E. story of Apollo and Daphne. Although one modern translator assures us that Apollo wanted to "marry" Daphne (Humphries 18), the god clearly wants to mate for an afternoon, not cherish for long years. When she says no, he chases her, with what nowadays would be called intent to rape. Far from considering Apollo a criminal, however, Ovid's culture grants the pursuer a godly, one might say upper-class, masculine prerogative to demand sex. Boasting that he is the son of the top god, no mere "shepherd or wild-haired stable boy" (Ovid 45), Apollo is ready to take Daphne by force. Ovid describes Apollo as a violent hound racing a hare, the dog's "teeth, his black jaws" about to clamp down on her ankle (46).[8] When Daphne sees that she cannot outrun her attacker, she asks her father, a demi-god, to turn her into a laurel tree. Technically, Daphne escapes Apollo's sexual advances, but she does so only at the cost of her humanity.

As Apollo sidles disconsolately up to the laurel, he announces his "love" as a direct inspiration for military conquest, proclaiming that war heroes parading in Rome will henceforth wear Daphne's laurel crowns (46). Although Apollo claims to be honoring Daphne, he is still treating her violently, for he must strip her leaves to make wreaths for himself, wearing them as the "sign of all I own" (46). The story neatly condenses three long-surviving views of the relationship of men to women: *the hunt, ownership*, and the claimed *homage* to women through war. The god does not explain how killing the men of some other city and raping their women will honor Daphne any more than does Apollo's own warring against her.

In the twentieth century, the most influential proponent of the Apollo Syndrome is Sigmund Freud, who drew heavily on classical mythology and combined it with the (by then) omnipresent and almost unconscious military vocabulary of nineteenth-century imperialism. Just as Ovid characterizes the relation of man to woman as the hunt, Freud declares in *Three Essays on the Theory of Sexuality* (1905) that the sexuality of most human males "contains an element of *aggressiveness*—a desire to subjugate" (23). Biologically, he says, such a tendency must have developed from an ancient "need" to break down what he assumes will be women's resistance to sex (24). In the face of feminine reluctance, he understands why men should take an "active," even "violent attitude to the sexual object" (*Three* 24; *Drei* 57). Already eclipsing the human partner under the word "object," Freud slips in violence too as perfectly normal.

Freud suspects that girls might have a hard time growing up, but he blames this difficulty on biology, the nature of women, not on social causes (*Drei* 123). He proclaims, incredibly, that women must shift from a "childish" interest in the clitoris to a mature focus on the vagina only (*Three* 87). Although he grants that this change might confuse a woman, Freud still traces any resulting hysteria or lack of enthusiasm for heterosex to a woman's personal failure in her important task of "renouncing" the clitoris ("Female" 5: 252). He advises a woman to resign herself to her bodily "deficiency," the "fact of [her] castration" ("Female" 5: 261). He warns that if she persists in a "defiant" desire to stimulate the clitoris, through masturbation, for example, or active moves in intercourse, she will become too "masculine," an unnatural and unattractive state for her ("Female" 5: 260).

When women passively hang back from intercourse, for reasons Freud cannot fathom, active men can resort to force; after all, he says, cruelty and the sexual instinct intertwine (*Drei* 58). In "Why War?" (1932), he repeats unchanged the idea that, in men, an erotic instinct is linked to an aggressive one, which drives men to "destroy and kill," and he reiterates that men's sexual desire needs "some contribution from the instinct of mastery if it is in any way to possess that object" ("Why War" 280–81; "Warum Krieg" 20–21). Freud gets close to saying that human males, like the god Apollo, are perfectly justified in ignoring a Daphne's refusal.

The *OED* defines "aggression" as "the first attack in a quarrel, the making of an attack or assault," hardly a promising picture for a love affair, and traces the word to its military root: "to aggress, to march up to," in ranks (1989 ed.). To call someone "aggressive" would seem to be uncomplimentary, but gradually in the nineteenth and twentieth centuries the word took on some positive connotations (as applied to men, not women), including initiative, assertiveness, and confidence. Certainly Social Darwinists played a role in this shift. By the 1880s, they had adapted the phrase "survival of the fittest" for a variety of programs: everything from arguing free trade to touting master races, from denying aid to the poor to promoting eugenics. A "handful of extremists" among Social Darwinists used their theories to glorify war, imagining "the joyful prospects of apocalyptic military confrontations" (Gay 41, 53–54).

In the twentieth century, although the competitiveness accepted in business and sports gave "aggression" a further positive edge, the discipline of psychology played a part in making "aggressive" seem like a compliment. Significantly, the *OED*'s first listing for a positive connotation is A. A. Brill's 1912 translation of Freud's *Selected Papers in Hysteria*: "We no longer deal here with sexual passivity but with pleasurably accomplished aggressions" (1989 ed.). This language construes male sexuality as not just confident but assaultive. Conversely, and just as dangerously, the new psychological association of aggression with a supposedly inherent, violent sexuality tends to validate fighting as a kind of preparation for sex, or even a substitute, strengthening the view that when men march to war in serried ranks, they are just fulfilling another "natural" part of life.

Freud's views of sexuality percolated from academic treatises to middlebrow magazines and other outlets.[9] Although the doctor's voice always carried a tone more cautionary than celebratory, his notion of the inevitability of sexual motives behind all aspects of life translated into an expanding sense of license. Apparently influenced by popularized Freudian legacies touting both indulgence and male forcefulness, one "ranking U.S. navy medical officer" argued in a 1941 review of training that to fight well, a man must also show "sexual aggressiveness":

> The men in a successfully trained army or navy are stamped into a mold . . . . They cannot, they must not, be mollycoddled, and this very education befits nature, induces sexual aggression, and makes them the stern, dynamic type we associate with men of the armed force. This sexual aggressiveness cannot be stifled. Recently, I read an article by a man who bewailed the effect army life would have on his son. Imagine, if you can, an army of impotent men. This very sexual drive is amplified because of fresh air, good food and exercise, and exaggerated by the salacious barracks talk. It cannot be sublimated by hard work or the soft whinings of Victorian minds. (Qtd. in Costello 76–77)

Although the officer does not elaborate on a soldier's sex life, typical requirements for the time period might include strict heterosexuality, multiple partners, payment, a focus on penetration, and a short amount of time spent with the women. (In wartime Honolulu, for example, men received a grand total of three minutes with a prostitute at initially segregated brothels, eventually reserved for whites only [Enloe, "More Than Two" 145–47].) Costello's medical officer assumes that every aspect of such historically specific scenarios equally "befits nature," but he contradictorily reveals that a serviceman's actions must be "trained" and "induce[d]." The officer's striking image of stamping men in a "mold" further acknowledges that his ideal of manhood is not natural but social, not spontaneous but coerced.

In a second contradiction characterizing this officer's version of the Apollo Syndrome, he claims that a military man's sexuality "cannot be sublimated by hard work or the soft whinings of Victorian minds," but he himself is hoping to sublimate or displace a good portion of a man's energies into fighting instead of copulating, since the two are deemed interchangeable. To prove this equivalence, the officer points to the past:

How important this libido was considered historically can be gathered from the words of Gian Maria, Duke of Milan, who after his defeat stated: "My men had ceased to speak of women, I knew I was beaten." The Mongol hordes, who conquered all Asia and most of Europe, recognized this fact too. "He who is not virile is not a soldier. He who lacks virility is timid, and what rabbit ever slew a wolf." (Qtd. in Costello 77)

When the officer equates slaying with mating, he also casts the female mate as the quarry, and, just as this premise predicts, Costello finds that barracks talk expresses no gratitude to sex partners but only "contempt for women" (77). While this outlook ignores a woman's own sexuality and offers her up as a sacrificial victim, it less obviously curtails a man's sexuality too. As any pet-owner knows, rabbits reproduce prolifically; maybe it's more fun to be a sexy rabbit than a lone wolf. For Ovid, the hound's jaws predominated in the picture of Apollo's aggression, and here too the wolf's teeth take precedence over genitals. The naval officer, for all his bluster about sexuality, subsumes pleasure under power.

It's not only Freud and military men who think that "instincts" to copulate and to master, even to kill, are inextricably connected in men. One minority strand within contemporary feminism agrees. Catharine MacKinnon, for example, seems to assimilate all intercourse to rape. Rightfully skewering laws that fail to recognize rape as a crime unless accompanied by visible bodily injury, MacKinnon tries to figure out this blindness. She concludes, in 1983, that "coercion has become [so] integral to male sexuality" that "forced sex" has become "paradigmatic" (618). While she bravely exposes an often hushed up abuse from husbands and lovers, she sometimes seems to extend this experience from many women to all women in heterosexual relationships. And whereas MacKinnon does call any male coercion "conditioned" (628), other feminists seem to regard abuse as inevitable. Andrea Dworkin, for instance, believes that in the sexual desire of men, "hostility always plays some part" (178). Although she usefully argues that intercourse makes up such a small fraction of women's sexual pleasure that it should not be taught to women as central to all sex (138), she implies, throughout her book *Intercourse* (1987), that any male hurtfulness is not a similarly trained ignorance but an innate intention. In this view, the Apollo in all heterosexual men goes on slaying his male enemies and mating with women, after wrestling *them* down too.

The Apollo Syndrome, which assumes that "a sexually aggressive man makes the best fighter," does, then, have a long history, but it is by no means "universal" (Costello 76). In some traditional cultures, such as the New Guinea Trobrianders, elders tell warriors to avoid, not consort with, women before a battle (Huston 121–23). Men learn that retaining semen, not releasing it, will increase overall power. Male characters in William Shakespeare's *Antony and Cleopatra* similarly worry about losing manly power through contact with women. Caesar, Enobarbus, and Philo fear that Antony's ostentatious sex life, which might suggest to the World War II navy officer Antony's prowess in battle, will instead feminize him—to the point that he plays at wearing Cleopatra's "tires [attires] and mantles," far from the fray (2.5.22).

In part, Antony's peers disapprove of him because he has turned his "devotion" from public war-making to private, emotional exchange with a specific woman, whom he is loath to leave (1.1.5). However, these peers differ from the modern officer not only in their attitude toward emotion but also in their view of sexuality itself. Whereas mid-twentieth-century military culture usually attributes a stronger libido to men, Renaissance (and medieval) audiences assigned women the greater "lust" (1.1.10). Once Antony enters a realm of sexual voraciousness, assigned exclusively to women, Cleopatra's other supposedly inevitable, feminine characteristics—cowardice in war, tears, inconstancy—might somehow rub off on him too. His "love of Love—her soft hours" must render him soft in return (1.1.46).

Nevertheless, what really bothers Antony's peers is not that Cleopatra suffers from (and might spread) too much feminine weakness, but rather that she does not display *enough* femininity. Caesar worries that Antony "is not more manlike / Than Cleopatra, nor the queen of Ptolemy [Cleopatra] / More womanly than he" (1.4.5–7). After buckling on Antony's sword in a game, she storms to the real wars, commanding her warship from its deck. Antony's wife, Fulvia, similarly directs military campaigns, and Antony admits that her strategy does not lack "Shrewdness of policy" (2.2.74). Like Caesar, Enobarbus objects that women's participation in battle crosses prescribed gender barriers and threatens the standard hierarchy. To Cleopatra's face, he argues that her presence in war will "Take from his heart, take from his brain, from's time / What should not then be spared," but in an aside he frets more about image than practical success: "If we should serve with horse and mares together, / The horse were merely [utterly] lost; the mares would bear / A soldier and his horse" (3.7.7–12). Apparently, women's recognized ability to give birth, plus this newly claimed prerogative to give commands, would, for Enobarbus, add up to too much power for women, leaving men "lost."[10]

The view held by Antony's peers, that heterosexual activity potentially clashes with a man's fighting ability, still sways proponents in the modern world. In the small "wars" of the playing field, coaches still occasionally advise football players to abstain from intercourse before a game. And an editorial in the *Guardian Weekly* from February, 1999, wondering why President Clinton suddenly proposed a ten-and-a-half billion dollar increase in "Star Wars" research, speculates that "post-Monica [Lewinsky], he has become a pushover [to Pentagon hawks] . . . . A large part of the rhetoric of the impeachment case has focused on the disjunction between a promiscuous commander-in-chief and the strictly enforced military codes governing those whom he nominally commands" (Kettle 6). This editorial implies that at least some of the public characterize masculine military men as sexually restrained—in striking contrast to Costello's World War II naval officer who claims sexual *un*restraint as the sure sign of a fighter. To placate that segment of the public which would hold commanders to rigid sexual codes, Clinton must be trying to counter a "feminine" promiscuity (contracted from his Cleopatra) by sending up more "masculine" missiles. Such a picture depends on the interlocking pieces of the Antony Syndrome: sex belongs more to women than to men, too much sex will render a man feminine, femininity means weakness, masculinity requires constant proof, and only war-making or war-mongering validates manhood.

Now, to assume that climbing into or staying out of a woman's bed on one day can affect the accuracy of the spear throw or the missile aim on the next is entirely illogical. Yet both the Apollo Syndrome and the Antony Syndrome persist side by side in Western culture, for all their mutual incompatibility and irrelevance to battle. So too do other incompatible assumptions about sex muddle along together. Britons and Americans in the twentieth century have contradictorily believed that heterosexual men have a more urgent sexuality than women *and* that sensuality belongs to an inherently feminine realm. Homosexual men are lambs who cannot fight, *and* they are beasts who fight more naturally than other men. Desire is part of "fallen nature," deserving punishment in itself, *and* soldiers are perfectly justified in demanding sex. War fortunately can provide extra sexual treats, *but* unfortunately sexual indulgence causes all the wartime losses. However, if the contradictions among these murky beliefs could become more visible, they might provoke questions and revisions to our sex/gender systems that so favor war.

Chapter 2

World War I: No Half-Men at the Front

(a) I Fight to Prove I'm Not My Sister (but I Suspect I Am)

Since the European rivalry for colonies centrally contributed to World War I (Thomson 219), it is not surprising that the definitions of manliness compelling men to fight were inextricably bound up with constructions of colonizer and colonized, civilized and savage.[1] The soldiers in Henri Barbusse's novel *Under Fire* (1917), Wyndham Lewis's "The French Poodle" (1916), and William Faulkner's "All the Dead Pilots" (1931) dread the label "womanly," which the characters define as emotional, lusty, primitive, animal-like, and dependent. These definitions overlap with stereotypes from colonization and slavery, which construed Africans as "lusty" and "animal-like" (D'Emilio and Freedman 35). However, the fear that African men might be stronger "animals" led some European men to start envying a "real savage," as opposed to the "sham" savages to which Europeans had supposedly degenerated (Lewis 170). Although white males detected in themselves the same desires and helplessness that they projected onto women and darker-skinned people, many Europeans and Americans denied their own emotions and vulnerabilities and signed up for war to confirm manhood. Ironically, American black men often used war to prove manhood on the same terms as their oppressors, as shown by playwrights Alice Dunbar-Nelson in *Mine Eyes Have Seen* (1918) and Mary Burrill in *Aftermath* (1919).

In one scene from Barbusse's *Under Fire*, French soldiers watch Africans from the colonies sent past them to the front lines. Allowed to rest for once, the white soldiers discuss among themselves the gossip they have heard: that their African counterparts always enthusiastically prepare for battle, fight fiercely, and take no prisoners. "In fact," one Frenchman sums up the Africans, "they're real soldiers" (45). This conclusion poses a dilemma for his comrades. One *poilu*, bristling at the inference that Africans have proved themselves soldiers on the same terms as whites, retorts confusedly: " 'We are not soldiers,' says big Lamuse, 'we're men' " (45). Now, according to the status quo, the quintessential "man" in France is a soldier, whereas an African is a subhuman savage. However, if Africans make good soldiers too, the squad will have to admit either that Africans are not savages—and should not be colonized—or that all soldiers are savages. While Barbusse's first speaker does indeed seem willing to praise colonized men, the second, poised on the brink of admitting that war dehumanizes everyone, suddenly scrambles to reserve manhood for whites only. This effort to reaffirm that "*we're* men," exclusively, then distracts him from questioning any further the definition of manly as belligerent, although Barbusse's antiwar novel as a whole is headed toward just that criticism.

Like Barbusse, Wyndham Lewis served as a soldier, first with an artillery unit and then, from 1917, as an official war artist (Tate 296). In Lewis's story "The French Poodle," social conceptions of masculinity pressure the British soldier Rob Cairn, on sick leave for shell-shock, to return to the front: not for any political cause he could name, but solely to confirm that he is not a woman. In a survival of the Antony Syndrome, Cairn's friends fear that if he spends too much time with a woman, her supposedly intrinsic traits will somehow rub off on him and diminish his effectiveness in any active walk of life. Cairn has learned that he should not get too close to Dolly, a former sweetheart, or to Carp, his new French poodle. Though Carp is male, the whole breed was considered suited to ladies; a newspaper in 1914 lampooned men who supported women's suffrage as "poodles of the male sex" (qtd. in Rowbotham 13). Lewis's story clearly parallels Carp with Dolly. In the past, when Cairn took the advice of his business partner, Fraser, to leave his "lady-love," Cairn guiltily thought of her as a "mascot abandoned" (171–72); when the soldier now worries about the dog's fate if he returns to the front, Fraser again scoffs, "Damn you and your mascots" (172). Like the label "mascot," the name "Dolly" belittles her, an eternal child or plaything. Although the recommendation to leave Dolly depressed Cairn, he could not ignore it, nor does he question his society's assignment of women to the level of subhuman pets, heedless children, or objectified trinkets.

As the link between Dolly and Carp reduces women to a minor recreation, it also assumes that they are more animalistic than men. Carp's attributes turn out to be the same as those that Cairn's culture associates with women in general: "servile good nature," "hysteria," and "amorous proposals" in every direction (170). Like the cheerful Carp, women serve, whereas men are expected to command. Women may express emotion, from affection to hysteria, whereas British men are supposed to remain reserved and calm. Finally, just as Carp throws himself against any stray dog, women are assumed to be naturally promiscuous, interested in sex as their main characteristic.

If Cairn had been on speaking terms with the German enemy, he might have discovered similar views; a German pamphlet from 1900 declared, "Instinct makes woman animal-like, dependent, secure and cheerful" (qtd. in Gay 327). This vocabulary, making women more "primitive" than men, has threaded through Western culture at least since Aristotle (Lerner 206). The doctrine continued to attract adherents in the Middle Ages, though earthy Eve, akin to the beastly snake, now had to compete with asexual Mary, to create the Whore/Angel dichotomy still prevalent in the Victorian age. In the grip of this muddled inheritance, Cairn regards women as more excitable and sensual than men.

Since Cairn's society constructs gender as a strict binary, men must avoid anything women are supposed to be: sexual, emotional, or objectified. If nineteenth-century manliness meant strict control of one's sexuality, a new twentieth-century masculinity would increasingly require just the reverse: demonstrable sexual exploits, now carefully designated heterosexual. Cairn can see this promised land ahead; he envies his dog the "amazing physical catholicism of its taste," but he cannot quite make his way into the new erotic freedom (170). Still imbued with an Aristotelian notion that men possess all the "spirit" and women, all the "matter" (Lerner 206), Cairn expects to be almost ethereal, springing actively into higher realms. Unfortunately, because he did not respond correctly to the prospect of being blown up, Cairn has failed a masculinity test:

When the shell came he had not bounded gracefully and coldly up, but with a clumsy dismay. His spirit, that spirit that should have been winged for the life of a soldier, and ready fiercely to take flight into the unknown, strong for other lives, was also grubbily attached to the earth. It, like his body, was not graceful in its fearlessness, nor resilient, nor young. All the minutiae of existence mesmerised it. It could not disport itself genially in independence of surrounding objects and ideas. (167)

Men, Cairn had thought, live closer to the heavens than to the earth. There they fly gracefully, free of "surrounding objects and ideas." Men are cold, fearless, and fierce. Whereas Cairn expects women to form attachments as instinctively and slavishly as his dog Carp, he envisions himself indifferent to everything: other people, dogs, his own life.

When Cairn cannot attain that detachment, he supposedly betrays a biological insufficiency in maleness, which in retrospect had already manifested its telltale signs:

> Even as a boy he had never been able to learn to dive: hardly to swim. Yet he was a big red-headed chap that those who measure men by redness and by size would have considered fairly imposing as a physical specimen. It requires almost a professional colour-matcher, as a matter of fact, to discriminate between the different reds. (167)

Here the narrator derides a scale of manliness calibrated on redness and size, implying that such inferences are outdated and comical. The arch tone further insinuates doubt that such "winged," angelic soldiers could possibly exist (167). Yet if the observer–narrator mocks this notion of non-corporeal men, he does not seriously question the accompanying ideal of emotional remoteness. Instead, he pokes fun at Cairn and sometimes at himself, as if to show independence even from his own judgments—meanwhile honoring the ideal of detachment all the more. He still tries to read womanhood and manhood along a scale from lowly dependence to lofty self-sufficiency.

Whereas women supposedly seek stasis, and men, activity, men may not really desire all kinds of motion. Cairn did not want to fly up into the air. He had thought that only women were weak and objectified, but then the shell tossed him around like a flimsy object. He has discovered that he would be content after all to settle down in a safe niche on earth. Even more than the fear of death, the threat of "renewed monotonous actions" deters Cairn from returning to the front (168). He prefers not to be turned into a bored robot, manipulated by an even bigger, robotic war machine, which will finally pulverize him, after playing with him as its doll. However, instead of recognizing the falsity of the old gender divisions, which would put all passivity onto Dolly, Cairn keeps the dividing lines in place, but then secretly worries that he has strayed to the womanly side.

Nevertheless, Cairn has begun to notice that it is impossible for a man to behave as expected—actively, fearlessly—in this particular war. He knows that the old male model of "a century ago," the strong yet gentlemanly officer hero, has been "superannuated" by the mechanization of battle in World War I (168). "Gentlemen" die in droves. Yet to compensate for the lost ideal, Cairn revives an even older model, something he calls a "real savage" (170).

Cairn explains this ideal by way of a confused theory of animals and the problems that he says urbanized men experience without them. At first it appears that men could learn from the example of animals' good sense, but then Cairn wishes that he had grown up not so much observing animals as killing them. On the one hand, he suggests that the "patient backs of beasts" could receive the human "instinct" to give blows, as if animals could deflect the aggression of humans from other people (169). On the other hand, maybe the hunting of animals does not replace the beating of humans so much as prepare for it. For Cairn implies that if he had been taught to hunt, now as a soldier he would be better able to transfer that violence to the enemy, without the scruples that evidently plague him. Here Cairn echoes a turn-of-the-century craze for hunting as a prescription for recovering manhood. One American congressman, William Kent, could give a sigh of relief after bagging the quarry: "It's good to be a barbarian . . . and you know that if you are a barbarian, you are at any rate a man" (qtd. in Kimmel, *Manhood* 136). Cairn, who regards modern men (including himself) as only "sham" barbarians, envies the "real" savages in the hazy past (170). Presumably, "real" savages were "real" men, who knew how to kill both men and beasts without a qualm (170).

Caught in several contradictions, Cairn does his best to resemble this earthly savage, though earlier he sought to soar as an unearthly, winged, free agent. Moreover, this savage must hail from primitive times, though Cairn initially condescended to women (and dogs) because they were more primitive than civilized men. But Cairn ignores these contradictions and barrels off toward savagery because he imagines his ideal caveman never worrying about the future, never regretting the past, never caring about a soul. Cairn himself does all these things, but, because he has assigned such feelings to women, he thinks that he has to deny them.

In fact, Cairn is so afraid of admitting his need, and so unwilling to face grief if the object of his affections should be taken away, that he pushes away his own loved ones. To end the suspense of a possible future rejection from his sweetheart, he dismisses her himself. To end his anxiety that Carp might be abused if left at home or shot if taken to the front, he undertakes a kind of preemptive strike. Just before he returns to the trenches, Cairn gets the dog out of his life—by savagely shooting it. Although this turn of events appears to shock

Fraser, the shooting logically concludes his advice all along, to harden one's heart.

Because Carp's name resembles his master's, Cairn appears to be trying to blast away parts of himself. Yet when he targets emotions such as anxiety, love, and grief, supposed to be present exclusively in doglike women, Cairn commits some fundamental violence against himself as well. After he breaks off his relationship with his sweetheart, he bitterly regrets his decision. Similarly dissatisfied when he shoots the dog, he is so upset by its screams that he has to postpone his return to his unit for two more weeks. When he finally does go, he is resigned to die, as if death were the only fit retribution for Carp's death. He thinks that he deserves to be punished, but he cannot admit the reason. He frets that he "aimed too low," not that he aimed at all, acknowledging only lack of technical skill, construed as manly (172). Confronted by the prolonged suffering of his pet, however, he compounds his failure as a marksman (in his friend's eyes as well as his own) when he "sobbed in a deep howling way, that reminded Fraser of a dog" (172). Recounting the story of Cairn to the narrator with a "wealth of friendly savagery," Fraser presumably ranks himself with the real savages (safe at home though he is), whereas he condescends to Cairn, despite affection for him, as sham and sick (167). Because Cairn misses Dolly and sobs at the pain of the dog, his business partner brands him weak, doglike, womanly.

Less censuring than Fraser, the narrator finds Cairn interesting, but only as an oddball. Unlike another soldier whose dog is a "suburban appendage" and whose destiny therefore had "nothing sultry in its lines," Cairn attracts the narrator by his rare exoticism (167). Nevertheless, despite this relegation of Cairn to the status of anomaly, one could see in him a startlingly typical case. Cairn may well reveal a common motive pushing Western men, Allies and Central Powers alike, to consent to World War I. To prove that he would remain emotionless if Carp were to die, Cairn kills the dog himself. To stop the agony of waiting for the world to blow up, he will, paradoxically, help blow it up himself. Contemporary definitions of manhood lead men to kill creatures whom they might have cherished, simply to prove they don't care. But then, because they do secretly care, the lie of masculine detachment contributes to war in a second way. Cairn feels guilty and hence accepts death as a necessary punishment. Unable to express love—not for woman, man, or beast—since love is a "feminine" feeling, Cairn is left to pursue his "sultry" affair with the war itself. And, a mere two weeks after his return to the front, death will embrace him.

Like Lewis's "The French Poodle," Faulkner's "All the Dead Pilots" shows men fighting solely to prove manhood. When World War I ended before Faulkner could finish his air force training in Canada, he apparently regretted this missed test so much that he falsified information about his service (Tate 294). In the story, the American Sartoris joins the Royal Air Force and at least gets shipped overseas, where he directs his antagonism not toward the German enemy but toward his squadron commander, Captain Spoomer. They compete over two women, Kit in London and 'Toinette in Amiens; yet, despite the supposed centrality of these prizes, the men actively focus on the only relationship of real importance to them: the tussle with the other man. In specific imagery, each pilot strives to reduce his rival to a symbolic woman. Such a transformation will, they think, confirm the victor as "the" man.

As the supposedly treasured goal of all intrigues and battles, the women remain denigrated objects. This status emerges indirectly from the core of Faulkner's comedy, a yarn about Spoomer's beloved pet. In both Lewis's and Faulkner's stories, men's affection for dogs parallels and even surpasses any closeness to women. Yet as Carp in his similarities to Dolly only reminds Cairn of the woman whom he fears he might turn into, here too Spoomer's dog serves as a kind of alter ego. When the captain leaves the base, he locks up the dog; Sartoris lets it out and observes its behavior. If the dog trots off to Amiens, Sartoris knows that its owner has gone there too, to sleep with 'Toinette. If Spoomer is only loitering somewhere near camp, the dog, with almost psychic attunement, bides its time before the master's return by rooting in a nearby refuse bin for "plebeian food" (33). The link with Spoomer implies that the officer, trotting off to the bed of a woman who usually entertains only enlisted men, must himself be rooting in the leavings of "plebeians." 'Toinette, nominally elevated to a pedestal, first loses all individualized personality and then, a shell, sinks to the level of the rubbish bin.

This disdain for women under a superficial veneration is further revealed by Sartoris's method of marking his victories over men. While Captain Spoomer lies in bed with 'Toinette, Sartoris steals his clothes, so that the captain has to creep back to base wearing her skirt and shawl. As a preliminary punishment, Sartoris had already dressed a drunken ambulance driver in Spoomer's tunic, maybe to get Spoomer accused of drunkenness. Yet the real *coup de grâce* is to make Spoomer dress as a woman. Sartoris similarly marks a victory over a French corporal, yet another suitor, by feminizing him. The Frenchman kicks at Sartoris, "striking for his pelvis"; Sartoris can tell that he has won the fight when the corporal begins to "scream like a woman" (39). Although the chivalric language elsewhere in the story paints women as superior beings, for men to dress like a woman or sound like a woman reduces them to obvious inferior status, the ultimate demotion.

All the pilots desperately try to deny socially designated feminine traits. Both men and women in the story seek out multiple sexual partners, yet the men cannot accept this similarity. Sartoris resents 'Toinette if she has "betrayed" him with Spoomer, whereas he does not worry at all that by copulating with 'Toinette, he has betrayed Kit, "one of those three-day wives and three-year widows," acquired in England (34, 31). Any affinity, once recognized, would upset his trained sense of gender difference and hierarchy. The one real distinction between their drive for multiple partners, 'Toinette's likely economic need during the war, never occurs to him.

Yet even as the characters seem to accept the apparent fixity of gender assignments, the prevalence of dress-up in the story suggests an alternative understanding. Perhaps people can don and doff gender roles that are much more fluid than the pilots' society assumes. Sartoris's very name, sounding sartorial, argues that the man is the clothes, or that the gender is "performative," as Judith Butler says, putting *everyone* in permanent drag (95). In addition to the scenes where Spoomer has to slip on a woman's skirt and the ambulance driver finds himself wearing Spoomer's uniform, Sartoris dresses an English corporal in the tunic of a captain (Spoomer's rank) to practice boxing. For this practice match, Sartoris also attaches a woman's garter to the tunic, presumably to signal that Spoomer might now be wearing the colors of his lady, and that Sartoris intends to win back her garter and her allegiance for himself (31). Combined with Spoomer's costume changes, however, Sartoris's boxing apparel looks ambiguous. Is the man with the garter a medieval knight advertising the colors of his lady *for* her? Or is he a human being close to recognizing that he—or any man—could *be* her?

If such similarities between men and women—in vulnerability, or multiple partners—cannot quite be admitted to conscious attention, the story nevertheless lays bare gender ideologies that may help fuel wars. First, the story reveals that men may not be fighting for the public good but solely to bolster private egos trained to be unsure of manhood. Second, in a revival of the Apollo Syndrome, each man uses sexual brashness with women to convince others (and himself) that he will later muster adequate aggressiveness against the enemy: in the process characterizing women as enemy too. Third, the role reversals explode the expected polarizations of feminine and masculine—skirts versus trousers, colored ribbons versus plainness, chastity versus sexual prowess—into human possibilities, available to men and women alike.

Just as Lewis's "The French Poodle" tries to bracket Cairn as an exotic freak, Faulkner's story also isolates Sartoris and Spoomer as humorous bumblers. Nevertheless, in both stories of supposedly rare oddballs, the authors may inadvertently provide a key to understanding a much more widespread consent to World War I. Because the men have been made desperate to prove manhood according to social definitions that no human being can (or should) meet, such as detachment from caring, the soldiers agree to launch the shells and try to dissociate themselves from the resulting damage. Yet those shells come home, as both Cairn and Sartoris discover, when they meet their appropriately distanced, offstage deaths.

While Cairn and Sartoris were dying for a by-no-means certain status as "the" man in Europe, whites back in America were busy dismissing Negroes as "half-men" (Du Bois 13). As we saw in chapter 1, "half-men" also occupied an ambiguous turf between sexual "inversion" and cowardice. Weighing how best to parry this all-purpose slur, W. E. B. Du Bois debated whether Negroes should answer a call to fight to make a faraway world "safe for democracy," when America made life neither democratic nor safe for Negroes at home (Hatch and Shine 92, 94). His impassioned question was taken up by Alice Dunbar-Nelson in her wonderfully open-ended play *Mine Eyes Have Seen*. When Chris receives his draft notice, he angrily asserts that he owes more duty to take care of his dependent sister, Lucy, and crippled older brother, Dan, than to fight for a country that has "let my father's murder go unpunished" (171). Protesting against horrific lynching—5,000 Negroes murdered between 1880 and 1930 (Jennings)—Chris further resents America for giving him only the "fragment of an education" and no "chances for making a man out of myself," burdening him instead with the hated label, "only half a man" (171).

To help Chris decide whether to accept military service, Dunbar-Nelson provides him with examples of other marginalized groups confronted by similar dilemmas in the war. An Irish immigrant neighbor, Mrs. O'Neill, cannot let herself dwell on the irony that her husband died for the same British government which refused to grant the couple's native Ireland independence. A sickly Jewish youth, Jake, knows that both Jews and Negroes have suffered persecution, but he hates hearing the downtrodden complain and wishes that the army would accept him too. Chris, unimpressed by either example, insists that his duty is to family, not to politicians who deal out "a hand here, in the Somme—a hand there, in Palestine," then, when the game goes wrong, lay out and "discard" a million new men (171).

As Chris contemplates resisting the draft, his sweetheart Julia at first encourages this rebellion. However, when she hears atrocity stories, that Germans "crucified children" and raped women, she switches her opinion (173). Lucy too begins to urge her brother to fight, for "humanity" and the "good name" of his race (173). All along, Dan has pushed Chris to don a uniform, proudly recalling Negroes' participation (often unacknowledged) in America's earlier wars (172). Yet, ironically, Dan's concern for race duty is bound up with a conception of manhood that exactly duplicates the oppressor's definitions.

That is, whenever Chris says he'll stay home with his disabled brother, a poor "shell of a man," Dan's own sense of manhood is so threatened by this characterization that he furiously refuses to be "the excuse, the women's skirts for a slacker to hide behind" (171). Dan deflects onto Chris his own fear that his status as invalid might dress him in skirts, an analogy available because his Victorian inheritance places all women on a hysterical edge of invalidism. If Chris hesitates to fight, Dan sees only passiveness, not active choice. This insinuation angers the younger brother in turn. At the end of the play, Chris again clenches his fist hearing the "two names" that "no man ought to have to take" (173). Although he means "slacker" and "weakling," it's clear from "skirts" that the two slurs boil down to that most terrifying name of all, "woman," assumed to be indolent and weak.

The play ends ambiguously, with Chris's family and neighbors leaning rapturously from a window to drink in the martial music from a passing band, while Chris stands apart in the center of the room: not yet with them, but perhaps swayed by their arguments to fight. Nevertheless, Dunbar-Nelson shrewdly hints that if Chris does indeed accept his draft, he will be going to war not primarily out of concern over a specifically German threat, but out of a need to establish Negro manhood identical to Caucasian manhood. He seems able to consider himself a "whole" man only on whites' terms, which require fighting for fighting's sake.

Ironically, when Negroes did enlist in World War I, white officers often denied them the chance for the all-important proof of manhood through fighting. Unlike the French, who, as Barbusse's novel shows, habitually sent soldiers from the colonies to the farthest forward lines, American officers kept Negroes mainly behind the lines, in supply work. Both treatments, of course, deeply denigrated blacks, as undependable or expendable. When American Negroes came home, their bitterness—at military attitudes and at increased Ku Klux Klan attacks—broke out in rioting in the "Red Summer" of 1919 (Hatch and Shine 175). Responding to these developments, Mary Burrill's play *Aftermath* depicts a soldier, John, who returns to find his father lynched. John's desire for revenge frightens his family, but Burrill sardonically has him summarize the lessons of war for both black and white manhood: " 'But I say unto you, love your enemies'. . . That ain't the dope they been feedin' us soljers on! 'Love your enemies'? It's been—git a good aim at 'em an' let huh go!" (180). The "her" "let go" is the gun, mechanism of destruction personified as feminine and proudly controlled by the man, while real women are let go from the equation for worth, which now requires armed violence as the infallible test of both manhood and citizenship.

As Hazel Carby argues in her study *Race Men*, novels by angry black North Americans and Caribbeans in the postwar 1920s and 1930s imagined rebellion as both violent and specifically male: "the energy that a male revolutionary hero needs for an act of rebellion is the same he uses in the sexual act; it comes from a reservoir easily depleted by women, who therefore threaten to be a potential drain on the power of manhood" (Carby 127). Like Lewis's Cairn, who must distance himself from the feminizing influences of Dolly, these revolutionaries are caught in the Antony Syndrome, which holds that intercourse with women hinders the fight. At the same time, however, the black fighters assume, like Faulkner's Sartoris in his Apollo Syndrome, that violence advertises and ensures male heterosexual potency; one character, for instance, "knew the feeling of warm blood . . . knew, as well, that his scythe-sword was ready to drink. He could feel the thing getting stiffer and stiffer in his hand" (qtd. in Carby 128). Eerily, if the radical "race man" can do without the depleting female body, he also seems able to do without his own male body, which the weapon replaces. Meanwhile, as Lewis's story shows, some white soldiers were revising their old epithet for Africans, "savage," into a compliment for bold fighting. Yet whites who appropriated "savage" as armor for themselves could not, any more than black men, stomach comparison to that most primitive creature, woman.

(b) I Fight to Prove I'm Not Attracted to Men (but I Do Want to See Male Bodies)

If recruits such as Lewis's Cairn, Faulkner's Sartoris, and Dunbar-Nelson's Chris went to war to avoid the taunt of "sissy" ("sister" construed to mean cowardly and weak by nature), men were also beginning to fear another connotation for "sissy," homosexual. After the sexologists at the turn of the century declared that male "inverts" all "approach the feminine type" (Ellis 119), any man brave enough to accept the emerging label "homosexual" would find it already stigmatized with the inferiorizing connotation "effeminate." To counter that taint, poems by Wilfred Owen carefully link homoeroticism with social codes for manliness—especially fighting.

Yet even as men were enlisting to prove that they were not womanly, including no public erotic interest in male bodies, mobilization ironically provided many opportunities for viewing beautiful male flesh. In a scene that occurs almost ritualistically in the literature of World War I, writers such as Erich Maria Remarque, Frederic Manning, and (much later) Pat Barker ceremoniously disclose an assembly of naked men: at latrines, baths, lice-picking sessions, or medical examinations. Interestingly, an ability to find a wartime comfort in the sight and closeness of comrades' naked bodies seems available to all soldiers, regardless of primary sexual orientation. In fact, this reaction puts in doubt the strict categories that the sexologists were busy codifying, suggesting instead a malleability of sexual responses.

Nowadays, critics sometimes associate the British war poet Wilfred Owen with homosexuality through facts of his life, such as frequenting the circle of Robbie Ross, known as "Oscar Wilde's champion" (Hibberd 59–61). References to homoeroticism in the poetry itself are rare but powerful. However, even as Owen sketches a few bold, if indirect, expressions for his desire, the poetry remains imprinted by conventional notions of manliness. The persistence of contemporary gender terminology in "Storm" and "Apologia Pro Poemate Meo" ("defense of my poem") complicates Owen's protest against the war, for it is the war that permits him to fulfill some of the requirements for manhood, and it is military life that throws him into a new intimacy with men.

In one of Owen's few clearly homoerotic poems, the striking sonnet "Storm" (written in October, 1916, after a year's military training in England), the speaker compares the beauty in the face of another man to lightning in a cloud. He likens himself to a tree "shadowed" by that cloud and by its "brilliant danger" that could blast him open (60). Although he knows that contact with this man could call down the scorn of the community, the speaker quietly accepts his *coup de foudre* (French for love at first sight): "So must I tempt that face to loose its lightning" (60). Even when he pictures the kind of spurning that Oscar Wilde endured twenty years earlier, the speaker daringly embraces risk: "What matter if all men cry out and start, / And women hide their faces in their shawl, / At those hilarious thunders of my fall?" (60). In an incredible rush of power, he recoups his anticipated social downfall by transforming the sound of the tree crashing into a new thundering, which can then answer the lightning of the lover, in a sky-wide hilarity of erotic play.

This thunder simultaneously elevates the earthly lover to the level of a god, like Zeus the thunderer, for at "the opening of my heart" and the consuming of "my sap," the speaker asserts that the "Great gods, whose beauty is death, will laugh" (60). Whereas a Christian God might be presumed to laugh at him, perpetrating a bad joke by making his creature desire men instead of the scripturally more acceptable female helpmate, the Greek and Roman gods laugh *with* and delight in their own male lovers: Apollo with Hyacinthus, Jove with Ganymede. Just as John Addington Symonds tried to gain respect for modern homosexuals by pointing to the ancient Greeks, who approved some same-sex practices, so too does Owen find backing in the classics, especially mythology.

In Ovid's *Metamorphoses*, the gods themselves have affairs with men, yet disaster hounds even these heaven-blessed liaisons. Apollo accidentally kills Hyacinthus with a discus. The thunderer Jove, as a "flashing, warlike eagle," ravishes the handsome Ganymede and carries him off to Olympus (278–79). Ganymede may ascend to the realm of the gods, but he must also die to his life on earth. Ovid further reinforces the sense of threat accompanying homosexuality by assigning these stories of the gods' fatal affairs to the singer Orpheus, whom the Maenads soon tear apart—out of jealousy, Ovid claims, because Orpheus slept only with boys after Eurydice's death (276, 299). Like Ganymede, Owen's speaker in "Storm" experiences "unearthly brightening" from his Jove's lightning bolt, but he senses danger (60). Nevertheless, this poem alluding to the classics declares that homosexuality is a god-made ecstasy, not a sin.

In this celebratory vein, the poet dreams that along with the lightning will come rain, and the "land shall freshen that was under gloom" (60). While he may suggest that his gloomy life anticipating the trenches will improve with the advent of this unnamed man with the beautiful face, he also briefly envisions the renewal of a wider land. Mythically, some ancient cultures interpreted the life-giving rain as the semen of a sky god (Graves, *Greek Myths* 1. 31). Socially, Owen may echo the contemporary reformer Edward Carpenter, who hoped that his long-term relationship with the laborer George Merrill would light the way to others seeking the "New Life" of more humane sexual and economic relations in England (Rowbotham and Weeks 27). Yet even the forthright Carpenter, who made "no secret" of his sex life to pilgrims flocking to his cottage, still had to camouflage his printed defenses of homosexuality in "vagueness" to avoid illegality, and he faced alarming harassment, particularly between 1908 and 1910 (Rowbotham and Weeks 88). If Owen can, like Carpenter, at moments optimistically herald a future freshening and flowering for all lovers, the poem also realistically admits the havoc of present-day persecution. Moreover, the poem grimly acknowledges Owen's own limited prospects, as a soldier in 1916, for love or life at all.

In fact, when the last stanza begins, "And happier were it if my sap consume," the line shimmers through a spectrum of moods (60). By inviting the lightning to strike him, the speaker may agree to risk his reputation for this liaison, to let his semen flow and be spent. Yet he may also despairingly imply that it would be better to be killed in the war, for after the taste of an affair like this one, afforded by military conditions, what kind of civilian life could he return to? If the speaker is acquiescing in his own death, in part because his society makes no place for these godlike lovers at home, then the war horribly reappropriates the "hilarious thunders of my fall," which he had bravely wrenched from catastrophe (60). A puritan society can make even the thunder of the lethal shells welcome in some ways, and so drown out any further protest, against sexual discrimination or war.

When the defiantly "hilarious thunders" of "Storm" reappear a year later in the "glee" of Owen's "Apologia" (November, 1917), the unexpected "laughs" amidst the slaughter carry some of the same erotic currents, under the overt focus on emotional camaraderie. These ties between men are said to be better than the bond between traditional lovers: "For love is not the binding of fair lips / With the soft silk of eyes that look and long, // By Joy, whose ribbon slips,—/ But wound with war's hard wire whose stakes are strong" (101–02). Yet if Owen boldly uses hilarity and laughter as a kind of code for a vivacious kindling of erotic interest between men, newly conceptualizable, he maintains his society's old gender hierarchies quite conservatively. Like Ellis, the poet links women with passivity (they can "look and long," not act), weakness (their "ribbon slips"), and decorativeness (even their animate features, "eyes," become indistinguishable from inanimate, status-bestowing objects, "silk"). He keeps women "soft" and men "hard," with all the positive connotations for hardness that the English literary tradition bequeaths: muscular, unsentimental, disciplined. Whereas John Milton had borrowed classical images of a delicate vine winding around the hard tree to represent Eve's clinging to Adam (Sammons 117), Owen refashions the conjugal trope to apply to two male partners, by endowing both the wire and the stake with phallic hardness; a slang dictionary of 1893 lists "hard-bit" or "bit of hard" for an erection (*OED*, 1989 ed.).

However, as soon as Owen even hints an erotic embrace, he must, like Symonds in "A Problem in Greek Ethics," scramble to spare these two men the "taint" of effeminacy. To do so, he must adopt the whole manly baggage of *hard*: not only erect but uncaring.

Hence, the poet can rejoice that in battle men achieve the remorseless disdain for life that has been designated masculine: "power was on us as we slashed bones bare" (101). Yet he is honest enough to admit that the soldiers are really engaged in "murder," which cannot be construed to serve any higher purpose: "death becomes absurd and life absurder" (101). The speaker exults to have "dropped off Fear," yet he shrewdly recognizes this courage as really despair, since men attain that state only beyond "the entanglement where hopes lay strewn" (101). He further thrills to have "sailed my spirit surging light and clear" over the carnage, as Lewis's Cairn expected his Aristotelian manly spirit to soar free and detached above the battle. Yet Owen is again perceptive enough to locate the origin of this masculine freedom in the numbness of fatigue, "dead as my platoon" (101). Nevertheless, although he can identify all bravery as a kind of optical illusion, an exhausted not-caring-any-more that simply looks like caring-for-some-cause, Owen (along with the rest of the soldiers) still needs these tricks of supposed power and fearlessness and active agency, to validate manhood.

If early-twentieth-century men could not refrain from the fight or show mutual erotic attachment, because their society defined both making peace and loving men as womanly, the war ironically provided many opportunities to view male nakedness (Bourke 129). Such closeness seems to comfort not only men who are aware of their homoerotic interest, but also quite a few other soldiers—no matter what their sexual orientation. In a striking convention, many novelists of World War I ceremoniously present nakedness at latrines, baths, and lice-picking sessions. Erich Maria Remarque's description of common latrines in *All Quiet on the Western Front* (1928) sets out the contradictory tone that governs such scenes. On the one hand, authorities seem to be stripping bodies so as to impose surveillance, control, or humiliation. On the other hand, soldiers who find themselves exposed may not feel cowed after all, as they discover the joys of being naked men together. Yet this enjoyment may not defy controlling authorities as much as it appears. The men may simply be yielding to an even more insidious manipulation, for the war machine appropriates sensual pleasure into a further lure to war.

Remarque's narrator, Paul, describes a common latrine, roofed, and individual boxes that can be lined up outdoors for the same purpose (7–10). In the first case, twenty men sit side by side on a pole. The builder has omitted partitions and doors, not for lack of material, but to ensure that "they could be reviewed all at one glance, for soldiers must always be under supervision" (7). Yet if the goal is to prevent something—theft of army goods? escape without leave? masturbation? clandestine homosexual encounters?—the system does create some pleasures not obtainable in civilian life. Especially outside in the open air, the men shed their trained modesty and learn to appreciate common physicality: "I no longer understand why we should always have shied at these things before" (8).

Remarque makes this scene especially idyllic, as the friends draw up their toilets in a circle, gossip, play cards. The "three boxes stand in the midst of the glowing, red field-poppies" and the "wind plays with our hair," while the recruits gloat over Kemmerich's "good" wound, which will let him go home, and watch the "little white clouds of the anti-aircraft shells" (9–10). After just a few pages, Kemmerich dies of his wound, and incoming shells turn out to be not so innocent. Nevertheless, if Remarque magnifies the gentle sensuousness of the boxes to highlight the later horrors, some of the delight survives as a genuine, valued memory of the war. Defecating together outdoors is better than sitting privately, even in a "palatial white-tiled 'convenience.' *There* it can only be hygienic; *here* it is beautiful" (9). That beauty derives from the countryside, but also from the solace of being unashamed bodies together.

Another World War I author who dwells on the pleasures of communal nakedness is Frederic Manning. Encouraged by the success of Remarque's novel, Manning finally wrote his long ruminated *The Middle Parts of Fortune* in six months, publishing it privately and anonymously (1929), as well as in an expurgated version, called *Her Privates We* (Marwil 253, 259). Manning's *Middle Parts* shows the British soldiers experiencing the war in much the same way as their German counterparts: enduring boredom in the trenches, fending off rats, resenting their own officers as the most visible enemy, pilfering food, and slogging on in order to defend immediate buddies rather than preserve some grand principle blazoned by governments. Just as Remarque includes a comforting scene of physical togetherness at the latrines, Manning depicts a playful, naked group at divisional baths, in the cut-down casks of a brewery.

> At first the taunts and pranks at the baths may seem designed to humiliate neophytes:
> "Dost turn thysen to t' wall, lad, so's us 'ns sha'n't see tha dick?"
> one man shouted at a shy young newcomer; and when the boy turned

a red and indignant face over his shoulder, he was met with derision, and another man pulled him out of the tub, and wrestled with him, slippery as they both were with soap. (53)

If the young man feels indignant, Manning insists that, "Rude and brutal as it was, there was a boisterous good-humour about it" (53). The "indecent horseplay" does not so much threaten real attack as it allows the sensuous contact of slippery bodies (53). Others join in to rescue the shy one:

> and laughing at his show of temper and humiliation, some other men intervened, and they let him slip out of their hands back to his tub, where he continued the washing of himself as modestly as he could. Finally, after fighting for the showers, they dried, dressed themselves and marched away, another company taking their place. (53)

While the lad wants to shield his body and his embarrassment, the taunters' "riotous noisiness" seems to cover over an equal nervousness at their own delight, a feigned hostility that hides enjoyment (53). In retrospect, Manning endows the scene with a healthy, diffused eroticism: "They were distinctly fresh" (53). Even the repetition of the word "and," linking clauses in a biblical cadence, reassures the reader that men's wrestling naked is just one of those things for which there is a "season" and a "purpose under the heaven" (Eccles. 3.1), despite the qualms of peacetime prelates.

Manning highlights another scene of nakedness when enlisted men strip to pick lice silently. The soldiers have just been discussing reasons for the war (141–56), as Remarque's soldiers also sit around and try to fathom why the nations of Europe are slaughtering each other (203–07). Participating in what became a whole trope of scorn against "Big Words" (Hynes, *War Imagined* 285, 296), Remarque's characters finally abandon verbal explanations as futile—"The best thing is not to talk about the rotten business" (207)—and Manning's talkers decide that high-sounding abstractions cannot justify the war, nor can verbal warnings convey its horrors to ignorant civilians back home (152).

Instead, in Manning's scene of lice-picking, the ineffectual words subside before the unanswerable preciousness of bodies, like the demonstration of the host at communion:

> Glazier took his tunic and shirt off, and began to hunt for lice. One after another they all followed his example, stripping themselves of trousers, underpants and even socks, until the tent held nothing but naked men. They would take a candle, or a lighted match, and pass it along the

seams of their trousers, hoping that the flame would destroy the eggs. A hurricane lamp hung by a nail on the tent-pole, and after it was lighted they still continued the scrupulous search, its light falling on white shoulders studiously rounded as they bent over the task. (Manning 156)

The men know that basking in the glow of flesh is better than shredding it for duty, and that naked bodies are better than perpetually armored ones. Yet when a "wailing sigh" and a nearby explosion interrupt the men, causing them to dress and disperse, the author almost seems to need the whining shell to legitimate his idyll (156). If a room of naked men had lounged together by candlelight back in England, the police would probably be raiding it; a series of laws in 1885, 1898, and 1912 against "gross indecency between men" increased prosecutions for vague infractions (Weeks, *Sex* 102). If camaraderie is better than killing, killing seems to be the only context in which England allows a fleeting, doomed warmth of bodies together.

Paul Fussell finds such scenes of naked soldiers picking lice or bathing so prevalent in World War I literature that he designates them a "set-piece" (*Modern Memory* 299). He traces the convention to poetry by Uranians (a movement recommending pederasty) and to Walt Whitman's lines about male bathers (304). He then speculates that war poets adapted this already popularized tradition for two reasons: to underline the poignant contrast between vulnerable flesh and the iron that will tear it (299), and to continue the sensuality that Fussell calls "homoerotic rather than riskily homosexual" (305). Writing a fictional trilogy of the Great War in the 1990s, Pat Barker pays homage to earlier writers by alluding to these set-pieces, yet she significantly varies them. Whereas for Fussell the display of skin allows the men to escape the war for a moment and heightens the contrast with slaughter, for Barker the State horrifyingly appropriates the naked body, exciting but then rechanneling sexual energy to fuel the war.[2]

Just as Manning has his soldiers review reasons for the war, then abandon words as they strip together, Barker pointedly juxtaposes the men's discussion of possible causes for the catastrophe with their observation of a nude comrade floating in a garden pool. Barker's characters—Prior, Owen, Potts, and Hallet—speculate about official or ulterior motives for the conflict, using many of the same arguments as Manning's characters (149–56) or Remarque's (203–07). In Barker's version, Potts blames economic greed, "feathering the nests of profiteers" and ensuring "access to the oil-wells of Mesopotamia" (*Ghost* 143). Prior, by contrast, finds even Potts's "conspiracy theory" too "optimistic," as it assumes that *someone* is benefiting; actually,

"Nobody benefits. Nobody's in control" (143–44). Shocked at the cynicism of his companions, Hallet points to the defense of "Belgian neutrality" and "French independence" and insists, "like a little boy," "This is still a just war" (144).

Barker, however, adds to her predecessors' explanations an interesting further cause for war, in attitudes toward the body, a connection that hovered over earlier World War I literature but only implicitly. Her character Owen comments mysteriously, "You say we kill the Beast [Germany] . . . I say we fight because men lost their bearings in the night" (*Ghost* 144). In 1918, Sassoon wrote a poem containing the lines "You swear we crush The Beast: I say we fight / Because men lost their landmarks in the night." He sent the poem to Owen, who could quote it by heart (Hibberd 120). Barker uses these lines to condense the implied argument in all three novels of her trilogy. Because men have lost their way to the bed and the heart, which they cannot reach unashamed or express unhindered, they are more likely to be flailing at each other in a war. That is, external prohibitions and internalized repressions (of all sex, but especially of polymorphous attractions) have contributed to war: by displacing eroticism into any available intensity and by offering the brief compensation of a male intimacy rarely allowable in peacetime.

Just as in Manning's novel verbal explanations for the war fade into irrelevancy before silent bodies, so too in Barker's novel abstract speeches dissipate in the face of physical human presence. Owen's last, cryptic assessment about lost bodies in the night is immediately illustrated when Owen, Prior, and Potts discover Hallet in the familiar World War I set-piece of observed bathing: "As they watched, not calling out a greeting as by now they should have done, he stepped out of his drawers and out of time . . . . He was going to lie down in the overgrown goldfish pool with its white lilies and golden insects fumbling the pale flowers" (*Ghost* 146–47).

Barker prepares this interlude by sending the observers through the back gardens of abandoned houses, telling us outright that the men are leaving the "comparative normality of the road" (*Ghost* 145). There, one assumes, prudent and prudish citizens trudged to commercial jobs and kept buttoned up. Now, however, the trampers reenter a primitive, sensual "labyrinth of green pathways" (145). Yet if they have broken down literal fences and some figurative boundaries marking out industrious job and modest privacy, so that Hallet can float idly and his friends gaze appreciatively, other barriers remain rigidly in place:

> They strolled across the tall grass towards him and stood looking down.
> Legs bloated-looking under water, silver bubbles trapped in his hair,

cock slumped on his thigh like a seal hauled out on to the rocks. He looked up at them lazily, fingers straying through his bush, freeing the bubbles.

"Enjoying yourself?" Prior asked, nodding at the hand.

Hallet laughed, shielding his eyes with his other hand, but didn't move.

"I'd be careful if I were you," Owen said, in a tight voice. "I expect those fish are ravenous."

And not just the fish, Prior thought. (*Ghost* 147)

Owen tightly represses any sexual overture toward Hallet, or even toward the omnisexual Prior; both Owen and Prior must remain incognito before their friends.[3] The insects might be "fumbling the pale flowers," but the men have learned that they should not be fumbling each other (147).

Nevertheless, whereas Hallet's society officially forbids any of the men to enjoy their sexuality with him directly, Barker hypothesizes that this same society often smuggles disapproved pleasures back into its midst, as long as they appear in disguised or displaced form through the military machine. Somebody seems to be getting a secret thrill out of assembling all that male flesh. The military doctor Mather at Prior's medical exam starts with the rectum—"They always went for the arse, Prior thought"—and the doctor makes another "unduly intimate gesture" when Prior turns around (*Ghost* 9). Is the search for hemorrhoids and venereal disease really all that motivates Mather? As Prior grumbles in the privacy of his mind, "Better men than you have paid for this" (9). Perhaps Prior misjudges Mather, who may be entirely professional, but it is not so much individuals who misuse Prior, but rather a whole system that manipulates both doctors and soldiers to obtain touch in surreptitious ways. As Michel Foucault speculates, a vast apparatus of surveillance spies on its charges' sexuality not so much to stamp out "perversions" as to savor the forbidden sexuality voyeuristically, by "caressing them [bodies] with its eyes" (*History* 1: 42, 44):

The medical examination, the psychiatric investigation, the pedagogical report, and family controls may have the over-all and apparent objective of saying no to all wayward or unproductive sexualities, but the fact is that they function as mechanisms with a double impetus: pleasure and power. The pleasure that comes of exercising a power that questions, monitors, watches, spies, searches out, palpates, brings to light; and on the other hand, the pleasure that kindles at having to evade this power, flee from it, fool it, or travesty it. The power that lets itself be invaded by the pleasure it is pursuing; and opposite it, power asserting itself in the pleasure of showing off, scandalizing, or resisting . . . all have played this game continually since the nineteenth century. (*History* 1: 45)

Certainly Prior, during his stay at Craiglockhart Hospital for shell-shock, gains back some of the power and dignity he loses to the doctors by "showing off" and "scandalizing" Dr. Rivers, flaunting a sexual allure which he senses that Rivers is attracted to but determined to ignore. Yet Prior's little "game" of survival does not distract Barker from the much more dangerous games played by a militarized society, which sneaks itself some pleasure within "perpetual spirals of power and pleasure" (Foucault, *History* 1: 45), a substitute "screw" which also ensures that soldiers get "screwed."

Barker creates several other important scenes where military routine offers its participants secret erotic pleasures. Her description of divisional baths belongs to the same genre as Manning's divisional baths in the brewery casks or Remarque's latrines. Whereas the intimate medical exam put Prior, unasked, in the position of the observed and penetrated, the baths reverse the roles and let him, as officer, observe the naked men. Although he touches no one, he feels guilty because he has in the past entertained a sexual fantasy of approaching a naked man while himself remaining clothed. At the baths, Prior thinks at first that other officers, presumably exclusive heterosexuals, or homosexuals with a different fantasy life, do not feel his discomfort at occupying a voyeuristic, unequal, and intrusive position. However, it suddenly dawns on him that for everyone, no matter what his imputed sexual orientation, the scene may well be exciting: "Whole bloody western front's a wanker's paradise" (*Ghost* 177). The military situation provides a convenient excuse to exhibit the vista of naked male bodies. Such a spectacle may then entice an otherwise inhibited society to go on recreating the gratifying scene: that is, to go on recruiting, drilling, and unclothing its specimens. Again, the agent of manipulation is not a few individuals but a whole hypocritical society.

At the time of Prior's epiphany about a "wanker's paradise," it also occurs to him that "Whenever a man with a fuckable arse hoves into view you can be quite certain something perfectly dreadful's going to happen" (*Ghost* 177). By allowing Prior to take this apocalyptic view, Barker implies that the Judeo-Christian West has so insistently associated guilt with sex that for many it can only be enacted sadomasochistically. War, which authorizes hurting and self-hurting on a grand scale, serves as a remarkably efficient sadomasochistic machine. This machine allows the people in it, as in all sadomasochistic situations, to express a deep but forbidden desire, yet at the same time to receive the punishment thought necessary for even the most fleeting, unsatisfactory pleasure. Military men, whatever their putative sexual orientation, can ogle the naked troops at their baths, fantasize an erotic encounter, or grope under cover of medical exams—as long as the bombs instantly blot out the evidence, prevent further development of a relationship, and punish the participants. War becomes a gigantic, culture-wide, sadomasochistic response to the unnecessarily instilled guilt of being born sexual creatures.

If Prior, of all Barker's characters, most boldly defies his society's ban against homosexual behavior, he still cannot entirely escape the coercive gaze of what Foucault calls the "disciplinary apparatus": "a perfect eye that nothing would escape and a centre towards which all gazes would be turned" (*Discipline* 173). This center defines and controls expectations for sexuality and—issues that Foucault largely ignores—gender, as well as class. Barker literalizes such an "eye in the door," the title of her second volume, in the peephole of the prison cell in which Prior's friend Beattie has been incarcerated as a pacifist. More figuratively, Beattie warns Prior that the eye is not so bad as long as it "stays in the door"; he need worry only if it gets inside his head (*Eye* 36). As Foucault theorizes, the coercion of sexuality since the Enlightenment has operated less by law and more by norming (*History* 1: 89). Through a sense of being watched and judged, people internalize the dominant ideologies of sex (and gender), along with the gaze.

Unfortunately, as Beattie suspects, the "eye in the door" does take up residence inside Prior's head, making him see as the government sees and do what he himself regards as reprehensible. In fact, when Prior turns his childhood friend Mac over to the police as a fugitive "conchie" (conscientious objector), the case bears out Foucault's contention that authorities no longer have to punish transgressors if they can induce them to police themselves (*History* 1: 89). Interestingly, the regimented students at the eighteenth-century orphanage that Foucault studies seem already headed for the army: "We found all the pupils drawn up as if for battle, in perfect alignment, immobility and silence" (qtd. in *Discipline* 177). Whereas Foucault names the military camp as the *origin* for the panoptic system of "hierarchized surveillance" used in schools, families, prisons, and asylums (*Discipline* 171), Barker underlines the camp and military service as important *goals*. Prior may have scorned all social institutions, but once he has the dominant "eye" in his own head, he ends up carrying out the bidding of the stolid Ministry of Munitions better than its most zealous supporters.

Ironically, once Prior realizes that he has conformed to the society he hates to the point of handing Mac over to the police, this recognition just consolidates his desire to get back to the war, away from an England that is corrupting him. Surprisingly, as he says good-bye to an acquaintance, he declares that the front is "the only *clean* place to be" (*Eye* 275). For all its mud and wastefully spent gore, the front is still cleaner than home, with its hysterical intolerance against suffragists and homosexuals (epitomized in the Pemberton Billing trial), its shoddy, police-state surveillance, and its disdain of the body—to the point of misinforming teens that masturbation causes tuberculosis of the spine (*Eye* 73). In this farewell conversation, Prior predicts that he will rue the day when such a "*bloody* fool" as he willingly returns to the trenches (*Eye* 276), but, in the event, he discovers, "What an utter bloody fool I would have been not to come back" (*Ghost* 258). He returns for "the fug of human warmth" and "all these faces" together (*Ghost* 256, 258). Society at home denies such closeness among men for two reasons: because emotion is supposed to be feminine and sex with men, effeminate. The front qualifies as "the only *clean* place" because it is at least honest about these needs for emotional warmth and physical touch (*Eye* 275).

Unfortunately, the war may also draw Prior because he now needs to wash himself clean. Like the cow that slips in its own feces on the way to the slaughterhouse (*Eye* 106), Prior knows that he has sullied himself by betraying Mac. As a consequence, he craves expiation, and so willingly returns to the "slaughterhouse" in France. As Foucault suspects, if a society can shift guilt inside a person, it no longer has to coerce him openly: "Finally, after long hesitations, they saw him come of his own accord to join the society of the other patients" (qtd. in *Reader* 151). In doing the penance through suffering or even death that Prior may now think necessary, he is also, conveniently, doing the bidding of the "other patients," the mad war-makers.

Discovering just how mad those war-makers are, Prior's unit must cross a canal on exposed duckboards, only days before the rumored peace; all Prior's fellow officers agree that the order is "insane" (*Ghost* 252). Barker no doubt models this situation on the death of the real Wilfred Owen at Oise-Sambre Canal, a few days before the armistice (Owen xvii). However, for her fictional version, she carefully contrasts Prior's attempt to cross a canal bank with another canal bank incident a few pages earlier, when a French teenage boy solicits sex with Prior, and he obliges (*Ghost* 248). Prior records in his diary that while he plans to tear out the account of the sexual encounter, he can leave undisturbed the pages anticipating the needless encounter with German machine-guns. If anyone found out about the teenager, prosecutors could throw Prior in jail for unlawful "indecency" (the charge against Oscar Wilde), priests could condemn him as immoral, or psychiatrists could attempt to "cure" him of "mental illness" (Weeks, *Sex* 102, 104). By contrast, Prior suspects that any civilian readers of his diary would consider the second canal bank rendezvous with the guns legitimate, moral, normal, and manly—despite its character as suicidal, murderous, and insane.

Although Barker clearly prefers the first canal bank incident to the second, she does not present the sex scene as ideal. For one thing, Prior pays the young man in cigarettes, even though he knows that paying humiliates both partners. For another, the necessary furtiveness means a bed of knotty tree roots. But if the setting is uncomfortable, at least Prior treats the boy considerately, ensuring that he experiences pleasure too. Barker further makes the coupling positive by suggesting a drive toward an almost mystical, collective unity. When the lad tries speaking German, Prior realizes that this French boy has been entertaining all the armies with his sexual favors. Although Prior thinks at first that this knowledge ought to disgust him, instead it excites him—not as a way of triumphing over his German predecessors, but as a symbolic means of merging with them. Only partly in jest, Prior quotes from Friedrich Schiller's "Ode to Joy" to express his yearning: "Oh ye millions I embrace you, / This kiss is for the whole world" (qtd. in *Ghost* 248). The mystical, exuberant offer to *kiss everyone* sounds a lot more inviting than the mandate to *kill everyone*, which must have seemed the operating principle of the World War in which Prior is caught up. Because his society wants to blot out the sexual exchange—either obliterating the record, as Prior does in his diary, or inhibiting the enactment, as Dr. Rivers has in his life—denial helps fuel wars. When a culture scarcely allows people to try even for small sexual encounters, let alone the Big Embrace of everyone, then its frustrated citizens head off toward the Big Death.

As Barker interprets them, the views of sex and gender generated by the new disciplines of psychology and sexology, along with the old attitudes fostered by religion and empire-making, contributed to World War I by making all men suspect their possible effeminacy, by locating the proof of manliness primarily in soldiering, and by combining sexual lures with training in guilt, which in turn induced a need for self-punishment. To the man (of any sexual orientation) who seeks sexual comforts but believes chastisement appropriate, war offers both; "happier were it if my sap consume," says Owen, ambiguously picturing both the tryst and the execution (60). And for the man who hopes to be accepted as "manly" but betrays his own ethical standards, precisely by meeting gender expectations (as in the case of the fictional Prior), war abundantly supplies both the perquisites and the punishments.

(c) I Fight to Prove I'm Not Emotional (but I Do Love My Comrades)

When Lewis's character Cairn goes to war to prove manliness (section (a)), he feels that he has to deny emotion, calling it womanly. Ironically, many World War I soldiers, even those disillusioned by the war, look back on a deeply emotional camaraderie as one of the most valuable experiences of their lives. Although this love defines itself as a fellowship rather than a sexual attraction, it often displays a physical dimension. Remarque's narrator Paul, for example, greets his fellow soldiers, "I could bury my face in them, in these voices" (212). He claims that comrades stand "nearer than lovers" (212), echoing the biblical bond, "passing the love of women," between David and the slain warrior Jonathan (2 Sam. 1.26). Such fierce superlatives persist in accounts of military friendships throughout the twentieth century.

An odd ambivalence charges the scenes of camaraderie in World War I literature, as if the characters were claiming, "I embrace my buddy and he dies" (death as a random intrusion), but also, "I am allowed to embrace my buddy because he dies" (death as a needed justification for the embrace). This uncertainty permeates the emotional bonds in Henri Barbusse's *Under Fire* (1917), Erich Maria Remarque's *All Quiet on the Western Front* (1928), Frederic Manning's *The Middle Parts of Fortune* (1929), and J. M. Barrie's "The New Word" (1918), as well as memoirs and poems. Frank McGuinness's much later play set in World War I, *Observe the Sons of Ulster Marching towards the Somme* (1985), is able to examine this usually unconscious ambivalence much more explicitly. Only the existence of danger seems to license the intense feeling that might otherwise invite the charge of "sissy," so that, in a horrifying way, soldiers come to love the war they hate.

Henri Barbusse's *Under Fire* sets the archetype of all such scenes that permit an embrace only in proximity to the death of one of the men. Chapter XII, "The Doorway," in the prominent center of the book, details a single day, which the first-person narrator spends with his comrade Poterloo. In the early morning, the pair slip away from their squad to visit Poterloo's demolished village, Souchez. When the two regain their trench, the narrator records their solidarity as almost

magical, punctuated by "confused delight . . . as though we were
meeting after absence," and by the modulation of Poerloo's singsong
accent into a kind of song (169). On the evening march through open
trenches, Poterloo repeatedly encourages the narrator, laughing at the
wind and rain. They learn to prize each other's physical presence,
expressed through a resonant voice, a hand to the shoulder. Finally
the book allows the two men an embrace, albeit an inadvertent one:
"We pull up sharply, and again I am thrown upon Poterloo and lean
on his back, his strong back and solid, like the trunk of a tree, like
healthfulness and like hope. He cries to me, 'Cheer up, old man, we're
there!' " (173). Just at this moment, however, the fatal shell explodes,
and the narrator sees his friend's body rise: arms outstretched, head
replaced by a flame (173).

On the one hand, for Barbusse to place the men's brief physical
contact immediately before the attack heightens the poignancy of
Poterloo's death. The apparently invincible, tree-like strength of the
back contrasts with its actual fragility, and the comfort of touch
contrasts with loss. On the other hand, this sequence uncomfortably
implies not only poignant randomness but also a kind of necessity.
The narrator seems able to report the only embrace in the book
because Poterloo dies. A doomed man deserves a little bending of the
rules of propriety.

This sense that closeness might break unwritten rules of decorum
and so require some special dispensation is reinforced by insistent
details of the physical setting during the long day. After the narrator
and Poterloo look at each other with "confused delight," they first
catch sight of the "doorway" of the chapter title:

> Two posts lean one upon the other, with a confusion of electric wires
> between them, hanging down like tropical creepers. It looks well. You
> would say it was a theatrical contrivance or scene. A slender climbing
> plant twines round one of the posts, and as you follow it with your
> glace, you see that it already dares to pass from one to the other. (169)

The slender plant that "dares" to pass between the two mutually leaning posts suggests the line of affection and touch beginning to reach
out from the narrator, who will soon lean against Poterloo's tree-like
back. Yet immediately before that closest touch, the narrator again
notices a trench doorway: "and there, rising before my eyes all at once
and towering over that rim, is something like a sinister doorway, made
of two black posts that lean upon the other, with something hanging
from the middle like a torn-off scalp" (173). The leaning posts and

hanging wires make this doorway similar to the earlier one, yet now it is "sinister." The ominous "torn-off scalp" prefigures Poterloo's decapitation in a few moments. Unfortunately, in the process of association, even the "tropical creepers" of the earlier Edenic sensuality have become implicated in danger (169). The narrator can only paint a first blush of "confused delight" and strong embrace, before the inevitable sundering (169).

Like Barbusse's narrator and Poterloo, close pairs in Remarque's *All Quiet on the Western Front* (Paul and Kat) and Manning's *The Middle Parts of Fortune* (Bourne and Martlow, Bourne and Weeper Smart) support each other emotionally, even though they have learned to scorn emotion as womanly. On home leave, Paul privately questions this assignment of stoicism to men: "Why have I always to be strong and self-controlled? I would like to weep and be comforted too, indeed I am little more than a child" (183). Nevertheless, in his mother's presence, he remains impassive. He flees her, back to the front, declaring wildly, "I ought never to have come on leave," intimating that he would rather confront the guns than the minefield of emotion, his mother's and his own (185). When a second parting from his mother hurts "much worse" than this first visit, he abruptly breaks off the chapter (269). Ten years after the war, when Remarque can finally write about horror, he still cannot find words in which his character Paul might face tenderness.

In a self-protectiveness much like Paul's, Manning's Bourne appreciates a village woman's "clear, logical, and hard" manner, which he takes to be rare; if she had been as demonstrative as he expected, her emotion might crack his own reserve (62). Bourne is surprised at her "tranquil" laugh as she listens to shells falling (62), for the soldiers more commonly class all women as cowardly and hysterical. If they find that a man displays anything less than phlegmatic, unquestioning endurance, his pals deny that he *is* a man; Bourne's companions slur a deserter, Miller, as a "twat" and a complainer as a "cunt" and a "Weeper" (208, 147). Probably because they fear that they themselves could so easily duplicate Miller or Weeper, with good reason to complain, weep, and walk away from the carnage, the rest of the men furiously name even the bodies of these outcasts womanly, to bolster the vain hope that misfits could bear no resemblance to themselves.

Although the soldiers try to foist off emotion onto women, dismissing calm or independent examples as exceptions, the men nevertheless crave the comforts of shared emotion. When Paul and Kat steal and roast a goose together, they find "a more complete communion with one another than even lovers have" (Remarque 94). Half asleep before the fire, Paul sees himself in the third person: "if anyone were to caress him he would hardly understand, this soldier with the big boots and the shut heart" (95). Yet if the war has armored Paul's heart, a moment in the firelight finds a chink through which to send a caress: "Is my face wet, and where am I?" (95). He cannot name crying directly, although he manages to honor Kat quite simply: "I love him," he says, as Kat's "gigantic, stooping shadow falls upon me, like home" (95).

In *The Middle Parts of Fortune*, Manning employs similar strong terms for "comradeship," rising "on occasion to an intensity of feeling which friendship never touches" (79). Bourne later judges, "These apparently rude and brutal natures comforted, encouraged, and reconciled each other to fate, with a tenderness and tact which was more moving than anything in life . . . they put their hands on each other's shoulders and said with a passionate conviction that it would be all right, though they had faith in nothing, but in themselves and in each other" (205). He reveres a sign proclaiming the help of "THE EVERLASTING ARMS," not because Bourne believes in God any more than he trusts women, but because he believes in this new communion through men's arms (207–08). The ambiguity of "arms" lets the eternal martial arts mask and justify the human arms stretched out toward one another.

In part, male camaraderie appeals to the soldiers because it seems to break down the class divisions of peacetime. Weeper marvels that "gentle-folk an' all, we all stan' the same chance now" (Manning 201). Nevertheless, this boon is illusory, for if death levels the ranks, the army does not. As old class barriers fall, a new, rigid pecking order separates the men. Manning's account records in oppressive detail an endless jostling for prestige, while Remarque also exposes a tyrannical exercise of power: "A non-com. can torment a private, a lieutenant a non-com., a captain a lieutenant, until he goes mad" (44). As soon as Manning's Bourne, who has steadfastly refused a commission, considers a promotion after all, his comrade Martlow bitterly complains, "That's the worst o' the bloody army: as soon as you get a bit pally with a chap summat 'appens" (133).

If promotion parts Bourne from Martlow, wounds and death far surpass commissions as the great separators (133). Remarque's Paul admits that exhaustion and repeated losses stupefy and isolate the men: "We have lost all feeling for one another," as they step indifferently over the wounded (116). Similarly, Manning's characters may prop each other up for a time, but "then, one by one, they realized that each must go alone" (209). Official hierarchies belie the promise of equality, and, even within a single rank, the band of brothers can fracture all too easily.

Death hovers at the edge of such scenes not only because it may soon put an end to emotional bonds, but also because the imminence of death authorizes the expression of emotion in the first place. In J. M. Barrie's story "The New Word," a British, middle-class family welcomes the war precisely because it prompts a display of affection, which, father and son agree, would brand them "effeminate" in peacetime (238). When Mrs. Torrance prods her husband to "show more warmth" to Roger the night before he reports for duty, Mr. Torrance still pretends only disdain: "Two men show warmth to each other! Shame, woman!" (228). Although father and son have clearly desired more ease and demonstrativeness with each other for a long time, only Roger's departure allows Mr. Torrance to admit grandly, "I'm fond of you, my boy," and Roger can venture a relatively effusive "Good-night, dear father" (234, 240). Even now, however, the men need to mask their rare chat as a sop to please Mrs. Torrance: "Of course you and I know that display of that sort is all bunkum—repellant even to our natures" (238). As a matter of fact, confronted by her actual rather than symbolic presence, father and son again hide their warmth, claiming that they discussed "tactics and strategy, wasn't it, Roger?" and consolidating their new bond by excluding her (239).

Although Barrie's story gently mocks the men for their awkwardness, it never rebukes their need to play out their reconciliation against the blankness and forgiveness that Mother must provide, nor does Barrie undercut the assumption that war offers Roger his only "chance of seeing whether I was a man" (236). Instead, the story earnestly endorses two oddly contradictory, sought-after opportunities given by war: proving stoicism in public, while still sneaking emotion in private. Yet permission to utter the "New Word" of the title, a long censored "fond" or "dear," is expensively bought, since the war could cost the son his life.

This uncomfortable sense that only sacrifice can unbuckle the expression of caring intrudes into the accounts of officers and their subordinates as well as family members. Historian Michael Adams, trying to explain a "continuing affirmation" of the war even when anonymous slaughter had overturned early dreams of chivalric battle, examines a surprisingly satisfied tone in the memoir of Vivien Gilbert (*Great Adventure* 101). Just as this officer has learned to admire his servant, Sale, a shell rips off both Sale's legs; Gilbert holds the head of the dying man in his lap. Adams sees that the officer finds "compensations" even in this horrible death: "Gilbert had been moved to cry, a massive emotional freeing for a respectable Englishman. And he now felt that he and Sale were equals" (*Great Adventure* 102). Adams adds sardonically, "It is odd that it took war to suggest their common humanity to many British people" (102).

In fiction too, only dying seems to legitimize the expression of love between comrades. Through a superhuman effort, Paul carries Kat under fire to a dressing station, but by the time he gets there, Kat has already died (Remarque 288–91). Manning creates similarly powerful scenes, as Bourne holds the blasted Martlow, and Weeper Smart carries Bourne, who dies anyway (216–17, 246–47). The cryptic words of love and the generous but futile actions make these episodes the most moving of the two books. Certainly the characters do not want these scenes, but somehow their societies seem to require the violence in order to slip in the togetherness. The cover drawing of the inexpensive Ballantine edition (1982) of *All Quiet on the Western Front* signals this linkage. Under a brilliant red sky, a wounded young man sits with his back and head against the chest of a man whose hands cuddle the lad's shoulders. Even the crassest advertiser knows that tenderness sells. Yet the cover is unlikely to announce "two men find love," unless shell fire gives an alibi for the sunset glow of romance.

This tension between coveting and condemning men's mutual tenderness usually remains under the surface in the literature of World War I; however, playwright Frank McGuinness can in 1985 finally make the contradiction explicit in *Observe the Sons of Ulster Marching towards the Somme*. Imagining the motives of a Protestant Irish regiment that fought for the British Empire in the Great War (Keegan 223, 254), the play demonstrates how camaraderie may reward soldiers, but also how the rhetoric of dying for a brother may hide a fear of loving him alive. Like Pat Barker, McGuinness blames the carnage on social restrictions that prohibit men from sharing either feelings or bodies in peacetime, in turn creating despair and masochism which governments can then appropriate to run their wars.

Observe the Sons features four pairs of soldiers, in a barracks during training, at home on leave five months later, and, finally, in a trench before the catastrophe of the Somme. Some viewers in 1985 might be tempted to interpret Pyper and Craig as "the gay couple" (using modern terms) and the other three pairs as straight friends, but McGuinness shrewdly scrambles such categories. The play breaks down strict divisions between hetero- and homosexual by showing that all the men fear to seem womanly, all repeat each other's lines and actions from one scene to another, and all crave some sort of mutual touch.

While the volunteers strive to differentiate themselves from women as a lower order, the play makes it clear that their learned gender distinctions do not hold up. Moore boasts, "You don't join the army to do woman's work," but the recruits spend the first third of the play making beds (18). Millen interrupts any "silly chat" about dying as "more fit coming from crying women," implying that women chatter and take fright, whereas men keep silent and face facts (20). Inadvertently, of course, he only illustrates that men don't face the fact of outrageous mortality rates, and they can certainly gab. Although these recruits assume that the sexes are born with fixed traits, they contradict themselves by acting as if they themselves could turn into a woman at any moment. Anxiously maintaining a hierarchy of possible womanliness, Anderson introduces himself and McIlwaine to the other recruits, "No cause for panic, ladies. The men are here" (33). Each of the eight men wants his family to approve a brave, returning son—"Made a man of himself in Flanders" (76)—but instead all the soldiers gradually discover, "There are only cowards, and the worst learn to hide it best" (50).

Indoctrinated with the need to avoid so-called feminine traits, the volunteers are startled when Pyper twice insinuates, "I have remarkably fine skin, don't I? For a man" (17, 34). He can use the reference to women's supposedly finer skin—and women's status as sex objects—as a quick code to advertise homosexuality, precisely because sexologists such as Havelock Ellis were insisting that male "inverts" resemble women. Actually, men's and women's skins do not differ naturally at all, only socially, if custom keeps middle-class ladies from rough work, nor does sexual orientation correlate to skin type. However, Pyper is not interested in deconstructing cultural assumptions, only in manipulating them to announce sexuality as a central part of his life. Nevertheless, if he deliberately hints some kinship to women to activate the code *sensual*, he still needs to counteract the taint of femininity by cultivating an image as tough, even ruthless warrior (35). Indeed, the ploy seems to work, for Pyper garners a measure of acceptance from his skeptical companions only through battle: "He's some fighter though. Pyper. Who would have thought it?" (44).

Whereas McGuinness has Pyper adopt the contemporary association of male "inversion" with "female germs" (Ellis 133), an admixture that Pyper will flaunt but still compensate by fighting, the playwright, from his 1980s' perspective, keeps questioning any special link of male homosexuality to womanliness. He suggests that *all* men resemble women (i.e., they're all human), by having other characters repeat Pyper's "feminine" come-on. McIlwaine, for instance, echoes Pyper by joking to George Anderson, "I have remarkably fine hands for a man," and adding "Georgie" as an endearment (44). Although discomfited by McIlwaine's drunken affection, Anderson too, by the end of this scene, affirms yet again, "Remarkably fine hands," as McIlwaine completes the refrain for the fourth time in the play, "Aye, for a man" (58).

Unfortunately, McIlwaine's hands are now bleeding from beating the lambeg drum, so that he and Anderson have twisted Pyper's line to imply that only men do things wholeheartedly: to the point of self-sacrifice. However, this social notion of what a real man does contradicts another of their society's stereotypes: self-sacrifice belongs to *women*'s essential nature. Moreover, McIlwaine is not shredding his hands for any particular cause. He is drumming in a purely ceremonial display, and, since they missed the public holiday, their ceremony remains entirely private. In defining what is appropriate "for a man," Anderson and McIlwaine go beyond self-abnegation for a communal cause, to require sacrifice in and of itself—that is, masochism—as the definitive stamp of manliness (see also Savran 10, 24–25).

The play boldly suggests that these men must receive pain and inflict it because their society has tried to prevent them from giving pleasure or help, which might betray "fallen" nature or "feminine" nature. As a consequence, they substitute fighting as the only contact allowed. As if to prod the audience to question these substitutions, the main visual image throughout the play contrasts hurting hands with touching hands. In Part 3, where pairs of soldiers occupy the stage in separate scenes, all seek mutual touch. Pyper moves Craig's hands over carvings, to teach him that to "Touch" is to "live" (46). Millen gets Moore to believe that he takes his hand (though they are not actually touching), as he rebuilds Moore's shattered nerves by coaxing him across a rope bridge (50). Anderson grabs McIlwaine's fists to help him beat the Orangemen's drum (52). After Crawford trips Roulston, "spread-eagling him," their touch extends from hands to whole bodies (55).

Whereas the first three pairs offer helping hands, the fourth couple seems to be hurting each other again. Yet Crawford too claims that he is just helping Roulston realize his own harshness, teaching Roulston to rejoin the group as an equal member, not a superior but isolated Christ. As Crawford spreadeagles Roulston, McIlwaine earlier greeted the newly arrived Crawford by hurling him onto the bed, claiming he can "smell a Catholic" (33). McIlwaine may be "snarling" as he throws himself onto Crawford, but he actually presents a very graphic picture of one man taking another to bed—but *of course* it's attacking, not loving (34). The multiple examples of tussling, however, begin to suggest that attacking is just the way men get away with physical contact in this culture.

Although an interest in other men's bodies pulses through all McGuinness's characters, they cannot express it openly. At one extreme, any long-term sexual relationship would be impossible. Pyper hints that he enlisted in the army to get himself killed and thus escape the futility and reputed sordidness of being homosexual in 1916; he seems even to have regarded himself as "evil" (47). Ironically, however, meeting Craig has made Pyper want to live, as he realizes that a relationship with a man could be good, not evil. In a further irony, Craig is now risking himself recklessly, because, he asks, "What kind of life do you see for us when we're out of here? It might be many things, but it won't be together" (77). Maybe they could love furtively now and then, but Craig has too much dignity to settle for anything less than a completely visible commitment.

In addition to pushing Pyper and Craig to despair, such a repressive society also restricts the "polyvocality of desire" of nominal heterosexuals (Weeks, "Hocquenghem" 693). As Pyper explains in the prologue, his whole regiment let themselves "be led to extermination," even "led ourselves," claiming "we would die for each other in battle" (12). In retrospect, however, he protests, "That is not loyalty. That is not love. That is hate . . . . Hate for one's self" (12). He implies that a Christian denigration of the body and a more general fear of tenderness lead men to hate themselves, to the point of self-immolation. Both these aversions, to the body and to emotion, may be traced to social definitions of gender, which assign sensuality and nurturance to women only, when men too could enjoy these feelings.

In the literature of World War I, whether written during the war, during the spurt of creativity ten years after the armistice, or much later in revival literature such as McGuinness's, camaraderie does console soldiers beset by exhaustion and fear. Certainly no one would begrudge them that comfort. Nevertheless, the books also show that strong male bonding may not just contrast with a surrounding hell but may help keep the horrors going. First, as McGuinness suspects, men may use the intensity of fighting to substitute for the intensity of pleasures not allowed. Second, soldiers may need further war to avenge fallen comrades. Manning's Bourne, for instance, rages after Martlow's death that he will "kill every bugger I see," whether the enemy is attacking or attempting to surrender (217). Grief for slain friends also drives Siegfried Sassoon, yet his berserker behavior only leads to guilt. In his large-minded poem "Enemies," Sassoon imagines the ghost of a German soldier whom he killed, now taking the hand of his dead British mate. The smiling Britisher makes the German understand how the destruction of such beauty could have deranged Sassoon into murderous frenzy (66). Here the poet manages to sidestep the enmity of governments, but he can envision this larger camaraderie of former enemies only in the underworld.

Third, intense male tenderness may prolong the war by enforcing a kind of solidarity of imitative suffering. In her memoir *Testament of Youth*, Vera Brittain reveals that her brother Edward, though not charmed by the same "heroism in the abstract" as his friend Roland, nevertheless schemes to be shipped to the trenches after Roland's death (129). In the grip of a "bitter humiliation even less endurable than his grief," Edward earns a Military Cross, then dies, basically to show himself worthy of his friend (245). Drawing on such contemporary examples, Pat Barker has her fictionalized Wilfred Owen quietly return to France when he hears that Sassoon has been invalided to England (*Ghost* 14), as the real Sassoon feels ashamed over the faraway deaths of his troops (*War Poems* 94, 108). Esteem and longing for wounded companions translate into the "honor" of not escaping when others did not. Such scruples create, however, a purely symbolic togetherness, as new sufferers share what others must have gone through. The returnees to the front display a perhaps admirable but entirely abstract fairness, on the analogy of a child who decides, "If Daddy beats you, I'll try to be beaten too"—without questioning why anybody is getting hit in the first place.

A 1915 British recruitment poster explicitly plays on this sense of obligation to comrades, in case glory does not tempt men to cross the channel in sufficient numbers (Fairman 7). The words "Your friends need you. Be a man" border a chaotic scene where one man gestures frantically for help, another remains calmly glued to binoculars, and their companion lies wounded on the ground. The poster does not examine whether it might not be more helpful to friends to stay home, push for a negotiated settlement, and work against imperial competitions, rather than add oneself and more friends to the next million men stuffed into the meat grinder.

In addition to prolonging a present war, camaraderie may even lure societies to want or allow future wars. The depiction of male bonding in literature or, especially, in oral tales may invite reenactments. As Sassoon began to suspect as early as 1918 in his poem "Song-Books of the War," each new generation may sign up at hearing "a snatch of soldier-song" (126). Envying even "blind regret and haggard mirth," simply because they are shared, the young men will heed the bright "marching rhymes," not the old veteran's warning, "War was a fiend who stopped our clocks" (126). Perhaps Sassoon wondered if his own angry but tender poems would bewitch rather than warn distant readers. For in an odd parallel to propagandist Barrie, who dangles a sentimental moment between father and son as a bonus of war, Sassoon offers a "grace" that can only be received through comrades' eyes, in a military setting (122). It is not so much the young recruits who anticipate that they will learn to value intimacy with comrades. Rather, the culture as a whole (leaders and citizens) prizes these scenes of closeness and so accepts war as not entirely reprehensible.

As Sassoon and Barrie promise that war allows the deepest possible affection, Remarque and Manning, for all their antiwar rage, similarly seduce us with touching scenes, as Paul and Kat roast a goose or Weeper Smart carries Bourne. McGuinness inspires us with an exchange of orange sashes, when the men movingly accept Pyper as "one of our own" (77). Memoirist Gilbert and novelist Barbusse beguile us with tears for a servant, or the embrace of a strong back, like the "daring" reach of a plant bridging the two strong planks of a doorway (Barbusse 169). In a society which will not in peacetime allow men that solidarity, that embrace, that supposedly frivolous mirth, or those tears, because all are deemed womanly, only war opens this precious door.[4]

(d) I Fight to Protect My Sister (but I Hate My Sister—So as Not to Be Her)

Propagandists pushing America to join World War I pictured their country as "a beautiful young mother going out in a gauzy costume . . . . Her sons will arm her and clothe her" (qtd. in Cooperman 25). Although these sons did not really let mother bear arms, they provisioned themselves as if the chastity of American wives faced immediate threat. The European Allies similarly depicted the initial German invasion as a figurative rape of "Poor Little Belgium" (Winter and Baggett 66), with no mention of poor Congo or poor India, long ago violated militarily by Belgium and England. Rather than identify oneself as an imperialist whose ambitions clashed with the greed of a rival imperialist, it was easier for Europe and America to draw on pervasive medieval revivals (Adams, *Great Adventure* 63) and cast one's own nation as a noble knight, who would cross swords with an evil "Teutonic Beast" (Cooperman 13) and rescue damsels in distress.

This story of rescuing damsels omits, however, the resentment against women that many men felt. Underneath an announced intention to shield womanhood, soldiers often epitomized exasperatingly gung-ho civilians as ignorant ladies. Siegfried Sassoon, for example, accuses factory girls of an almost sexual titillation from "heroes' " suffering: "You make us shells. You listen with delight, / By tales of dirt and danger fondly thrilled" (100). Even the ambulance driver Nellie in Helen Zenna Smith's *Not So Quiet* (1930) reserves her greatest fury at complacent patriotism for "Mother and Mrs. Evans-Mawnington," although the two fathers equally rally their children to war (90). Although jingoists such as Jessie Pope did urge men to the slaughter and some girls handed out white feathers for cowardice (Gullace, "White" 182), all women at home did not fit the tiresomely repeated stereotype of "fat and incredibly bloodthirsty" valkyries, as novelist Rose Macaulay grumbled (50). Ironically, British feminists who tried to stop the bloodshed by protesting the war were censored by the Defense of the Realm Act, and even their history (as opposed to that of suffragettes who joined the war effort) was for a long time suppressed (Tylee 257).

Men secretly irritated that the burden of fighting fell only on them could also envy their girlfriends' moving into vacated jobs. With millions of men mobilized, women in unprecedented numbers took over farming, factory work, and tram conducting. These new workers made more money than they had as domestics, conferring a sense of promise: "a revolution in economic expectations, a release of passionate energies, a (re)union of previously fragmented sisters, and a (re)vision of social and aesthetic dreams" (Gilbert 223). Nevertheless, the benefit may have been only apparent. In the short term, war "devastated" more than it liberated women's lives (Marcus, "Asylums" 57), and, in the long term, militarization may only have reinforced age-old roles for "prolific mothers" and "admiring wives," who must gladly send sons to battle and silently suffer at home (Thébaud 23). Women continued to be seen traditionally, "as either threats to or supporters of men and morality" (Grayzel 3–4).

When women at least *seemed* to be thriving—inheriting jobs, supposedly discovering a new sexual freedom—soldiers might well bridle at risking their lives. However, another cause may have fueled men's rancor even more. If soldiers found themselves similarly wanting to stay home, harvest their fields, and make love, then they would have to admit that, under the circumstances, they were *just like women*. If the designated warriors could not live up to the expectation that they would fight on untiringly, they were only proving themselves human, but their society had scarcely prepared such a subject position for men. The resulting impossibility for men to admit this glimpse that they resembled women contributed to an underlying fury. Four fictional works—Frederic Manning's novel *The Middle Parts of Fortune* (1929), Pat Barker's trilogy (1990s), Wyndham Lewis's short story "Cantleman's Spring-Mate" (1917), and D. H. Lawrence's novella *The Fox* (1923)—show soldiers chafing because men act "like women" or seething because women act "like men." These resentments belie the official ideology that boys eagerly marched off to guard cherished sisters.

In Manning's novel, a corporal shrewdly redirects the anger of an enlisted man away from a potential target, the war itself, toward an absent, safer target, women. Pritchard recounts how his bed-chum, Swale, had both legs blown off, heartbreakingly asked to be helped to his feet, then died. As he remembers, Pritchard cries, openly expressing the intense emotions of camaraderie. Yet Corporal Tozer, interrupting, instantly sets about defusing and managing this grief. First reasserting discipline ("Get those blankets folded"), Tozer then doles out a bit of sympathy (15). However, when Pritchard rejects the platitudes ("Bein' sorry ain't goin' to do us 'ns no manner o' good"), folds his blanket as if "he would never use [it] again," and scoffs at a promised letter of condolence from a captain to Swale's mother, Tozer senses that Pritchard's grief is turning to rage, not so much against the Germans as his own officers—and perhaps against his own government (15). However, instead of addressing this incipient mutiny directly, Tozer simply asks, "Have you a wife and children of your own?" (16). The corporal may appeal to a duty to defend them, but even if Pritchard does not believe in his family's immediate danger, their memory will help Tozer to lure his men from dangerous thinking. Taking Tozer's bait, Pritchard mentions a daughter, dead at age four, then concludes furiously: " 'The wife can look after 'erself . . . . Th' bugger were never any bloody good to me.' He lapsed into a resentful silence, and the corporal was satisfied that his emotion had been diverted into other channels" (16).

A complicated cultural misogyny enables Corporal Tozer to redirect anger that might strike against a futile war into an already prepared scorn against women. Pritchard does not explain his grudge against his wife; is he reproaching her for supposedly needing him to protect her? for giving him a sickly child? for producing no sons? for not copulating with him more often? Or he may be faulting his wife for his present pain in a different way. The epitaph to this chapter announces Pritchard's crying by quoting Shakespeare: "But I had not so much of man in me. / And all my mother came into mine eyes / And gave me up to tears" (qtd. in Manning 12). Instead of calling grief human, the lines blame a matrilineal legacy and the mother herself, for wounding her son and for "giving him up" to tears, which is the same thing as surrendering him to the enemy. Since Pritchard now feels a great deal of emotion at Swale's death, he may be accusing the nearest "mother" in his life, his child's, for infecting him with "her" sentiment in the first place, leaving him doubly exposed: to the pain of caring and the loss of face, "so much of man" as he thinks he ought to display.

If Pritchard is in part complaining of his wife's distance from his bed, he might well hold the war responsible for separating them, but Tozer has already sidetracked such rebellious thoughts to more stereotypical betrayals. A woman's fickleness, not the war, must be the source of his loneliness; a woman's emotion, not his own, has unhinged him. In effect, his wife, not the war, has killed Swale. The other men are similarly encouraged to dissipate horror at Swale's dismemberment by laughing at Pritchard's difficulties with his wife (they "grinned a little"), stripping their tunics in the heat, and smoking together (16). As Corporal Tozer damps down Pritchard's troublesome, "motherly" tears, the brotherly band reestablishes an all-male family, with its more surreptitious emotional comforts, and hence deflects any thoughts of mutiny against the father.

Taking her cue from Manning's Pritchard, who attributes his own painful grief to women's pernicious influence, Pat Barker has her character Prior translate his helplessness in war into a determination to feel powerful over a helpless woman. On leave in England, Prior bitterly resents the blitheness with which holidaymakers frolic at the beach, while his buddies are rotting in the trenches. At least one motive for his complex desire to seduce Sarah Lumb is, then, to use her because he has been used by the war: "They owed him something, all of them, and she should pay" (*Regeneration* 128). Even when he becomes fond of her and insists that he "no longer felt hostile to her, as he'd done back there in the crowd," he still mixes military terminology with erotic contexts, worrying that the "first time was almost always a disappointment. Either stuck at half mast or firing before you reached the target. He didn't want to think about Sarah like this" (*Regeneration* 130). He doesn't want to anticipate a poor "performance," but he fails to notice that his vocabulary still reduces her to a demolishable "target."

If Prior's confusion of the vocabulary for war and sex sounds exaggerated, one need only point to Wyndham Lewis's story "Cantleman's Spring-Mate," originally published by *The Little Review* in 1917, to find a contemporary soldier disdainfully referring to the woman he seduces as "a sort of Whizbang. With a treachery worthy of a Hun, Nature tempted him towards her" (*Blasting* 310). As a newly commissioned officer about to leave for France, Cantleman knows that he may not survive. However, instead of admitting the danger that this manmade war poses to him, he follows a Hegelian line of thought and names "Nature" his enemy. Like Hegel,

Cantleman then personifies "Nature" and life as feminine. Hegel thought that nature insulted men by meting out random death and advised them to reclaim the initiative by waging war (Lloyd 73), ignoring the logical contradiction that this ruse just adds more death into the world. Cantleman similarly pretends to be "indifferent to Nature's threat," trying to counter nature by "making war within her war upon her servants" (*Blasting* 310). He makes war on the Germans, as if that effort will somehow ensure his immortality, but then he further transfers his war to Stella. He displaces the threat of German weaponry onto her, calling her "Whizbang," perhaps because he can impose his will on her more easily than on a shell. To convince her to submit to him sexually, all he has to do is present her with a ring, which he never intends to honor.

Certainly Cantleman infuses their coupling with all the resentment that he might more reasonably direct against German bombardments:

> That night he spat out, in gushes of thick delicious rage, all the lust that had gathered in his body . . . . He bore down on her as though he wished to mix her body into the soil, and pour his seed into a more methodless matter, the brown phalanges of floury land. As their two bodies shook and melted together, he felt that he was raiding the bowels of Nature. (*Blasting* 310)

An inheritor of the nineteenth century, Cantleman calls Stella an "unconscious agent" of nature, whereas he claims all consciousness and agency for himself. As we saw in the Introduction, Victorian men were supposed to maintain control at all times, over others and over their own emotions and bodies. If Cantleman feels "drugged with delicious appetites," he yields briefly to his body, but only if he can blame Stella and only if he can keep "deliberately aloof," to maintain a supposedly all-important control (*Blasting* 310–11).

A striking expression of this projection of one's own condition—Cantleman's threatened loss of control, Pritchard's grief, or Prior's helplessness—onto a feminine Other occurs in Barker's *The Ghost Road*. Since Barker is writing many decades after the war, she can use the influence of feminists and of Foucault to help her digest and analyze the examples from earlier works, which she deliberately invokes. When Prior glimpses the "shuttered face" of a prostitute and thinks, "The only way not to be her was to hate her" (41), the narration makes explicit the hostility against women and also posits a reason for it: a feared resemblance. Prior sees in the prostitute's boredom a mirror of the expression that he suspects covered his own face as a child, when Father Mackenzie habitually sodomized him. As an adult, Prior enjoys both male and female sexual partners and finds this whore exciting in part because he can imagine solidarity with other soldiers, "sliding in on another man's spunk" (*Ghost* 43), but during that year with Mackenzie, he remained, like the prostitute, unpleasured. Since Prior does not like to recall that childhood episode, his aversion to the "shuttered face" is understandable, yet his response—hating her—fails to solve the problem. He says that he does not want to "be her," but it's too late; he has already recognized an identity.

Prior's encounters with the prostitute and his girlfriend Sarah locate the root of his misogyny in distaste for his own vulnerability: as a child, to the priest's whims and, as an adult, to the guns of the western front. Prior tries scorning Father Mackenzie or his boss at the Ministry of Munitions, Major Lode, but when an attack on these authority figures proves impractical, he shifts disgust onto weaker figures outside officialdom: working-class Sarah or outcast prostitute. However, Prior misplaces his hatred when he turns it against individuals: either women or the priest. Even Mackenzie, Prior recognizes years later, "loved me, the poor sod" (*Ghost* 176). Instead, Prior (or the reader) should question the social systems that exploit them all: Major Lode's imperial hierarchies, the Christian condemnation of homosexuality that sends Mackenzie to furtive and hypocritical satisfactions, the economic structure that makes it difficult for women to earn money except by selling their bodies or making munitions, and the war-making that uses young men and discards their mangled corpses.

The imperial-military hierarchies that bolster the ego of Major Lode denigrate women as weak and, at the same time, idealize them as saintly. However, instead of worshiping women, as this ideology prescribes, men embittered by the war and fearful of change may resent women—to the point of murder, as Lawrence fantasizes in *The Fox*, written in 1918–1921. Regarding himself as a force opposing conventional English views, Lawrence nevertheless remained deeply entangled in them. Although he resisted the sexual constraints of the middle class, he perpetuated many rigid gender roles. Participating in "a general upsurge in male insecurity" after World War I, Lawrence complained in the 1920s that the tone of "the post-war world was feminine—not, however, a true femininity of instinct and feeling, but a perverted femininity of will and idealism—and that a masculine renaissance was necessary to restore the balance" (Simpson 17). Ironically, although Lawrence denounced the war as a "blasphemy which we are all committing" (*Kangaroo* 225), many of his carefully guarded gender divisions proved useful to the militarism that he otherwise disdained.

Whereas Lewis's Cantleman hates nature, Lawrence claims that his philosophy of sex reveres nature. Yet the two stories are alike in the male characters' need to keep women inferior. Demobilized from Salonika, Lawrence's soldier Henry cannot accept that two lone women, Banford and March, now own his grandfather's property and work the land, and he does not approve that they may be living together sexually. When March informs Henry that the women may later hire themselves out as land-workers, he insists that there "won't be any demand for women land-workers, now the war's over," but she further buffets his hope for reestablishing the old ways: "Oh, we'll see" (17).

Henry is infuriated not only by the ability of the new owners to make their own money, but also by their household without men. Banford's father thinks that his daughter won't ever marry, hinting at her lesbianism; in the most open reference of the story, Henry asks March, "Do you wish you'd gone to bed with her?" (54). When March "waited a long time" before answering, "No," her hesitation lets Henry worry that she did sleep with Banford or wished she had (54). Henry hysterically repeats two contemporary misapprehensions: that all independent women must be lesbians and that lesbians are monsters. The omniscient narrator backs Henry by indirectly chiding Banford and March through their hens, which display an "obstinate refusal" to lay eggs (8). Conflating the hens with the women through an ambiguous pronoun "they," the narrator complains that "They had a beautiful home, and should have been perfectly content," but instead "they" possess a "tendency to strange illnesses" (8). Reflecting the turn-of-the-century "medical model" for homosexuality (Weeks, *Sex* 104), the narrator concurs that Banford is both ill and "unnatural" (55). Independence and homosexuality, the story implies, both sadly denature a woman. Lawrence himself seems to endorse this narrator's view, for in his essay "Cocksure Women and Hensure Men" (1929), he warns that women moving into new political and literary arenas will never be satisfied having "laid a vote" or even an "ink-bottle" of talent (555).

Henry hopes to reassert his supposedly natural title to the land and to women-as-property in one blow, by marrying March. As he tries to outmaneuver the present owners, the story underlines again and again his parallel with the fox. Both have ruddy, glistening hair, bright eyes, and a masculine, "penetrating" stare that mesmerizes March (16). At the same time, the narrator dismisses March as a "helpless, fascinated" rabbit, and Banford looks like a "sick bird" (62, 34). Because Henry is so clearly scheming and manipulative, the comparison to the predatory fox seems to condemn him. However, this Nietzschean, Darwinian vocabulary may simply praise the stronger animal.

As its chief asset, the fox displays a powerful tail, "full and frictional," with which to make a "fiery coverlet" for women, suggesting the medieval phrase *feme covert* for a wife "covered" by her mate (41). Unfortunately, Henry is not fashioning a comforting fur with which to protect March. Instead, like the fox raiding the henhouse, Henry shoots rabbits and birds. Henry accepts shooting as an adequate image for ejaculating, not bothered by the destructive connotations. Reviving the old Apollo Syndrome of the classical story "Apollo and Daphne," Henry believes that the sexual relationship of men to women resembles the hunt, and no self-respecting hunter would beg his quarry, "Please fall to my gun" (24). Not stopping even to ask consent (as Apollo pretended to do only for a few moments), the sexually powerful man engages in "a subtle, profound battle of wills . . . a battle never finished till your bullet goes home" (24). Here Henry employs the same hostile erotic language that has Cantleman "devouring" his mate (Lewis, *Blasting* 310) or Prior aiming to hit the "target" (Barker, *Regeneration* 130). Meanwhile, Lawrence's narrator sympathizes with Henry and fails to undercut his desire to rule his partner, willfully hurting her on the way to ultimate conquest.

Lawrence's own views, as indicated in essays, similarly idealize men as hunter and fighter. For an author who detested the absurdities of Britain at war (harassing him because his wife had a German name), Lawrence ironically perpetuates a military vocabulary of competition, not cooperation. In 1928, he equivocates that England "has always been a fighting country, though never a military country," because a true Englishman

> hated being bossed or bullied. So he hated being a soldier or a marine, because as such he was bossed and bullied. And when he felt anything or anybody coming to boss or to bully him, he got up and prepared to place his fist in the eye of the boss and bully. Which is a real man's spirit, and the only spirit that makes a country a man's country. ("Is England" 557)

According to Lawrence, women are peaceful by nature and never feel any impulse to punch the boss. Men, essentially bellicose, never think of any way to contain the bully except the fist.

In *The Fox*, Henry regards women who just want to arrange their own lives as bossy, and they too can expect the fist. When he discovers

March cutting down a tree under Banford's direction, he takes over the axe and reasserts his own phallic dominance: "Then suddenly his form seemed to flash up enormously tall and fearful, he gave two swift, flashing blows" (*Fox* 65). Although Henry, full of malice, is clearly calculating the fall of the tree against Banford, the introducer of the 1994 Penguin edition of *The Fox* assures us that Lawrence has the "literary skill" to make his character's behavior "both understandable and acceptable *in context*" (xxvi; italics in original). That the life of a woman who farms the land and loves another woman should seem to this critic sufficient "context" to justify premeditated murder attests to an ongoing, powerful animosity toward independent women.

Moreover, Lawrence describes the killing of Banford by "flashing"/flasher Henry in terms that make the murder sound like a symbolic rape (65). The end of a bough "swooped down on her," reducing her to "a little twitching heap" like "a wild goose he had shot" (65). Henry demands his pleasure, but he grants her only such pleasure or "twitching" that he can claim to produce and control; he can then steal away her separate physicality forever by eliminating her life entirely.

When Henry goes on to marry the bereft March, his relationship to her duplicates his antagonism to Banford. His wife must lie back like "seaweeds," which he insists are stronger than "resistant oak trees" (67). March's strength must reside only in passivity, not in the recalcitrance of tree-like Banford (67). March must "sink" her will and become "submerged in him" (69). In a series of late stories and essays, Lawrence repeats Henry's diatribe against modern women who annoyingly want to "*do* something, to strain herself in some direction" and "*exert* herself in love" (*Fox* 67; see Phillips, *Dying Gods* 143–53). Characters with whom Lawrence seems to sympathize specifically condemn the "frictional, ecstatic Aphrodite" as too active (*Plumed Serpent* 463), though Henry can move his manly, "frictional" tail as much as he likes (*Fox* 41). The gentle seaweed imagery for a woman who must renounce both a public voice and her own orgasm masks an extreme hostility. Keeping March underwater, Henry secretly wants to drown her, as he has murdered Banford.

Actually, Henry may be hoping to drown out aspects of himself that he has been taught to regard as womanly. His excessive need to prove his power betrays a deep suspicion of powerlessness, supposed to be intrinsic to women but all too available to everyone. That the war might be exacerbating Henry's hysteria appears from a description of ducks, surrogates for birdlike Banford, right before he kills her. Though led by a drake, the ducks (female) stupidly refuse to keep in the background, away from the tree. "[W]agging their rumps," the flock go "stemming away downhill from the upper meadow, coming like boats running on a ruffled sea, cockling their way top speed downwards . . . cackling as excitedly as if they brought news of the Spanish Armada" (64). "Cockling," the ducks look like cockleshell boats but also edge out male phallic prerogatives; at the same time, these uppity ladies are "cackling" their titillation over an English naval victory, which they themselves did not have to fight and die to achieve. Like Sassoon faulting factory girls for shivering deliciously over war talk (100), Henry accuses Banford of flaunting her "rump" and gloating over news of a battle. Not only do his female ducks exult over the Spanish Armada, but their boatlike description also turns *them* into an armada, ready to sink. Nevertheless, if the narrator tries to foist off all weakness onto women, the present war has brought home to men such as Lawrence's Henry, Manning's Pritchard, Lewis's Cantleman, and Barker's Prior their own physical and emotional helplessness: frail boats easily swamped by machine warfare. Mistakenly taught that all vulnerability is womanly, these characters then blame women for the men's own human fragility, which could pull down not only death, but an even more fearful consequence, the charge of "sissy."

Chapter 3

World War II: No Lace on His Drawers

(a) I Fight to Prove I'm Not My Sister
(but I Suspect I Am)

World War II, in contrast to later doubtful causes such as the Vietnam War, often glows in American memory as a heroic endeavor whose fighters could all discern, believe in, and eagerly pursue their noble mission. Certainly Nazi atrocities against Jews and other scapegoats demanded intervention, but the U.S. government "did not enter the war to save Jews" and impeded Jewish immigration even when it knew of the death camps (Shalom 113–17). Similarly, few GIs at the time cited persecution as their reason for serving in the armed forces. Instead, this conflict may have been one of America's "least ideologically motivated" wars, where a depressingly scant five percent of enlisted men possessed any "clear understanding of the threat to democracy posed by fascism" (Adams, *Best War* 88). So why did they fight?

Just emerging from the Depression, many men simply needed a job. Some wanted adventure, travel, an escape from boredom or domestic entanglements gone wrong. A significant number, however, were seeking the same elusive stamp of manhood that had lured World War I soldiers. Studies of American combat veterans recorded that if a majority scoffed at "patriotism" as sentimental bunkum, most valued group loyalty and a "code of masculinity" (Stewart 146). Infantrymen and bomber crews resisted their desire to run away because of "friendship," "machismo," "sense of honor," and the fear of being seen as a coward (Stewart 148). German soldiers slogged on for much the same reasons. Researchers hoping to show the usefulness of Allied propaganda in demoralizing the Wehrmacht instead discovered that soldiers' "political" and "ethical" beliefs—any original ones or new leafleted notions—did not affect zeal (Shils and Janowitz 143). Regardless of German soldiers' adherence to or doubts about Nazism, the "conditions of primary group life" kept a unit going: "the capacity for intimate communication, the provision of paternal protectiveness by NCOs and junior officers, and the gratification of certain personality needs, e.g., manliness" (Shils and Janowitz 143).[1] Even within conscription by all sides, the association of fighting with manhood played a role in ensuring that men accepted the draft and persevered through the trials of their service, since the threat of shame to oneself and one's family helped prevent rebellion (Adams, *Best War* 87). No one wanted to run the gauntlet of comparisons to a woman: "Christ, he's acting like an old maid" or "Whatsa matter, bud—got lace on your drawers?" (Stouffer et al. 2: 132).

Although the social science researchers seem to accept as inborn a "personality need" to prove "manliness," they might question how cultures manage to forge this unlikely link between adult powers and the courtship of early death. Most importantly, because societies routinely confuse gender (social) with anatomy (biological), the codes imply that if a man transgresses *any* gender prescription, the infraction will literally emasculate him. In *Goodbye, Darkness: A Memoir of the Pacific War* (1979), William Manchester makes explicit such fears and confusions, not usually articulated. Caught in the old Apollo Syndrome, which assumes that sexual "performance" augurs well for performance in battle, the soldiers in Manchester's work act out a kind of sympathetic magic. When A. L. Barker satirizes the irrationality of such rituals to establish masculinity, her story "The Iconoclasts" (1947) can reject contemporary gender indoctrination so completely perhaps because, as a woman, Barker is already excluded and has nothing to lose.

Can men under pressure to serve in the military also step outside their gender training? Norman Mailer in *The Naked and the Dead* (1948) and Joseph Heller in *Catch-22* (1961) do question specific military operations and petty "chickenshit" (Fussell, *Wartime* 80). Nevertheless, if their mockery inadvertently jostles the contemporary sex/gender system slightly, in the end, both authors would preserve that system. By contrast, James Jones in *The Thin Red Line* (1962) and Charles Fuller in *A Soldier's Play* (1981) expose several contradictions in the World War II definition of "man." As time passes after the conflict, these two authors can tease out parallels and crossovers in genders and races thought to reside at opposite points on a hierarchy.

One incident in Manchester's *Goodbye, Darkness* highlights the irrational fear of emasculation, which makes gender prescriptions so effective. A recently assigned lieutenant, Tubby Morris, tries to make his men climb over a wall into machine gun fire by taunting, "I've got balls and you haven't" (276). He then needles his sergeant (Manchester), "You think we couldn't hear you back there in the squad bay, masturbating every night? Did you think they'd give a Marine Corps commission to a masturbator?" (276). As another man, Bubba, titters, Manchester seethes, "I'm sure Bubba had never masturbated. His father, the Alabama preacher in whose steps he hoped to follow, had shown him the way to what he called 'Nigra poontang' when he reached adolescence" (276). In the end, the men refuse to follow the order and Tubby clambers onto the wall himself, where he is, predictably, instantly shot.

Even among Manchester's group, "military misfits" who flunked officer training for anything from walleye to skepticism about military traditions, Tubby's tactics hit a nerve (161). Writing thirty years after the event, Manchester can present the lieutenant as a suicidal idiot and says he had no trouble recognizing the initial claim to the only "balls" as a mask of fear, for which he felt compassion. Still, the further taunt about masturbation humiliated the young Manchester and induced a desire that Tubby die, a fleeting wish for which he still feels guilty. Although these field-tested "Raggedy Ass Marines" mock Tubby, bits of his gender ideology have taken hold in men as diverse as Manchester and Bubba (143).

These socially implanted assumptions mutually contradict. Although the lieutenant may seem to have made sex his most valuable goal, he betrays a widespread cultural devaluation of bodily pleasure. Tubby scorns masturbation, and Manchester similarly learned that the practice causes "brain damage" (42); if he can in 1979 call this dictum from his father "malarkey," his response to Tubby in the 1940s shows that fear and shame do pressure him. Power, not pleasure, counts, and the only goal of sex is penetrating a woman. Failure to do so is regarded as far worse than racism, which scarcely registers on the men. Tubby's jibes further equate penetrating a woman with climbing over a wall, killing people, and risking one's life. Once his culture has connected fighting with sex, all other questions fade away. Is scaling this wall a good idea? Would it be better to wait until the flanking battalion takes out the machine guns first? The feat becomes necessary right now, solely to prove Tubby to himself.

In fact, Manchester did share some of Tubby's mindset, enlisting to prove manhood. His family and culture trained him to define a man as one who fights in a war, any war. His mother's side bequeathed him the Confederate ideal of the gentleman soldier, and the Victorian literature of imperial adventure nourished his youth (40). Manchester says that he liked to think his adolescent militarism meant that he presciently understood Hitler's threat, but, perceptively, he now suspects that both he and Winston Churchill were just Saint Georges looking for dragons (41). No one would dispute that their countries found a dragon in Hitler, but ideals that formed Hitler were part of America and England too. *Goodbye, Darkness* has the honesty to expose racism against Jews and Blacks in the Marine Corps. To be a man, a male must always win, no matter what the cause; Hitler learned that precept in World War I, and his opponents imbibed the same priorities. Manchester, Churchill, and Hitler all needed an enemy, dragonish or not, to prove manhood.

Manchester also shares some of Tubby's Apollo Syndrome, assuming a link between sexual "performance" with women and "performance" in battle. For complicated motives, it is important to Manchester to try to lose his "virginity" before he is shipped overseas (176). On the one hand, he may feel that civilians owe him a rewarding experience before he dies (especially if masturbation is prohibited). On the other hand, if the penis "stands up" in what becomes essentially a departure rite, attended by "wild gaiety and rollicking despair" (J. Jones, *WWII* 151), then the successful accomplishment of the prescribed actions will ensure that the initiate can "stand up" in battle. To equate the two meanings for standing tall makes about as much sense as a shaman sprinkling water from a gourd to let the sky know humans want rain.

Manchester does not seem to suspect the element of sympathetic magic here, but A. L. Barker shrewdly dissects the masculinist traditions invoked in World War II as a kind of self-enclosed, ineffectual series of rituals. In her story "The Iconoclasts," focalized through a five-year-old British boy, Marcus ceremonially avoids the top step in the garden, and it is clear that his ten-year-old companion, Neil, serves as an equally fanatic neophyte in the temple of a nearby aerodrome, absorbing the aviators' esoteric language and urging Marcus to "pray" that the war lasts long enough for Neil to "pop them off [Heinkels and Messerschmitts] like paper bags" (252). The boys' need for ritual reveals the fear at the base of this small version of patriarchy, just as their vocabulary (following their elders'), reducing real events to a fairground game of popping bags, shows the inadequacy of the supposed solutions to insecurity, vested in two trained values in particular.

First, boys in this culture learn to take risks *for the sake of risk*, not to help someone else, but to bolster one's own self-image—even suicidally. Hence, Neil climbs onto a rickety old windmill to "test my nerve," hoping to ride one of its sails closer to the ground, then drop off in a pilot's perfect "four-point landing" (255). After he falls, the story ends eerily with the extent of Neil's injuries unspecified but apparently severe. Second, boys in this milieu learn not to show compassion. Earlier in their walk, Marcus feels sorry for a rabbit in a trap, but Neil scorns his pity. Later when the fallen Neil cannot move, Marcus, an apt pupil, suppresses his impulse to put Neil's leather jacket under the "sleeping" boy's head, so as not to make any further "womanish gesture," his mistake in wanting to help the rabbit (263). By telling the story from a child's viewpoint, Barker brilliantly underlines that training in manliness starts early, and that the persistence of the behavior (seeking danger, withholding compassion) into adulthood will make the hierophants not manly, as advertised, but still childish after all.

Just as Manchester's Tubby tries to boost his marines over the wall by calling their bodies female and Barker's Tubby-in-training avoids any "womanish gesture" (263), Norman Mailer's brutal Sergeant Croft in *The Naked and the Dead* drives his infantrymen by habitually scolding them, "Pack of goddam women" (521). When the fighting stalemates in one corner of a Pacific island, a boat drops off Croft's platoon, led by a newly assigned Lieutenant Hearn, on the undefended opposite coast. For the last third of the novel, the platoon reconnoiters behind Japanese lines, losing three men and transmitting no usable information. Finally picked up by another boat, the tattered survivors laugh hysterically at any remark, but when Croft sputters his usual refrain, "you're a bunch of goddam women," he sounded "funniest of all" (706). Why should his insult strike them funny now, at this culminating moment, delivering a kind of punch line for the whole book? Perhaps the men feel that they *are* women, in the sense that they have not lived up to manhood as defined. Presumably, men frame shrewd, rational plans and carry out heroic, effective deeds. In the experience of this platoon, however, nobody does either of these things.

Because the American troops on the other side of the island have already won the campaign, that victory transforms the platoon's efforts all along into irrelevancy. Within this superfluous assignment, to scout the pass, Croft makes up an even more preposterous task, to cross over, not through, the mountain; even if they had mastered the impossible terrain, they would surely have run into outnumbering Japanese guns. Further reducing their sense of manly combat, their own side causes most (perhaps all) of their casualties. Roth falls off a ledge during the needless climb, and, worse, Croft deliberately sets up Hearn for an ambush, to get rid of a rival. Registering Croft's murder of Hearn and recognizing the futility of the march, several of the exhausted remnants wonder if they ought to shoot their crazy sergeant; when they fail to do so, they feel ashamed, as if they have become the "goddam woman" to whom Croft once again compares anyone who dares protest (695).

If the uncertain survivors on the boat might be tempted to forget their shame by identifying with the larger group of Americans who have successfully wrapped up the campaign, they cannot take much comfort in manly rational plans and heroic feats in that direction either. Busily plotting, General Cummings is away badgering the navy to give him a ship for an unnecessary side assault when his soldiers blindly break through the Toyaku Line without him. Major Dalleson, no strategist, has the luck to guess right and urge the troops to keep going. Moreover, the infantry can defeat the Japanese not because the Americans fight especially valiantly against a worthily prepared foe, but because the Japanese have long since exhausted their supplies. The victors simply overrun emaciated, sickly opponents—and then don't capture them as they now could and should, but instead slaughter the masses (718–19). The whole campaign has been far from heroic.

Supposed to differentiate strong men from weak women, war instead exposes all human beings as naked, trembling, blundering. Nevertheless, the characters never comprehend that the gender expectations instilled in them were irrelevant to begin with. They simply feel humiliated that they haven't lived up to them. And although Mailer certainly grasps the absurdity of looking for rationality and heroism in modern war, he does not question, any more than his characters do, his society's basic gender divisions. Confining his female characters to a narrow repertoire of whining, nagging, and cheating, Mailer offhandedly blames women as the source of all unmet goals for manhood. He titles the biographical sketch that will explain Hearn's problems "The Addled Womb" (328), just as contemporary pop-sociologists were ranting against "momism"—mothers' coddling of sons—as the supposed cause of the large number of men who broke down in combat (Epstein 249). *The Naked and the Dead* gives no inkling that the need to name and polarize masculine and feminine traits, which in reality constantly blur, helps fuel war in the first place.

Another work which goes far to mock the expectation that war "makes men," without quite overthrowing it, is Joseph Heller's *Catch-22*. When a staff psychiatrist warns Yossarian, "I have very bad news for you. Are you man enough to take it?" Yossarian refreshingly spurns a century's efforts: " 'God, no!' screamed Yossarian, 'I'll go right to pieces' " (311). Women are supposed to go to pieces over trivia, whereas men keep stoic even in the face of serious threat. Yossarian, of course, is in danger of literally going to pieces, if his bomber explodes, and he is absolutely right that he would no longer be a man, living, no matter what stoicism he had mustered. Still, Yossarian does not throw a real fit over the escalating number of missions; he only feigns hysteria, as he cleverly tries to scheme his way to a psychiatric discharge. Probably Heller can get away with letting Yossarian even pretend to reject the usually all-important status "man enough" for two reasons: the sixteen years since the end of the war and, especially, the genre of the book. Comedy allows characters to blurt truths (who would want to be a man, as defined?) and scramble through sensible, unheroic deeds (Yossarian quests only to desert), which can be passed off as exaggerated or outrageous. Nevertheless, the novel must have gained its enormous popularity in part because Yossarian admits outright what millions of readers were thinking privately in their hearts: "Man enough? God, no."

Writing a serious work, not comedy like Heller's, and without keeping women at the bottom of the heap, as Mailer does, James Jones in *The Thin Red Line* locates and then criticizes a number of World War II gender expectations. The novel extensively debunks the notion of habitual and spontaneous bravery in "real men" and undoes a traditional dichotomy of martial man versus loving woman. Jones undermines this old division by validating Private John Bell's love for his wife (both sexual desire and strong emotional caring) and by reversing masculine and feminine personal names.

The Thin Red Line explicitly discloses that the need to prove manliness motivates men of all ranks to go to war and stay in it, edging out all other reasons. Corporal Fife, for example, admits that he is not fighting for God, freedom, democracy, or "the dignity of the human race," but only because "he didn't want anyone to think he was a nervous sissy" (122–23). Similarly, Captain Stein overlooks a raid that his soldiers are planning against a cache of marine guns, because he doesn't want to appear "an old maid, a wet blanket who ruined all the fun with overcautious advice" (100). Apparently, a man distinguishes himself from a "maid" by theft; what "fun" when the marines find their weapons gone. On another occasion, just as Stein is deciding not to bring charges of insubordination against Fife for a bit of uncharacteristic backtalk, a bird suddenly "whistled shrilly as though it had seen a woman" (117). Stein clearly regards himself as that woman, someone to whom forgiveness is supposed to be innate, simply because he has pitied Fife's fatigue. The captain then worries that he has "lost face" before his company, affronting the all-determining gaze of other men (117).

If the characters in *The Thin Red Line* dutifully try to demonstrate manliness, Jones boldly reveals that contemporary definitions of masculinity are both artificial and unattainable. Pfc Doll dimly recognizes that "everybody made up a fiction story about himself, and then he just pretended to everybody that that was what he was" (14). Significantly, no one may fashion a separate, private "fiction story" but must don one of a few socially approved costumes. Big Queen discovers that his peers consider him an aggressive bruiser, yet living up to his "myth" does not come naturally; remembering "how to act" perpetually "tired him" (63–64). After their first combat, the company similarly understand that a mantle has descended, conferring the title "tough veteran; that much had been explained to them, and they sought desperately to carry out the role—not only because they were egotistically proud of it, but also because there wasn't any other role" (355). To a degree of self-consciousness unusual in 1962, Jones knows that masculinity is a complex but strictly controlled social construct, imposed on men, who find no other subject positions available to them.

Whereas Jones's characters cannot seem to shuck off the social constructions of manliness, the book as a whole furiously deconstructs several of them. The myth of habitual masculine courage assumes that men never fear, strike the foe spontaneously and consistently, fight selflessly for others or a larger cause, and achieve active agency in their lives. In *The Thin Red Line*, however, all feel afraid, and a man who charges bravely one moment may inconsistently cower in another mood (330). Instead of supporting a public cause, here men undertake the most "heroic" feats only out of personal and petty motives. Dale volunteers for a raid solely to get out of the kitchen, and Doll goes along in a reflex to compete with Dale (225, 228). When Doll then disables a Japanese gun emplacement, he dashes forward not because he draws on the courage and brilliant planning with which he is later credited, but because he "simply could not stand it [waiting] any longer" (281). More self-aware but just as privately motivated, Bell joins special missions hoping to go home sooner to his wife (234). Bell further understands that while his comrades may vaguely claim to be fighting for their country, they struggle on as "tough" infantrymen only when they have developed a "rooted bitterness" against their own government (356).

Perhaps most damaging to the myth of innate and inexhaustible masculine bravery, Bell realizes that such tough soldiers possess no active agency at all. Just as Wilfred Owen in World War I recognized that men who "slashed bones bare" really derived their "power" from despair and their "exultation" from exhaustion (Owen 101), Bell, with more up-to-date chemical vocabulary, discovers that "adrenaline" propels "automatons without courage or cowardice" (305–06).

Whereas these robots "thought they were men" (275), in fact, a "numbness" has turned them into "something animal" (350).

Besides undercutting the myth of habitual bravery in men, Jones also upsets an old division of masculine and feminine into fighting versus loving. If the nineteenth century advised men to control their sexuality, the next century allows and indeed requires men to demonstrate specifically heterosexual desire; yet at the same time the ideal of self-control remains strongly residual. The resulting contradictions urge a man to find a female partner, but "too much" sensuality with her can still damn him as womanly. Similarly, if a man combines "too much" emotion with his heterosexuality, he again risks crossing his society's gender boundaries into perceived womanliness.

Bell has specifically offended such gender arbiters, incarnated in his superior officers, during a prewar stint as a First Lieutenant in a Corps of Engineers. After four months in the Filipino jungle, separated from his wife, Marty, in Manila, Bell resigns his commission, to spend more time with her. Bell's choice of love-life over military life so angers his commanders that they vow to see him both drafted and barred from future rank. These commanders represent a survival of the Antony Syndrome, the view of the Roman warriors in Shakespeare's *Antony and Cleopatra* that a strong sensual and emotional devotion to one woman will cancel out fighting ability. Bell's superiors manage, in fact, to get Bell drafted and parted from Marty after only eight more months together— and not just because of the exigencies of the time, for the government undertakes its vendetta against the couple even before war breaks out.

By the end of the novel, when Bell's competent soldiering has secured him a new commission to First Lieutenant after all, it may look as if his old bosses have failed in one part of their revenge, to keep him at low rank. However, Bell's revolution full circle, back to his beginning, does not mark a victory for him, as Peter Jones claims in *War and the Novelist* (140). Instead, the government wins, for Bell must again serve the state and its values. Showing no triumph, he takes the promotion only because "he would probably do as little harm there as he would anywhere else" (507). If he is still striving to do "little harm," his ideal blatantly snubs everything the state is expecting, that "manly" men destroy and do extensive harm to state enemies. Moreover, Bell's bosses score a main point in their original vengeful plan, because he is again separated from his wife. He cannot rejoin her for long years during the war, and, finally, she writes Bell asking for a divorce, saying she has fallen in love with another man.

Whereas Bell's commander assumes that he will retaliate against Marty (506), Bell himself feels no such vindictiveness and, in fact, believes that she has acted correctly in replacing him. For one thing, he suspects that after repeated coatings of protective "numbness," he (and most veterans) will return home after the war permanently altered for the worse (296, 466). Second, he agrees that she should choose another man in the present: "that powerful, perpetually affirming, female force for life that was in her would require her to go on living, even when she might not want to" (68). Although this wording falls into several contemporary stereotypes about women, Bell is also groping toward innovative conclusions. Like many men in the nineteenth and twentieth centuries, he erroneously assumes that a woman cannot experience her sexuality without a man to initiate it, and he calls an erotic "force for life" more "female" than "male." Despite these misconceptions, Bell untypically grants that his wife ought to enjoy sex and emotional support in the present, with another man if her husband is absent. And instead of labeling that "force for life" "female," he could more accurately call it "human," since such eroticism clearly inhabits him just as strongly.

One interesting way Jones praises Bell's wife is by reversing the feminine and masculine names of his characters. The only woman even referred to in the book, Marty has a masculine-sounding name; further, Jones assigns numerous male characters feminine-sounding names, such as Big Queen or McCron, whose sound *crone* is furthered reinforced by the nickname Mother McCron. (Even if "Mother" abbreviates "mother-fucker," the shortened form leaves his sex ambiguous.) Some of Jones's tags resemble items that girls might own, such as Doll and Bead, while others—Milly (Millard) Beck, Nellie Coomb, Dale, and Carol or Carrie Arbre—could designate men or women. When surnames conjure up musical instruments, they are not the bombastic drum or trumpet but a quieter Fife and Bell. By his unusual roster, Jones suggests that Bell and the other soldiers, pursuing the war solely to receive the imprimatur as active "man," end up "automatons," doing nothing on their own initiative (306). By contrast, Jones allows Marty, outside the war, to be the only "man" in the book. That is, by deciding what she wants, acting on her decision, and enjoying what she has, Marty lives out supposedly masculine prerogatives. And by combining that action with caring emotion, she gets to be a full person, which most of the soldiers do not.

If proving and reproving manhood are required of all American males the need may drive African-Americans, recent immigrants, and Native Americans most urgently. Participation in the world wars looked like a possible route to acceptance, since even the U.S. Constitution seems to predicate full citizenship on an ambiguous right/duty to bear arms (Adams, *Best War* 83). Negroes had enlisted in World War I expecting to claim that right, but they were, in fact, confined to menial tasks. Despite this bitter experience, the outbreak of World War II produced the same hopes. As Tech/Sgt Waters in Charles Fuller's *A Soldier's Play* exclaims, "The First War, it didn't change much for us, boy—but this one—it's gonna change a lot of things" (384). Unfortunately, the sole, magical elixir for transforming "boy" into "man" is fighting; "We are men—soldiers—," Waters asserts, exactly equating the two (390). He is optimistic that the desperation of the war will push the government to allow Negroes into combat. Ironically, however, even as America did finally ask Negroes to fight for democracy, the armed forces remained undemocratically segregated until 1948.

As Jones subversively parallels women and men, assumed to be different, Fuller questions some of the hierarchies of American culture by closely paralleling blacks and whites. Pushed to prove himself equal to a white man, Tech/Sgt Waters unfortunately duplicates the worst traits of the whites, as well as reproducing the same absurd notions of manliness. Just as whites have excluded him, Waters tries to exclude a "geechy," a Southern black soldier named C.J., whose "bowin' and scrapin'—smilin' in everybody's face" uncomfortably remind Waters of old stereotypes (382–83). Whereas the other members of the unit appreciate C.J.'s blues songs and his mild, accommodating manner, Waters excoriates the young private's willingness to say "yassah boss" and blames him for dragging Negroes down, rather than blaming the bosses themselves (383). When Waters deliberately provokes C.J. to hit him, so as to get this "Sambo" out of the way in jail (389), the sergeant even declaims, "Them Nazis ain't all crazy—a whole lot of people just can't fit into where things seem to be goin'—like you, C.J. The black race can't afford you no more" (384). Fuller does not shrink from exposing that Waters's acceptance of "power" as the highest value, solely because that's what "whites respect," only sinks him to the point of duplicating the lowest racism himself (385).

After C.J. hangs himself in jail, however, Waters's unintended contribution to that death weighs heavily on the sergeant. He discovers that imitating the worst of the white men has not made them accept him: "I've killed for you," he mumbles drunkenly to white officers, in guilty exaggeration, "And nothin' changed!" (380). However, Waters has no time to let his new regrets alter his behavior, for another black soldier, Pfc Peterson, finally shoots him, for "Justice," for "C.J.! Everybody!" (392). Correctly perceiving that Waters "can't look good unless he's standin' on you," Peterson adds nothing new by stomping on the sergeant in turn, dehumanizing Waters as an "it": "If this was a German would you kill it? If it was Hitler—or that fuckin' Tojo?" (383, 392). Just as the sergeant thought that he was opposing racist whites, only to turn fascist himself, Peterson believes that he counters Waters, only to mirror him exactly. Furthermore, by assimilating all enemies to just two leaders, Peterson also conveniently forgets that many Japanese and German soldiers remain as manipulated as he, often by the same taunt: that they have failed to become "men." Yet by accepting violence as the sure route to manhood, Peterson—like the men of all races and all sides—only hurts his own.

Confusing gender and sex, societies try to convince men that if they behave in an "unmanly" way, contrary to accepted gender prescriptions, the men will be literally "unmanned." The need to prove "balls" (as William Manchester's Tubby says) replaces larger community goals with private image-making. This irrational fear of emasculation tames even would-be rebels. Although Norman Mailer and Joseph Heller mock military "chickenshit," they cannot step back far enough to accomplish a larger critique of the sex/gender system that supports wars in the first place. A. L. Barker, James Jones, and Charles Fuller more thoroughly satirize that gender system, which trains men to seek danger for its own sake, take violent revenge, hide compassion, and deny even sexual passion, if it is combined with supposedly feminine tenderness.

(b) I Fight to Prove I'm Not Attracted to Men (but I Do Want to See Male Bodies)

Compared to the soldiers of World War I, men in World War II seem less able to enjoy the vista of male flesh. Writers still revive the World War I genre of naked bathing, but only to burlesque it or hedge it with despair, as seen in Keith Douglas's poetry (1942–1943) and Joseph Heller's *Catch-22* (1961). Although World War II soldiers engage in fairly common "deprivation homosexuality" (Adams, *Best War* 84), here too any literary accounts register unease, rather than the zest of Wilfred Owen's or Frederic Manning's eroticized camaraderie. Novelists who cast a character as a "confirmed" homosexual often portray him as a kind of enemy at home, or show him nervously retreating from his desires, as in Norman Mailer's *The Naked and the Dead* (1948), Alexander Baron's *From the City, from the Plough* (1949), and Dennis Murphy's *The Sergeant* (1958). Behind the hesitant characters, writers also seem to retreat from examining inherited notions about sex. In a striking exception, novelist James Jones in *The Thin Red Line*

(1962) daringly breaks down the polarization of heterosexual and homosexual, and he boldly blames a socially induced guilt over *any* sexuality as a major factor contributing to wars.

What happened to make World War II writers more wary of homo-eroticism? For one thing, American military services advertised more loudly than ever the harsh punishments for consenting sex between men. William Manchester recalls the theatrical procedure for lining up a marine company at strict attention, intoning the names of the accused, detailing the charges in a combination of legalese and slurs, and brandishing the penalty: eighty-five years in Portsmouth Naval Prison, for oral sex (120–21). However, at the same time that the military continued to prosecute homosexual *acts* as a "crime," service psychiatrists started to label homosexual *persons* "mentally ill" (Bérubé 133). The new approach did nothing to end insult and actually added to penalties. Between 1941 and 1945 alone, the services ejected at least 4,000 sailors and 5,000 soldiers, many more than the hundreds convicted of sodomy between 1900 and the start of World War II (Bérubé 147). And although authorities now considered these rejected men "ill," they still called them "dishonorable," subject to just as many disastrous consequences as under the old penal system, since dishonorable discharge seriously hindered civilian employment (Bérubé 128, 139).

The American government first turned to the relatively new discipline of psychiatry for help in screening recruits, as if better selection could prevent a repetition of the large number of "shell-shock" cases in World War I. Ignoring the obvious reasons for breakdown—the horrors of killing others, seeing friends killed, and anticipating one's own death in anonymous, mechanized warfare—psychiatrists pointed to homosexuals as most likely to fail in battle because of two presuppositions: "arrested development," an idea that came with an imprimatur from Freud (though not with proofs), and "effeminacy," a slur that came only with the imprimatur of prejudice (Bérubé 156).

Fastening on Freud's developmental model, which held that heterosexuals had as infants passed through a stage of bisexuality but abandoned it, World War II psychiatrists branded adult homosexuals eternally "immature," unable to take up proper mating or proper fighting (Bérubé 136–37). "Mature" men, by contrast, must crave women's bodies, and they must develop an equally eager "taste for battle" (Bérubé 176). Oddly, the whole society linked these two tastes, in an ongoing Apollo Syndrome. Although the doctors thought that all heterosexuals inevitably outgrew attraction to men, they still feared that some men might fall back, after all. The doctors continued to contradict themselves. If same-sex drives normally belong to most people, how can expressing them be "abnormal" (Bérubé 45)?

Just as the new idea of homosexuality as "arrested development" was mired in the very traditional Apollo Syndrome, so too did the notion of effeminacy derive more from conventional thinking than from empiricism. Like Havelock Ellis before World War I, military psychiatrists in World War II searched for signs of effeminacy, which they had already concluded by focusing on body type, mannerisms, and temperament, all dubiously assessed. Even when one of the army's own researchers, Major Carl H. Jonas, observed that the bodies of sixty homosexual soldiers, compared to those of sixty "normal" soldiers, were, on average, "no more masculine or feminine than the control group," his superiors discounted his findings (Bérubé 156). Jonas also wondered if some of the "feminine" mannerisms, in gestures or gait, that his colleagues were recording for homosexuals might derive in part from subjective opinions of the scientists, in part from in-group code, purposely cultivated. Effeminate temperament likewise depended heavily on shifting and gerrymandered categories of gender. If homosexual soldiers vigorously objected to hospitalization as "mentally ill," they were seen as "petulant," "like women," but others who resignedly went along with orders to report to hospital were similarly classed as "weak," "like women" (Bérubé 157).

If World War II psychiatrists intended to exclude homosexuals as useless for war, militarists discovered instead that the new, messy mix of concepts about homosexuality—*either* criminal *or* ill *but* dishonorable *and* always effeminate—proved very useful for recruitment. Society still defined effeminacy so broadly—everything from an aversion to killing to a penchant for pleasure, from a liking for books to a capacity for affection—that virtually all soldiers must have secretly suspected their own "femininity" at some point. And with the press of flesh at "heads" on transport ships so dense that marines stood "almost wedged against each other, a few inches from sodomy" (Manchester 193), many must also have felt an erotic twinge or two: all the more reason to worry if one belonged among the "lewd," "lascivious," and unmasculine "degenerates" so insistently publicized (Manchester 120–21). Whenever a culture locates masculinity preeminently in fighting, a constantly fanned uncertainty about masculine status helps push men of all sexual orientations to war.

Even within an atmosphere of draconian punishment for homosexuality (imprisonment with hard labor, witch hunts, interrogations, scorn, and dishonorable discharge), men may ignore official warnings, to find comfort in the closeness of male bodies, whether engaging in sex or just looking. For the pure pleasures of the gaze, one has only to relish Albert Murray's painting *A Lighter Moment during Arduous Training*, which features a crowd of naked men relaxing on a beach and diving off a ship in the background (Lanker and Newnham 174–75). Civilian life in the 1940s would not likely offer such a scene, except in nudist colonies, for a different clientele. Only the military setting licenses such widely communal, idyllic bathing.

Nevertheless, the frank telling of such simple pleasures, either in paint or print, encounters more obstacles in World War II than I. Franklin Boggs's *End of a Busy Day*, which pictures two medical corpsmen washing blood out of a sheaf of stretchers, met overt censorship (Lanker and Newnham 164). Originally, Boggs had painted the man in the shallows just as he saw him, naked, but government sponsors insisted that Boggs put drawers on him. Disgruntled, the painter complied: "That's weird. You can kill people, but you can't show one naked person" (qtd. in Lanker and Newnham 165). At the same time that the war loosens some inhibitions about the body, authorities may still drum in a message about immorality. This contradiction leads participants in wartime mores either to feel guilt (an idea taken up by Jones; see the end of this section), or else to feel no shame but still keep quiet about overseas experiences.

Official stoking of anxiety seems to have dashed enthusiasm for depicting wartime nudity in words as well as paint. Simon Featherstone suggests that Keith Douglas's poem "Mersa" (1942), named for an Egyptian town where British troops were stationed, invokes the World War I genre of naked bathing, only to bring it to a close. In the poem, an officer watches "cherry skinned soldiers" undress on a beach, but then he studiously focuses only on his own feet under the water, while fish alone "nip the flesh," as he sees himself dead (Douglas 99). Because the officer remains solitary at the end, the poem denies the sense of sharing and "military community" that consoled soldiers in World War I bathing scenes (Featherstone 93).

Like Featherstone in poetry, Paul Fussell finds in fiction only a last example of the bathing genre, announcing its future impossibility. He points to a scene from Joseph Heller's *Catch-22*, where Kid Sampson stands nude on a raft, while several dozen naked companions swim or lounge on the beach. McWatt, circling with his airplane, finally dips too low as Sampson jumps, so that a propeller slices him in half (347). When McWatt realizes what he has done, he flies his plane into a mountain and dies too. Fussell argues that if Sampson incarnates the bodily fragility important to bathing scenes of the earlier world war,

Heller's version arrests the tradition "because the homoerotic element has been purged away" (*Modern Memory* 307). Actually, Heller may still be imitating the conventional homoeroticism, but only to travesty it. Writing that "Kid Sampson had rained all over" (348), Heller echoes old myths that interpret rain as a sky god's ejaculation, to bless the earth (Graves, *Greek Myths* 1: 31), an image that Wilfred Owen had defiantly borrowed for his homoerotic poem "Storm" (60). Whereas Owen's version combined exuberance at the men's sexuality with despair at the war, Heller's scene can accommodate no blessing at all, only a horrible scattering of Sampson's flesh and blood.

As Heller shows simple bathing scenes headed toward disaster, homosexual characters in the literature of World War II commonly appear as "guilt-ridden, pathologically violent, or suicidal" (Gilbert and Gubar 250). Dennis Murphy's novel *The Sergeant*, for example, ends violently, after Master Sergeant Callan, winner of the Distinguished Service Cross, confusedly courts Pfc Swanson. Although Swanson is obviously drawn to Callan in return, the younger man cannot cast off his Manichean morality. While he talks with the sergeant, Swanson feels vivacious and joyous, but Callan's presence still turns "everything dark"; however, if Swanson puts his arm unenthusiastically around his patient French girlfriend, her company must signal a "beginning whiteness" (211). When Callan realizes that he cannot untrain Swanson's stark polarization of good and evil, the sergeant kills himself, so that his idol can breathe "steady and clear," never having to question his real desires again (254).

Nevertheless, on the last two pages, Murphy grants the two men a distant, purely symbolic mating, as if verbal pyrotechnics could somehow compensate the homophile reader for Callan's death. Seeking a sequestered place for his suicide, Callan "plunged into the clearing, leaping out toward the earth"; as Swanson hears the rifle blast, he seems to receive this orgasmic "bursting sureness" in his own body, which "caught and tightened with the intensity, the sorrow of it" (253–54). In another way of giving compensatory praise to Callan, the novel parallels the opening scene, where Callan bravely runs near a wood to kill German machine gunners, with the closing sequence, where Callan runs along the edge of the wood to kill himself. These echoes insist that the sergeant renounces Swanson nobly, duplicating his initial heroism. Yet this construct of noble sacrifice still unquestioningly accepts Callan *as* the enemy, since in the second scene he must replace the Germans in the position of target.

Two other World War II novelists, Alexander Baron (pseudonym for Alec Bernstein) and Norman Mailer, also cast a homosexual character as the enemy, by making him profess tenets of Nazism. In the British novel *From the City, from the Plough*, Baron treats a major's admiration for naked male bodies as reprehensible in itself. Since "mad" Major Maddison first watched nude men play volleyball in Germany, Baron hints that any homoeroticism, even among one's own citizens, must still somehow derive from foreign influence. Maddison also holds fascist beliefs. He "lives for war," exerts excessive discipline, loves violence for its own sake, slurs a "Jewboy," and reveres an abstract "mystic communion of soldiers," whose lives he negligently risks (71, 76–77). Although Baron seems close to admitting that racism and militarism exist among Britishers as well as Germans, he avoids examining these problems after all by diverting attention to the major's sexuality. When Maddison fantasizes himself in battle, "bleeding and smoke-blackened," feeling "delight" as his bayonet meets "the coy resistance of flesh," Baron represents homosexuality as inevitably sadomasochistic (80). He also makes war a homosexual pursuit—although, ironically, most of his British and American peers were assuming just the reverse, that homosexuals cannot fight.

Like Baron, the American Norman Mailer in *The Naked and the Dead* creates a compatriot who admires men's bodies at the same time that the character preaches a blatantly fascist philosophy. Only once, in Europe, does Cummings go home with a man who solicits sex, but the stranger only steals from him, and Cummings vows, "It must never come out": neither rumor of the incident nor expression of his own desires (426). He not only puts a tight rein on himself but also seeks the "route to control" others (718). By the time he receives a promotion to general, Cummings is certain that rigid ranks ought to govern the army and the whole society, with each man fearing the one above and scorning the one below—as if to ensure that hierarchy will lock men into safely untouching places (176). Although the social condemnation of homosexuality seems responsible for warping the general toward totalitarian control, Mailer indicts homosexuality itself.

For one thing, Mailer reproduces the contemporary, unfavorable association of male homosexuality with effeminacy, which means, of course, that he never questions what "feminine" means either. As a boy, Cummings likes to sew, imitating his mother, who "embroiders another golden stitch on the buttocks of the Cupid" (405). As if the buttocks weren't enough of an authorial sly signal, sewing too functions as code for effeminacy. In 1897, Havelock Ellis bizarrely declared that all inverted men and all non-inverted women innately love needlework (97). One of the bestselling American advice books for parents in the 1920s urged vigilance against a boy "who likes to sew and knit"; unless promptly curbed, he would surely turn into a homosexual (qtd. in Kimmel, *Manhood* 203).

Just as Mailer employs sewing as an infallibly gendered marker, he presents self-hurting as the spontaneous heart's desire of all women and all homosexual men. General Cummings, attracted to Lieutenant Hearn, prods him into elaborate power plays over trivial matters. In one example, Cummings tries to cow his subordinate into picking up a cigarette, which the latter has rebelliously crushed on the general's spotlessly clean floor. When Cummings first catches sight of the insolently ground cigarette (read "butt"?), he is said to feel "rage" but also "fear" and a "troubled excitement . . . as if he had been a young girl undressing before the eyes of a roomful of strange men" (318). In another instance of wanting to be overwhelmed by hostile force, Cummings commands Hearn to bring a heavy map board; when it falls against the general's shins, he wonders if he hadn't perhaps solicited that pain (398). Just as Havelock Ellis complacently defined masochism as "almost normal in women" (66), Mailer too sees only mastering and being mastered, hurting and being hurt, in *any* sexual relationship. Because Cummings has learned that a "girl undressing" is passive and inferior, and because he believes he must resemble that girl, he strives actively to master others, because he's been taught that mastery advertises masculinity.

Although Mailer seems to accuse homosexuals exclusively of harboring an excessive need to control others, the novel presents contrary evidence that the need to bolster uncertain superiority afflicts all men of this society. Croft, for example, the hard-driving sergeant, enacts on a more visceral, inarticulate level the general's more intellectual musings about power. Although Croft may seem to gravitate naturally to conquest, a process apparently different from Cummings's studied efforts, both men worry that they have detected some trait in themselves designated feminine: for Cummings, attraction to men, for Croft, paralyzing fear during a Japanese attack (155). This single moment of fright in his whole life haunts Croft for the rest of the book, as he tries to deny human vulnerability to death by assigning it to women only. In the past, sleeping with another man's wife, Croft had scorned all women as "deer to track," fuming, "I HATE EVERYTHING WHICH IS NOT IN MYSELF" (164). More likely, he despises feelings that *are* in himself and all people, but once his society arbitrarily labels some of his feelings feminine, he must struggle not to be found out as much as Cummings does.

Interestingly, both Cummings and Croft deride sexual desire of any kind. Whenever Cummings reaches out to Hearn, he regards his need as an "indulgence" and ever afterward wants to get back at Hearn for witnessing his "weakness" (319). Similarly, Croft, despite his whoring, is a trained puritan at heart. He taunts Goldstein, "you can beat your meat if you're gettin' anxious," equating masturbation with apprehensiveness or even sensible prudence (124). As Croft has foisted off fear onto women only, he now pushes pleasure-seeking into the women's camp too, since he assumes that only women could ever be timid or "give in" to desire.

Far from idiosyncratic, Croft shares this fundamental disdain for pleasure with most of the men in Mailer's novel. Brown, for example, thinks about how each man, alone on guard duty, is "beating our meat for company," but he judges himself "disgusting" (120). In his study *Virtue under Fire*, John Costello assumes that masturbation must have been fairly widespread among servicemen, but "masturbation guilt" still hounded men often enough to be spelled out as a "medical disorder" (101–02). The ingrained self-hatred of Mailer's masturbating characters hurts not only these men but the women they later seek out, because shared sexuality, no more than solitary, cannot privilege pleasure. Only power—not equality, not bodily delight—licenses sex. Such a system explicitly reduces women to ciphers and "gauges," by which men measure themselves "in relation to other men" (Mailer 322), and, paradoxically, it reduces the men's own male bodies to "disgusting" hindrances to manhood (120).

Once Cummings and Croft have learned to feel ashamed of their feelings and bodies, they seem able to experience pleasure only in displaced form. When Cummings fires the big guns, he thrills to their force and hears their sound as a "sharp detumescent roar" (565). Mailer dwells on the sexual nature of the general's love of weaponry (568), but he makes no such explicit link for the sergeant's. Yet when Croft wants to kill a Japanese prisoner so he can watch the victim's "quick lurching spasms," Mailer leaves the way open to interpret this voyeurism too as sexual (193). However, if Mailer brushes against an important insight about sadism in these two scenes, he never examines any social attitudes toward sex that might push men toward violence. Instead, he diagnoses their eroticizing of guns as the inexplicable, innate quirk of a rare few: Cummings, born to embroider on Cupid's buttocks, or a near-insane Croft, "whelped mean" (156). For Mailer, the danger emanating from these two powermongers derives from a biological flaw present at birth, not a warped social training.

By contrast, James Jones in *The Thin Red Line* is much more venturesome in exploring a culturally forged link between all kinds of sexuality and war. With unusual openness, the novel depicts a wide range of characters seeking out sexual contacts with other men. All fiercely deny, however, that *they* could be homosexual, because they have been taught to define "queers" as womanly (127). Yet even the more highly valued heterosexuality, if a man combines it with emotional attachment, may still transgress gender boundaries into an unacceptable realm of the feminine. However, when Jones portrays John Bell's love for his wife, Marty, the author undermines his culture's polarization of womanly and manly and, provocatively, questions the very divisions into heterosexual and homosexual. Finally, Jones illuminates the relationship between war-making and the fear and condemnation of *any* kind of sexuality—whether masturbation, homosexuality, heterosexuality, or whatever other names societies may fashion. The novel implicitly argues that war itself is a skewed reaction to a socially instilled and unnecessary sexual guilt.

By presenting several men who seek out male partners, Jones suggests that such desire is far from rare. Bead proposes to his tent-mate Fife that they have three choices: to "beat it" (masturbate), find a "queer," or "help each other out" (126). They decide to "help each other out," without having to readjust any labels for themselves. Later in the book, Doll attempts to seduce Arbre, but when both expect to be on top, they part in a huff. Yet each of the four men now feels he must prove that he is not one of the "fairies" (127). Fife, for example, thinks he is counteracting his sex with Bead by ordering his assistant in a more "authoritarian" style (127), apparently because he has learned to associate command, even arbitrary and stupid command, with masculinity. Defining manhood as conquest over a loser, the soldiers group "fairies" with women and then dismiss both as basically asexual, passive, abject, and cowardly.

Jones, however, debunks this stereotype of cowardice by making Bead the first of his company to kill any of the Japanese enemy, in the hand-to-hand combat that his peers have superstitiously set up as a test of manliness. Another soldier who pursued an interest in men's bodies, Doll, wins the Silver Star, one of the few medals in the book. Even as Jones is questioning all definitions of "courage" (section (a)), he shows that anatomy of a man's sexual partner, male or female, is irrelevant to his ability to clear society's sometimes foolish hurdles of "heroism."

When Jones's soldiers "help each other out" sexually, they face a bewildering array of terminology (126). Fife remembers that respected oldtimers may have "boyfriends," who in turn are expected to find girls later in life, but "None of this buggering was considered homosexual by anyone" (127). After his contacts with Bead, Fife does not know what label to apply to himself and is terrified that someone might unfavorably categorize him. Doll also draws on a whole taxonomy of "coke sackers, sock tuckers, and cork soakers," a kind of censor-evading code for sucking and tucking cocks (478). However, the widespread currency of "cocksucker" as "a familiar putdown among GIs during the war" (Bérubé 37) suggests that quite a few soldiers can visualize the possibilities of male–male sex, even as they distance themselves from it. When Jones allows his characters Fife, Bead, Doll, and Arbre to overstep heterosexual boundaries drawn for men in mid-century America, he calls into question the construction of such boundaries in the first place.

In addition, Jones strikingly blurs the divisions between heterosexual and homosexual through his most patently heterosexual character, John Bell. As Fife suspects, Bell worries about the possibility that his wife may take lovers in his absence, yet he still does not claim the exclusive dominion over her which Fife assumes. Bell agrees with Fife to the extent of feeling he *ought* to hate Marty if she replaces him with another man, but he continues to love her and believes that she is right to find someone else. Even when he tries to adopt what he regards as normal reactions, he significantly modifies them. After dreaming that Marty bears a black or Japanese baby, he tries to imagine murdering her, but he understands that he would be killing her only because he could not "admit" that he actually liked picturing the other man inseminating her (412).

Bell may not be admitting several truths about himself: that he is less territorial than a man is supposed to be, that he can identify with (and imagine himself as) Marty, and that he can identify with (and enjoy watching) another man—stances usually assigned by his contemporaries to homosexuals. Sexually, Bell can appreciate all positions and all body parts stimulated. Bell knows that Marty is active as well as passive, whether or not he accurately comprehends his wife's physiology; print discussions did not correct Freud's dismissal of the clitoris until the 1960s (D'Emilio and Freedman 312). Bell also understands that giving and taking pleasure can be alternating and reciprocal, not necessarily separated in fixed roles. In fact, he possesses an all-round sensuousness that allows the most comprehensive sexuality. By contrast, a man who insists on being exclusively "heterosexual" (defined as penetrator only) denies other possibilities for his pleasure, while a man who insists on being "masculine" denies the emotion and considerateness that are human, not exclusively feminine at all.

Bell recognizes that his generous sexuality is not acceptable in his society, according to two different standards: one set by these gender assignments, the other by a conservative Christianity. However, by making readers admire Bell and take his views seriously, the novel indicts the Christian devaluation of the body, not only for ruining private lives such as Bell's, but also for fueling the public disaster of war. One scene in particular intriguingly suggests this connection between the social condemnation of sex and a need to make war. As Bell finds himself volunteering again for an especially dangerous mission, to knock out Japanese gun emplacements, he incongruously remembers a sexual episode at age fifteen. On the edge of some woods, hearing voices but remaining hidden himself, the teenager had stripped and masturbated. He realizes that his present risk-taking in the Pacific war is motivated not only by respect for his captain, but also by a desire to experience again the pleasurable defiance of exposing himself, akin to the rebellion that he undertook in the woods. Bell asks provocatively, "Could it be that *all* war was basically sexual? . . . A sort of sexual perversion? Or a complex of sexual perversions? That would make a funny thesis and God help the race" (286).

Bell is not hypothesizing that any of the sexuality in itself is perverse. At fifteen, he stages a kind of righteous protest. Although the people on the road would be shocked and reproving, he knows masturbation is right and does it anyway, even if caught and punished. However, he cannot escape his training entirely, and once Christianity has proclaimed sexuality "fallen nature," several associations lock into place. Not only does the thought of sex provoke the expectation of punishment, but also the anticipation of violent suffering may now trigger the thought of sex. Ascribing shame to the genitals sentences people to accept that their arousal does not and cannot happen without chastisement, what Bell calls "this peculiar masochistic, self-destructive quality in himself" (284). Like Pavlov's dog, which hears a particular note every time it gets food, so that eventually the dog salivates at the sound alone, even without any food, people trained in a sex-hating society may feel excitement at suffering, even without any sex. John Bell discovers "perversion" not in sexuality per se but instead in its branding as wrong from the start, so that the need for a scourge must accompany sex and may even substitute for it (286).

In his nonfiction art book, *WWII* (1975), Jones remarks cryptically that U.S. servicemen should have understood Japanese obsession with "blood and violence and manhood," all tied in with "sexuality and sexual taboos and myths," because Americans have a similar tradition (110). Although he does not elaborate this provocative insight in his commentary on the artwork, Jones's *The Thin Red Line* does explore this trained linking of suffering and sexual response. In addition to Bell's memory of his teenage defiance, an earlier scene in the novel shows the still untested infantrymen, recently landed on Guadalcanal, stumbling upon a bloodstained American shirt in the jungle and whispering over their find in a "peculiar tone of sexual excitement, sexual morbidity" (66). They wear a "sullen look of sexual guilt," like that of "a gang of boys caught masturbating together" (69). Ashamed to be observing something so intimate as the unknown man's blood, they feel not only like "voyeurs" watching someone in "the act of coitus," but also like potential partners, "seducing him" (66). Significantly, Bell and the other men lump together masturbation, sex with a woman, and sex with another man as all, to some degree, transgressive in this culture.

In fact, seeing evidence in the bloodstained shirt of its owner's earlier "pain and fear" (66), the onlookers revert to a kind of primal scene: not, as Freud insisted, a child spying on parents, but a child discovering that one's own sexual experimentation with boys or girls or oneself has unleashed a parent's anger. Bead, for example, recalls a childhood incident when his mother found him "jerking off"—and was so horrified at this supposed uncleanness that she hit him (179). Although Bead resents his mother's fury, he still feels shame; even in the present, when ambushed while defecating and forced to defend himself hand-to-hand, he worries more about keeping his pants clean than killing (179). Similarly, when Bell and his pals finally abandon the bloody shirt to climb onto a mass Japanese grave with "lascivious masochism" (71), they disturbingly accept their own imminent ordeal and possible death, as if this suffering were the necessary consequence of being boys who might be "caught masturbating together" (69). Like Pat Barker's Billy Prior discovering World War I as a vast sadomasochistic machine to allow men a stolen sexual thrill before the wrath that they believe must inevitably follow, Jones's John Bell glimpses that men need World War II to complete a conditioned reflex. They have learned not only that sex will call down punishment but also, perversely, that the cataclysm all around them must have meant sex. The sex can then be surreptitiously continued, *if* it is accompanied by painful expiation, or even displaced into pain. Jones's *The Thin Red Line* boldly suggests that if Western society had not subjected its men to such indoctrination, which insists that all nonreproductive sexual arousal, by women, other men, or oneself, leads to damnation—either in a literal hell or in a denigrated realm of "feminine" sensuality—then perhaps soldiers would not acquiesce so submissively to the wounds of war.

James Jones's "funny thesis" that World War II soldiers have been trained to link sex and death is chillingly borne out in the poem "How to Kill" (1943) by Keith Douglas. The speaker, a British gunner, dwells on tactile and erotic words, but this vocabulary never applies directly to flesh meeting flesh. Instead, the gunner may "touch" the face of an enemy soldier only with the "wires" of his gun-sights, or a mosquito "touches" her own shadow (119). If the gunner notes, "They fuse," the antecedents for "They" can only mean a man and his shadow, blending, or "mosquito death" and the shadowy wisps of mere men, merging (119). At the moment of firing, the speaker cries out and claims to be "amused" to see "the centre of love diffused / and the waves of love travel into vacancy" (119). Eerily, the poem accepts the intense but distant relationship of two men trying to kill each other through machines as a substitute for an embrace. (See Douglas's wording in prose to describe a similar longing for "comradeship with the men who kill them and whom they kill" [Fussell, *Norton* 382].)

In the poem, Douglas's Faustian vocabulary that makes of this British gunner a "damned" worker of "sorcery," with death as his "familiar," implies the unlawfulness of his godlike power to destroy life—without, however, relinquishing that power (119). At the same time, the allusions to Christopher Marlowe's Renaissance play *Doctor Faustus* condemn the "waves of love" as part of the sensual pleasures that Faustus believes he should never have asked for in the first place. Once the modern soldier accepts this grim dictum, he stands far off from other human beings. Yet he still sneaks in orgasmic language, displacing it to the literal explosion of a whole body. Meanwhile, although it is males who are furiously killing each other and symbolically rubbing up against each other, he manages to blame a feminine instigator, by comparing lightweight, negligent death to a specifically female mosquito. The speaker reproduces unchanged the remnant of medieval Christian views in *Doctor Faustus*, which tied sensuality to femininity, inferiority, and death.

Simon Featherstone places Douglas in a group of World War II writers who no longer believe in "honour," "sacrifice," or "patriotism," yet who continue to participate in war as a way to cultivate masculine action, power, understatement, and detachment (109, 113, 114). The critic praises this existential self-making and believes that the poet's "objective" language keeps him from "complicity with brutality or militarism" (Featherstone 110, 113), but it is Douglas's very refusal to judge or protest which makes him an ideal tool for militarism. Caught at the stage of the ball-playing "child turning into a man" as he gazes up into the sky (Douglas 119), the gunner is still waiting for the descent of elusive manhood. Yet when the sorcery to transform child into man in this culture requires impossible feats— avoiding touch, damping emotion—then the frustrated necromancers of denied human attachment, including Jones's Bell and Bead, Heller's McWatt, Murphy's Callan, Mailer's Cummings and Croft, and Baron's Maddison, all settle for the embrace of death.

(c) I Fight to Prove I'm Not Emotional (but I Do Love My Comrades)

Even more self-consciously than World War I soldiers, World War II troops try to project a tough, stoical, "stern" image (Costello 77), to prove that they are not emotional—like women. Yet if World War II grunts and tommies find anything at all valuable in their alternately tedious and terrifying war experience, they again put an emotion-laden camaraderie at the top of the list. An interviewee in Studs Terkel's "*The Good War*" (1984) pinpoints the sense of special license: "There's a strange closeness of the men. You've had no sleep for several days. There's pouring rain and constant fire. It's over and everybody just goes to sleep in big piles. It's a weird sight. Guys in each other's arms. You never see that except in the army" (376). Within the general closeness, soldiers may express strong feelings of tenderness, although onlookers sometimes react uneasily (Alexander Baron's *From the City, from the Plough*). As in World War I literature, this caring may possess a physical dimension, not easily categorized (William Manchester's *Goodbye, Darkness*). For those left out of the bond, however, male camaraderie looks less splendid. Women may envy men's mutual intimacy (Dorothy Parker's "The Lovely Leave"), and minorities only sporadically cross the color line into the brother-hood (Gwendolyn Brooks's *Gay Chaps at the Bar* and John Okada's *No-No Boy*). Finally, a few rare voices hint that fellowship, when it occurs in the context of war, may not merit its privileged place, for outsiders or insiders, all caught in a myth of camaraderie (James Jones's *The Thin Red Line*).

In *From the City, from the Plough* (1949), a powerful novel of D-Day, Alexander Baron elevates tenderness among the men of the British Fifth Battalion into the one redeeming feature of their service. Even riffraff like Scannock, used to bashing the heads of cohorts, or tough-talking Charlie, devoted to black marketeering, surprise themselves by their kindness in the face of danger. Scannock steals a shipment of cigarettes but then, in a generosity unprecedented for him, decides to give his loot to "the lads." When the corporal thanks him, "you're a bloody great thievin' old bastard—bless your little cotton socks" (156), this praise bathes Scannock in "inarticulate delight":

> For the first time in his life the world—gone mad to his comrades—was coming right for him. In battle other men were close to you; they admired you; they talked to you; they passed a mug of steaming tea to you; they crawled under a blanket with you; you marched with them, you felt safe and strong with them, you were one of them. (157)

Similarly helpful despite his bluster, Charlie comforts young Alfie, who wets his blankets before the invasion, and defends Sergeant Shannon, who vomits after it.

In a chapter called "Shannon Ain't So Tough," the sergeant betrays his awareness of the coming battle only by unaccustomed talk about his orphaned childhood; when Baldy scorns Shannon for volubility, "'E ain't so tough, is 'e," Charlie corrects Baldy, "Shut your jaw" (134). During the invasion itself, Shannon plods on stoically, ignoring a limbless trunk flopped down a yard away and pausing only to help blinded Alfie, but at the end of the day he cannot stop replaying these scenes. Seeing the sergeant vomit in a delayed reaction of pity and fear, Baldy again judges, "Shannon ain't so tough," but Charlie again displays the greater understanding, "Quiet, you cowson" (145). Sonya Rose finds that British society during the war tried to combine the combat-soldier with a more domestic version of manhood; an ad to save more at home contrasted a German who "shouts and smashes everything" with a Britisher who would rather "talk to Ma—or mend things for the kids"(154). Yet sentiment in men must still yield to traditionally British "rationality and emotional reserve" (Rose 154). George Orwell goes further, explaining "toughness" as a spreading American influence. In his 1939 essay "Boys' Weeklies," Orwell concludes that, despite more gentleness and civility in the overall tone of the British writing, a "process of Americanisation is going on all the same": "The American ideal, the 'he-man,' the 'tough guy,' the gorilla who puts everything right by socking everybody else on the jaw, now figures in probably a majority of boys' papers" (300). In Baron's novel, although Charlie obviously admires Shannon's combination of competent action and strong feeling, their culture has come to an impasse in naming and evaluating the sergeant's behavior. The refrain about toughness seems unable to settle whether emotion cancels or redefines manliness. In neither case, however, is a man free to refuse violence.

Despite onlookers' discomfort at visible emotion, men need to express not only horror and pity but also love. Using the same exalted language as Remarque, who praised the bond between comrades as "nearer than lovers" (212), William Manchester in *Goodbye, Darkness* (1979) is "haunted" by memories of boot camp, "almost like recalling a broken marriage which, for one divorced partner, can never really end" (148). When he receives a slight wound, he goes AWOL from the hospital—to sneak back to the line. Perplexed at this alacrity in returning to danger, he decides that "an act of love" moved him, a desire to be with his men (451). Echoing many other soldiers who declare, "The reason you storm the beaches is not patriotism or bravery [but] that sense of not wanting to fail your buddies" (Terkel 37), Manchester concludes that marines fight not for glory or country or the corps but "for one another" (451). This discovery leads him to formulate a new definition of the still all-important manhood: "Any man in combat who lacks comrades who will die for him, or for whom he is willing to die, is not a man at all" (451). Instead of proving masculinity by acting tough or protecting women, a man now proves himself by protecting other men. Or rather, he proves that he needs war to allow him to express love for men. Whereas the gender ideology that influenced Manchester's youth had relegated love to the preserve of "woman" and made it her exclusive essence, now Manchester declares "man" the more complete being of love.

Equipped with a depth of feeling he did not expect, a man may well cry. Manchester's buddy Lefty is hit by a sniper, his groin "one vast bloodstain, crimson bubbles forming and breaking on his thighs" (240); when Lefty dies, all his comrades stand at or near tears. Only after the death of his friend can the author freely use the word "love" in his account (236). This love does have a physical component, as Manchester kisses the corpse on the lips and, looking at the gory crotch, muses, "In some obscene, unspeakable, vicarious but identifiable way, I felt that I had lost my virginity after all" (242).[2] Who has penetrated whom? Lefty is bleeding the way a woman bleeds when the hymen is broken? Or Manchester is the one who feels ripped up by loss? The scene may provide evidence for the "funny thesis" of the character John Bell in Jones's *The Thin Red Line*: that a socially induced fear of sexuality fuels wars by fostering displacements or by allowing embraces only in the context of attendant punishment (286).

How might this intense male camaraderie be viewed by the women of the time? Dorothy Parker's story "The Lovely Leave" (1943) shows the baffled exclusion and barbed jealousy that Mimi, wife of an officer, feels toward his fellow soldiers. Informed in a maddeningly brief call of his impending twenty-four-hour leave, she envies the "wild young voices" demanding a turn at the phone, for "he had heeded them and not her" (147). When he then spends the leave itself (reduced to only one hour) ignoring her and praising his "boys," she grants, "it's hard for you" in military training, but she grows painfully aware that "it's never lonely, that's all I mean. You have companionships no—no wife can ever give you" (160). Mimi herself never doubts that women's all-in-all is to love men, but the story nevertheless exposes deep contradictions in the construction of femininity. Such gaps and breaks in the ideology, on which Raymond Williams places any hope of social change ("Base" 38), did eventually lead to a revival of the women's movement a few decades after World War II. If the contradictions in the corresponding construction of masculinity, brilliantly brought out by Parker's story, could also come to more widespread consciousness, they might undermine some of the ideology of strict masculine–feminine opposites that helps shore up wars.

Unquestioningly, Mimi accepts her society's interpellation of her as hostess, particularly in its version as purchaser of goods. With a week before her husband's visit, she focuses entirely on décor, clothing, and sundries, buying "perfume and toilet water and bath oil. She had a bit of each remaining in bottles on her dressing table and in her bathroom, but it made her feel desired and secure to have rich new stores of them" (151). Imbued with the logic of capitalism that increased consumption is always better, she multiplies baubles and lugs home not one but six pots of fuchsia. To offer an opulence that she cannot afford, she goes without basics (lunch) to stock extras (whiskies-and-soda). Moreover, according to her society's expectations for middle-class women, she must not only purchase luxury goods but herself become one: the beautiful, alluring prize at the center of the advertising frame.

The story shrewdly records this identity between Mimi and the surrounding inanimate objects by describing them in terms that her peers might well apply to her. Mimi's view of the objects then varies according to her deteriorating evaluation of herself. Her new nightgown, for example, must be "delightful," "soft," with "little bouquets" and "innocent puffs of sleeves," just as a still operative Victorian ideology construes *her* as delightfully flower-like, innocent, little (insignificant, no matter what her size), and empty-headed, like the "puffs" (151). The "charming" fuchsia are likewise equated with her sexuality. At first she luxuriates in the "delicate parchment-coloured inverted cups" and "graceful magenta bells," but when Mimi revises her opinion of the blossoms to "dirty parchment-coloured cups" and "vulgar magenta bells," the language reflects her induced shame at her own "vulgar" desire, in the face of her husband's indifference (151, 158). Similarly, when the perfume she has sprayed lingers, "too present, too insistent," she feels that she herself insists too much on attention—even that she does not deserve to take up space in the world at all (158). All luxury items, so desirable from one vantage point, are from another completely superfluous, as she has been made to feel.

In fact, underneath the dominant ideology promoted by advertisers that everyone must acquire more and more commodities, a residual Christian ethic dictates self-denial. In either case, Mimi can be written off, as high, coveted gossamer or low, expendable fluff. She feels "unnecessary," to both husband and country (147). Although her society defines her as sex object, Steve does not need her body after all. When he saunters into the room naked, he is searching not for her but for a magazine to read in the bath. Ironically, she had earlier "laid bright-covered magazines about invitingly" among the pillows (151). In her role as hostess, she was supposed to put out attractive objects, with herself among them, but, unfortunately, he picks the wrong one—or, in a consumer culture, the right one, with the more obvious price tag. When he justifies his disappearance into the tub by contrasting its comfort with more spartan barracks showers, "a hundred boys waiting, yelling at you to hurry up," she again feels jealous, because the young men get to see him naked every day (158). While the story does not suggest at all that his sexual orientation turns to them rather than her, the men share the greater emotional tie and even enjoy an easier physical togetherness.

Interestingly, Steve's sexuality seems displaced entirely away from people, whether men or women—toward the "bright magazine" (158) and, more importantly, toward the violence of war. According to a wartime song, "Off we go into the wild blue yonder, / Climbing high into the sun, sun, sun, sun. / Here they come: zooming to meet our thunder—/ At 'em boys, give 'er the gun!" (151–52). Immediately before Steve's arrival, Mimi sings these words in a "sweet, uncertain little voice that made the lusty song ludicrous" (151). Lusty women might zoom to meet lusty men, but, caught between the contradictory requirements that she be entirely sensual but also sweet and innocent of any passion, Mimi hesitates uncertainly. Meanwhile, drill instructors teach the "boys" to divert their sexual energies to killing, as they "give 'er the gun" (152). Ominously for her, aviators personify airplanes as feminine.[3] Ominously for him, drill instructors substitute the gun for the penis, by teaching recruits to chant, "This is my rifle, this is my gun," with one hand directed to genitals (Gilbert and Gubar, "Charred Skirts" 226).

Feeling unnecessary when she hovers outside her husband's bath, Mimi also languishes uselessly without him. Although she works at an office job, she disparages it, "[d]ull as mud," and she possesses no friends but him (156). She deprecates her life and places it far beneath the soldier's: "I know you're doing the most important thing in the world, maybe the only important thing in the world" (155). Like her society, she elevates his killing as "most important," yet, in a self-abasement nowadays painful to read, she assigns destruction somehow more to her hands than to his. As she tries to stop lashing out at him for his neglect by redirecting her anger toward herself, she blames her own "nonsense" for the "ugly small ruin" of an earlier leave (147, 149). Such language enables them both to avoid the absurd nonsense of the much larger ruin wrought by war.

Yet behind Mimi's abjection, the story marvelously brings out contradictions in this construction of a masculine subject, supposedly performing the only serious work. For if Mimi fusses over superficialities such as dress, to please him, Steve spends most of his hour's leave obsessing over his belt buckle and uniform, to please his new commanding officer. As careful of accessories as she, he must adjust his flight cap "one inch over the eye, one inch above the ear" (149).[4] When he even asks for nail polish and "Shine-O" to polish the buckle, he surrounds himself with the same consumer items that supported her in her domains, the bedroom and the kitchen (159). He demands, in fact, one kitchen aid, a "Blitz Cloth," with a particularly telling name (159). Apparently marketers have borrowed the name of German bombing attacks on London to humor women for their skill in "attacking" grime. Yet the implied simile works in two directions. If women scouring pots with lightning energy resemble pilots pulverizing cities, so too the pilots, Axis or Allied, who drop bombs after "[c]limbing high into the sun" resemble women scrubbing (151). The name Blitz Cloth reduces the supposed heroism of fighting a war to a dulling routine.

Steve's preoccupation with arranging his "pretty suit" not only moves him into the "feminine" realm of dress but also makes him a childish "Boy Scout," as Mimi sarcastically remarks (159–60). According to contemporary sentiments, women and children cluster together because women take care of children but, even more, because women are assumed to remain inherently minors; appropriately, Mimi's nickname is "baby" (153). By contrast, war is supposed to make a "man" of him. However, Steve's military training infantilizes him too.

He worriedly performs the rituals of a scout, he pals with the "boys," and, most important, he refuses to feel and think at a mature level. He fears her emotion, "glimpses of your heart, and all that," nor can he handle his own adult emotion (156). And if Mimi seems impractical when she buys a nightgown that won't stand laundering, she manages to articulate some difficult truths about more basic vulnerabilities. She understands that it is "the knowledge of what you're all going into together that makes the comradeship of men in war so firm, so fast," and she perceives very clearly that the men might be "going into" loss of "sight" and "sanity" and "lives" (160). Contemporary cliché decrees that women cannot face facts; however, Steve is the one who cannot admit these horrors. He interrupts her vision of wounds and rubs his buckle, as if to scour away the reality of war.

It's not that Steve is a rare failure who has lapsed into womanly weakness. His government has commanded his preoccupation with nifty objects, yet this underlying parallel to women's situation—as consumer of goods, ultimately equivalent to them—usually remains invisible. When for one moment he looks unconfident and mumbles that he would prefer to be with her, he briefly acknowledges that much of his behavior is imposed, not natural, an assumed nonchalance that allows him to do the military training which he feels he must. Seeing this unexpected expression of his emotion, Mimi can rejudge the unsatisfactory leave "lovely" (161). Nevertheless, the ending does not mark a lasting honesty and understanding. Instead, like her earlier effort to reassess Steve's phone call from "horrid" to "lovely" (147–48), her final, studied optimism and his abrupt departure again gloss over the profoundly unlovely situations of both men and women. He cannot grasp how humiliating it must be for his wife to feel superfluous (157), but if he could see beyond the flattering ideology of active masculinity, he might realize that the premises of war define him as even more unnecessary—and expendable—than she. Despite the comforting emotional ties with the young men whom he clasps close to hide danger, the war may further reduce these GIs, already transformed into Government Issued property, to the ultimate superfluous object, corpse.

Like Parker, Gwendolyn Brooks detects many flaws in the vaunted male camaraderie of war. However, instead of taking the point of view of a woman left out of the club, Brooks puts herself in the position of a black soldier trying to be accepted among the troops. She knows that many blacks went to war to prove themselves men on the same terms as whites, and on this point she grants that World War II provided some positive experience to her peers. Gaining confidence for themselves, black soldiers also woke a few white servicemen to perceive the competence of blacks. As Brooks sardonically remarks in one title of her sonnet sequence *Gay Chaps at the Bar* (1944), "the white troops had their orders but the Negroes looked like men" (25). The whites may have been expecting "boys," but once General Eisenhower had allowed Negro units into combat, the latter performed well, and their fellows had to admit that equality or deny the evidence of their own eyes. Nevertheless, the races still rarely fraternized, and the U.S. Army—nominally fighting against the racism of fascists—itself remained segregated until 1948.

Brooks is brutally aware that camaraderie across the color line most frequently occurred only in a literal commingling of remains: "Such as boxed / Their feelings properly, complete to tags—/ A box for dark men and a box for Other—/ Would often find the contents had been scrambled. / Or even switched. Who really gave two figs" (26). Whereas Brooks's elegant sonnet form may at first seem remote from a GI's cavalier speech, the highly controlled structure aptly mimics the tightly boxed, apparently airtight categories in which bigots try to confine the races. The slightly uneasy rhymes of the poem ("fixed" and "perplexed," "taxed" and "boxed," "tags" and "figs," "Such" and "switched") yoke the lines together, as the regimentation of the armed services might line up a unit of rednecks next to the new "Negro Hero" (the title of another poem by Brooks). While the dead men *in* the boxes certainly don't give "two figs" what tags drape their coffins, those survivors of different races who discovered in battle that they could depend on each other may no longer give "two figs" either for the "boxed" feelings of bigotry.

If World War II only sporadically broke down barriers to soldiers' intimacy across color, the knowledge of discrimination against black servicemen did forge a new community among Negro relatives and friends at home. As James Baldwin recounts, the influx of different races into defense industries and the training of all black soldiers in the south, no matter where their birthplace, fueled racial tensions: "What happened in defense plants and army camps had repercussions, naturally, in every Negro ghetto" (82). Each resident had a husband or son or uncle, required to do the most dangerous transporting of munitions or forced to endure jibes and restrictions. Baldwin paints a vivid picture of the formation of a new civilian camaraderie of rage, as word from the troops propelled previously isolated groups onto the streets to seek news and commiserate. Matrons rubbed shoulders with "a girl in sleazy satin whose face bore the marks of gin and the razor," respectable older men hobnobbed with "sharpies," and "Holyrollers" stood on the same corner with "fanatical 'race' men" and "disbelievers" (83–84). These knots of common anguish and anger eventually coalesced into the Civil Rights Movement twenty years later.

As demotion to "boy" still oppressed African Americans during World War II, discrimination also bedeviled Japanese Americans. In John Okada's impassioned novel *No-No Boy* (1957), Ichiro returns to Seattle after four years of confinement: two in an internment camp, two in prison. The U.S. government had interned 110,000 Japanese residents (two-third of them American citizens) for no other reason than their ancestry (Harth 18). The government further punished male internees who answered "no" to two questions on a form: will you forswear allegiance to the emperor (in effect, deny all things Japanese and, for Issei, the immigrant generation, become stateless), and will you serve in the U.S. Armed Forces (Harth 18; Omori, video). Because Ichiro's refusal to be drafted has prevented him from bonding with either whites or Japanese, Okada's novel reads as a kind of anti-comrade tale. Once released from jail, Ichiro comes into bitter conflict with those Nisei (the first generation born in the new country) who did join the American military services and now resent the "no-no boys" as a supposed blot on their own record. Even Ichiro agrees with the abusive vets that he deserves to be beaten. In a repudiation of his initial protest now painful to read, he chooses to overlook the terrible irony that America was asking him to risk his life for democracy, while denying democratic freedoms to his family.

Primarily, of course, Ichiro fears that by spurning the army he has missed his chance to claim full citizenship, through a constitutionally established link between citizenship and arms' bearing. Yet in an important secondary fear, he worries that he has botched his chance to prove manhood. This concern surfaces on the very first page, when Ichiro dwells on the word "man" but then immediately casts his entitlement in doubt. He disdained to put on a uniform "when he was twenty-three, a man of twenty-three. Now, two years older, he was even more of a man. Christ, he thought to himself, just a goddamn kid is all I was" (1). Wondering if he might still be a child—or, worse, a woman in his mother's mold—he envies a Japanese American friend who died in the war "for something which was bigger than Japan or America or the selfish bond that strapped a son to his mother" (31). According to both his American and his Japanese heritage, men come into their own by distancing themselves from women and heading off to war.

Although Ichiro, like Jones's John Bell in *The Thin Red Line*, endorses a new sexual liberation for women, granting his friend Emi the right to extramarital relationships when her husband chooses to stay in defeated Germany, Ichiro would keep women traditional in other ways: focused primarily on love and subservient to men. Upset because his father has always deferred to an iron-willed wife, Ichiro still wishes his parents could reverse their behavior: "He should have been Ma and Ma should have been Pa" (112). Insisting on women's nonassertiveness, Ichiro differs little from white Americans expecting to solve all postwar social and economic problems by sending "Rosie the Riveter" submissively back to her bedroom and kitchen (Enloe, *Khaki* 174).

Not only must Japanese and American men stake out vast differences from women, but they must also come into their own by forming close ties with some men and fighting with others. To recoup the camaraderie he missed among GIs, Ichiro forms a friendship with Kenji, the only Japanese American veteran who will speak to him cordially. This friendship inaugurates Ichiro's healing, but equally important to that process, he must fight in a bar brawl, a kind of substitute for combat experience. He steps in to help Freddie, a troublesome former prison acquaintance who (rather too conveniently) soon kills himself, but only after providing Ichiro two important opportunities. Freddie gives Ichiro not only an excuse for battle but also an opening to brotherhood, for after the fight, Ichiro comforts even the confused attacker, Bull (250). While Ichiro may have defended Freddie admirably and forgiven Bull compassionately, he dangerously equates fistfights and warfare. This confusion does not enable him to question either the vastly different technology in the two kinds of fight or the much more complicated motives of governments, which seldom aim simply to protect the weak. However, because the association of the word "fight" with manhood is so strong, backing up the association with citizenship, Ichiro cannot claim even a partial rightness for his past refusal to go to war.

Whereas Okada seems to be reconstituting the fight as the sole arena for establishing manhood and camaraderie, James Jones in *The Thin Red Line* (1962) protests that for anyone, whether majority whites or minorities, camaraderie may be an illusory gain, not worth its price in the context of war. In fact, Jones deliberately invokes the grand scenes of World War I bonding—Paul carrying the wounded Kat in Remarque's *All Quiet on the Western Front* or Weeper Smart carrying Bourne in Manning's *The Middle Parts of Fortune*—only to undercut them. Throughout *The Thin Red Line*, Jones demotes camaraderie to a myth in three ways. In a satiric tone, he exposes the hypocrisy of officers who claim to love their men. In a comic tone, he caricatures eccentric devotees to C-Company. And, in a sadder key, he shows that ordinary men, more realistically presented than the caricatures and more likeable than the officers, still do not follow through on their fleeting impulses to help a friend.

As part of Jones's satire of officers, Lt. George Band rhapsodizes over "true comradeship . . . times when Band felt closer to the men in his outfit than he had ever felt to his wife" (101). Like Manchester, this fictional officer echoes the lyrical language of Remarque, who insisted that comrades were "nearer than lovers" (212). Yet Band's actions fail to bear out his words. He pushes his men when he should have rested them, and for all his claim to shepherd companions, he looks after his own career first. While Band is still dreaming of his "more-than-mated love," his men, filled only with hatred, are rechristening him "The Glory Hunter" (420, 456).

If officers no longer live up to the World War I ideal of paternal solicitude, perhaps soldiers of equal rank can manage old-style camaraderie. As if to affirm this possibility, Jones's Private Witt, shunted off to an outcast company for insubordination, keeps slogging back to C-for-Charlie Company like a dog to its human friend. However, if Witt at first seems to fulfill the Great War prescription for long devotion to one's group, here too Jones deflates loyalty. When the cantankerous Witt refuses to serve under successive commanders, stalks off in a huff, and then makes his way back through epic obstacles, his invective creates color and his travels offer humorous, private adventures, but his resemblance to a Faulknerian grotesque removes him from real life to the safety of a tall tale.

Like Lt. Band, Witt mouths the passionate language of World War I novels, as he proclaims an "almost sexual ecstasy of comradeship," yet only a few lines later he has tumbled into "second thoughts" (319). Even more important in demolishing his claim to love, Witt cannot brook any single companion, preferring the abstract notion of a company to actual people. And though he says he aims to save that company, he really wants to show them that they "needed him—whether *they* knew it or not" (304). Despite Witt's apparently outsize devotion, his self-serving motives—to get back at his superiors for his original dismissal and reestablish his reputation—cancel any genuine concern for others.

Witt's comic presentation cushions the jolt when Jones pulls the rug out from under his status as comrade. However, when serious characters fail to help each other, Jones unsettles the ideal irremediably. Faintly echoing the sacrifices made by Remarque's Paul or Manning's Weeper Smart, Bell "sacrifice[s]" his one clean handkerchief to Big Un

Cash, seriously wounded, and Thorne agrees to write a letter testifying that Cash "died like a man" (447). However, just one page later, Big Un's survivors recant their vintage World War I expressions of comfort: "'You going to write his wife?' Bell asked. 'Fuck no!' Thorne said . . . . 'Somebody ought to do it.' 'Then you write her.' 'I didn't tell him I would' " (448). Nobody keeps the promise.

Even more hurtfully, when Bead is fatally wounded, Fife hesitates to take his hand. Because the two were secretly sex partners for a time, Fife now fears that anyone observing a handclasp will brand them "Fairies" (259). Although he quickly corrects his momentary rejection of Bead, gripping the dying man's hand and cradling him, Fife still crawls away "hating himself" (260). He does not clarify if he is castigating his initial attention to social propriety rather than a friend, or if he is foolishly worrying that his present weeping at a death might look womanly too. Similarly concerned about appearances, Doll wants to put his arm encouragingly around subordinates, but he thinks better of it, as Witt "could have thrown his arms around his commander and kissed him on his dirt-crusted, stubbled cheek in an ecstasy of loving comradeship. Except that it might have looked faggoty" (406, 324). In fact, in Jones's novel, whether a man always chooses sex with other men, tries it once or twice, or never wants it at all, fear of *appearing* homosexual seems to have so increased since World War I that it becomes a major factor inhibiting mutual comfort among *all* the men.

When Jones debunks the possibility of camaraderie, his cynicism serves at least one good purpose, if it blocks the lure to future wars that Sassoon anticipated from accounts of intimacy in World War I. Even Alexander Baron, who believes, unlike Jones, that real camaraderie can still exist during wartime, seems intent at the close of *From the City, from the Plough* on retracting any suggestion that the men's tight interdependence somehow makes war worthwhile. In the last chapter, generals interested in their own reputations push the Fifth Battalion beyond exhaustion, until only a handful have survived the campaign. Surprisingly, the author neglects to tell us who escapes or dies among the characters we have come to care about. This blank anonymity in the telling brilliantly duplicates the brutal impersonality in the killing. The last few pages further erase any sense of triumph in victory or consolation in noble sacrifice. Instead, a major bitterly greets the last impossible order that will decimate the remnants with a laconic reminder, "this won't buy the frock a new baby" (223). His homey proverb, from a domestic context far from the battlefield, admits with rare honesty that tough men are as vulnerable to death in mechanized war as babies. The proverb perhaps also hints that frocks of glory, like the smart cap that so distracted Parker's Steve, are neither masculine nor feminine, nor are they worth a hoot without the life that animates them.

(d) I Fight to Protect My Sister
(but I Hate My Sister—So as Not to Be Her)

Although World War II governments, like those in earlier wars, still named the protection of women a primary cause for fighting, soldiers' actual attitudes toward women ranged more complicatedly. In Paul Gallico's story "Bombardier" (1942), an airman imbibes the official ideology of protection and idealizes his girlfriend, but she remains secondary to male idols. Russell Baker, in his essay "The Flag" (1980), recognizes that as a young man he sentimentalized women, though he also fled them to search for adventure in war. Ironically, even as soldiers were escaping entanglements with wives and sweethearts, some were seeking other women, for quick sex. The main character in Dan Davin's story "Not Substantial Things" (1947) celebrates war for ushering whores into the streets, and he laments the returning peace by epitomizing it in the grim townsfolk who now accuse women of sexual misconduct. Whereas Davin's soldiers indulgently shield a blonde harassed by a mob, William Manchester in *Goodbye, Darkness* (1979) bitterly invokes the biblical image of Whore of Babylon to focus intense hatred. However, this hostility may actually mask the male survivors' self-disgust, now projected outward onto women.

The ideology that claims war as the protector of women stands out clearly in Paul Gallico's story "Bombardier." "Salvo" Jenkins is a nervous, North Carolina country boy who desperately wants to succeed on his first sortie over the Atlantic in a B-31 bomber. He has blundered famously during training by hitting the lever "Salvo" instead of "Selective," wasting expensive bombs in the Pacific Ocean, and now he just wants to shoot straight and be accepted by the "team" (451). This idiom of *sport*, plus a vocabulary centered on *machines*, completely circumscribes Jenkins's conception of war. Both discourses unexpectedly foreground women: as the audience to whom men would supposedly dedicate victory in the game, and as the symbolic "she" embodied in mechanical ships and planes. Although these two discourses comfort Jenkins and the other airmen thrown into dangerous, anxiety-laden situations, the insulating words also rigidly stereotype the sexes, blot out the lethal nature of the fliers' task, and hinder many of them from ever examining the causes or alternatives to killing.

Conceived as a sport, war for Jenkins duplicates the hunt (he just wants to bring down another wildcat for his father) and substitutes for football (he was always too slight to play). Ostensibly, he takes up this new game of war to secure the attention of his college sweetheart and make her proud. By becoming a bombardier, he will outdo the three star football players, whose enlistment as pilots impressed her (455). Although Jenkins appears to elevate his girlfriend's judgment, he simultaneously denigrates it: "not even Mary Lou had quite understood him when he explained his great ambition to her" (454). Nor is she really his primary audience. He envies the three football buddies their regard for *each other* more than he covets their impression on her: "They did everything together. It was all for one and one for all, and everything for the team" (451). Once signed up with the prestigious sky team, Jenkins admits explicitly, "he would never want to succeed for anyone as much as he wanted to succeed for [Captain] John Strame, not even for Mary Lou" (454). He flies to please his new father figure, "Cappy Strame, the best pilot and the greatest guy who ever lived," and to join the band of brothers, "the greatest team in the world" (453, 451).

Just as impressing Mary Lou recedes before the more important goal of forging a tight homosocial bond, the ideal of protecting women glosses a world of machines from which real women have disappeared. Jenkins extensively personifies an Allied freighter as a young woman, "terribly lonely and nervous, pushing her way eastward" (457). Changing course to baffle German submarines, *she* has a case of the "jitters"; *she* is "helpless" and even "hysterical" (457–58). Poor Jenkins himself suffers the jitters throughout most of the flight, but the story does not undercut his habit of projecting his own, human responses onto the feminized freighter, as if fear and vulnerability really do belong exclusively to women. Instead of highlighting the irony that men can resemble the women from whom they distance themselves, the omniscient narrator seems wholeheartedly to approve a gallant Jenkins, who "felt a sudden pity for the solitary vessel. He wanted to call down to her, 'It's all right. Don't you worry. We're here' " (457). Jenkins, now invincible in his mind, will defend "her," the timid freighter, under his mighty wing.

When Jenkins then assures himself that his bomber will "spread her wings protectingly over the hysterical ship," he feminizes the plane as well as the freighter (457). Still, it is men who can "spread" her, ride her, and make her respond. The plane has a name, "Lumbering

Annie," and a temperament that men must humor; her "belly heavy with her load," she "took her own sweet time about getting into the air" (448). Ironically, this habit of calling all machines "she" turns Jenkins, this universal protector of women, into the ravager of a woman, when he feminizes the enemy submarine too. The language of bombing avoids the grisly details of destruction, carefully omitting even the word "bomb," as he successfully penetrates the body of the sub: "He put one right down her funnel from ten thousand" (457). All the airmen's accounts of their work seem designed to sound fun: "I'm playing a sport," "I'm snuggling a lonely woman," or (for some speakers) "I'm raping the bad woman"—never "I'm killing men." Once Jenkins finally explodes the submarine, the "bits and pieces of unidentifiable things" floating in a yellow oil patch only tacitly include the dead crew (462).

Although these evasions usefully cushion a basically decent young man from the immediate knowledge of his assigned, murderous task, the discourses available to Jenkins harm him and others in the long run. First, the pretense of sport or hunting does not allow him to examine for himself the causes of the war. Once his superiors tell him that he is the good farmer hunting the bad "wildcat" who got into the "chickens," his conscience is clear (456). Yet even if he is right to intervene now, he does not have the tools to think about preventing future wars. If Jenkins metamorphoses into a stealthy "cat," poised to strike, he cannot step back and ask whether it's a good idea for him to mirror the enemy's wildcat violence exactly (460). Second, the language of protecting hysterical women prevents him from noticing that he has polarized and excluded real women. When tears spring to his eyes as he overhears his idolized captain finally upgrade his nickname from "Salvo" to "Bull's-eye," Jenkins cannot see the similarities between men's own frequently frightened or love-starved emotions and these same emotions when they sometimes occur in the other half of the human race (463).

As Gallico's Jenkins idealizes Mary Lou, whom he does not really know, Russell Baker in "The Flag" sentimentalizes women and children but would just as soon extricate himself from their arms. Much more sardonic than Gallico, Baker can mock his younger self, yet he still musters a good deal of nostalgia for the excitement of his training. Although he laughs at his ignorance, he can still taste the regret he felt at eighteen: "When World War II ended in 1945 before I could reach the combat zone, I moped for months about being deprived of the chance to go down in flames under the guns of a Mitsubishi Zero" (44). He would gladly have died for "the flag," a tissue of "highly abstract political ideas . . . too complex to be easily grasped": that is, he cannot state any public causes (47). Instead, he signed up in a private bid to star in a good show. He pictured dying as floating translucently and painlessly before the cameras, with "June Allyson [an actress] and the kids" looking up worshipfully, "brave smiles smiling through their tears" (45).

Although June had some importance in this theatre—she was his audience—she certainly offered nothing very attractive, as he strove mightily to escape her: "As defender of the flag, I am able to leave a humdrum job, put June and the kids with all their humdrum problems behind me, travel the world with a great bunch of guys, do exciting things with powerful flying machines, and, fetchingly uniformed, strut exotic saloons on my nights off" (46). A peacock, he just wanted to look garish in a potent display, and he now candidly calls the rousing flag standing out in the wind a "male sex symbol" (46).

While a man ought to be able to celebrate such an emblem of vigorous life, Baker recognizes that flags often mask endeavors to multiply death instead. The dreams of the young Baker signal important problems at home, but he was unable to question why jobs were so boring, why war appeared as the only alternative, and whether June might also want to travel, fly, and pal around. However, the older Baker, thirty years after his war, more thoughtfully worries that if women agitate for "equality" by also doing "exciting things with powerful flying machines," they will go through training with no more notion than he had that those nifty gadgets drop bombs on people: "The question is whether women really want to start conditioning girl babies for this hitherto largely masculine sort of behavior, or spend their energies trying to decondition it out of the American man" (49).

That won't be easy. Men may be running away from women too closely associated with boring domesticity, but they may also be rushing toward other women, for the "saloons" that Baker mentions staff a few alluring bargirls in the background (46). In Dan Davin's story "Not Substantial Things," the I-narrator, Mick, pictures war as a time when soldiers can protect women: not innocent coeds like Gallico's Mary Lou, but desirable sex objects on exotic foreign turf. As peace dawns, Mick's New Zealand troops, moving into an Italian sector newly liberated from the Fascists, see some townsfolk harassing a peroxided blonde who "went in for a bit of horizontal collaboration" with the "local Jerry commandant" (467). Grumbling but sympathetic, the Kiwis rescue her, as they have already defended another woman that same day, joking, "her only sin is that she has loved too much" (467). In fact, Mick strikingly epitomizes the new peace, shabby and undesirable, in a habitual, foolish, and prudish hounding of "whores." Once peace fully arrives,

> We'd never bring the same energy to anything that we'd brought to things like the break-through at Minqar Qaim or the assault on Cassino. And we'd never be able to make friends again the same way or drink and laugh and die the same way . . . . The best was over with the worst. There was nothing left now except the dragging of some wretched whore through the streets in Avezzano yesterday, in Castel di Goriano today perhaps, and in the rest of the world tomorrow. (476)

Despite her apparent centrality, the individual woman in each scenario remains unknown. She serves as a *token* for the New Zealanders and a *scapegoat* for the Italians, and, as we will see, the troops finally shift their attention altogether from any real woman to a feminized *symbol* for the War itself.

As a token, the female companion in Mick's list of the vanishing "best" only sums up all the other compensations of war. The energy, travel, drinking bouts, and male camaraderie, which lured Russell Baker too, all seem to outweigh her in the end (476). Reduced to an abbreviation for other perquisites gone, the hounded whore remains a shadowy silhouette, not an individual. Mick never inquires into her real situation, her motives, her regrets, or triumphs. More observant, an English intelligence officer in 1944 records the desperate exchange of sex for food by Italian women; for example, one mother shocks the officer by trying to bargain money for survival out of limited sexual favors from her thirteen-year-old daughter (Richler 466). Mick, by contrast, gives no indication that he has grasped the economic plight of women in war.

Just as the New Zealanders see the peroxided blonde as an emblem for other, more centrally valued compensations of the war, so too the Italians substitute her for other problems, as a scapegoat. Mick shrewdly suspects that, without the Germans to provide the villagers an "enemy outside themselves," a "man'd soon have to start up again all the old fights with himself that used to go on in the days when there was no danger to his skin" (475–76). Some of these internecine battles, at the level of the community as well as the psyche, pit the "haves" against the "have nots." Mick notices, for example, that elderly Italians do not rush out to cheer the Kiwis because they have learned that no matter who drives the "fast military cars," whether

Germans or Allies, the poorest Italians would "never do any riding themselves" (469). Another social problem shows itself briefly when the departing Germans attempt to stir up fear of New Zealand "negri" (472). However, instead of questioning these power structures—economic, imperial, racial, and gender hierarchies—it's easier for the townsfolk to blame the old church-named evil, the Whore.

In fact, Davin's scenario of war-weary Italians hounding a scape-goated woman seems to have been duplicated all across Europe (Douzou 30). In his thoughtful World War II memoir *The Warriors*, Glenn Gray uneasily remembers French Resistance forces shaving the heads of women who had taken German lovers during the Occupation (74–76, 167). While Gray grants that some women were prostitutes and a few, perhaps, betrayed underground fighters for money, he strongly condemns the punishment of lovers in general, calling the public torment "not only unjust, but also unholy" (76). Like the French, the Germans directed post-war hostility against women who had supposedly given comfort to the enemy. Burghers raged against their own women for a range of "crimes," everything from giving food to a Russian prisoner, to having an affair with a Polish P.O.W. The vigilantes interpreted all help which a woman rendered as sexual; all sex was bad. Whether she met one steady partner or many, gave pleasure or turned a profit or simply survived, all her actions brought down the same label, whore (Banghard-Jöst 233). However, some of the tormentors seemed to be revealing their own hypocrisy. In 1942, when a man demanded that a woman who had taken a Polish lover be publicly "stripped and whipped" (Banghard-Jöst 237), he might be advertising his own sexual fantasies. One wonders if some of the jeering women among the mobs may likewise be hiding something: their own wartime affairs? a jealous regret that they didn't take advantage of relaxed mores when they could? Moreover, the same civilians who resented women's cohabita-tions, particularly with "the enemy," overlooked their own soldiers' sexual congress with women from various sides in the war.

As in Davin's example, where "one old dame" in Italy tries to yank out handfuls of the blonde's hair (466), punishment across Europe against female scapegoats typically took the form of shaving heads. A German boy eagerly climbed onto his bike to gloat: "My whole life I've always hoped to see a woman without hair . . . . It's just like I imagined it" (qtd. in Banghard-Jöst 237). He seems to be on the verge of discovering that a girl is like a boy and vice versa, but his social train-ing prevents him from consciously registering that men could grow long hair or women have sex outside marriage, as men do. However, instead of discrediting arbitrary gender divisions, any crossing of boundaries simply reaffirms for the boy a thrilling monstrousness.

Mick and his New Zealand troops, who protect the blonde, apparently differ radically from the vindictive Italians, who tear her hair. But actually the Kiwis ignore her individuality to an equal degree. Moreover, they soon forget real women altogether, as they transfer their allegiance to a feminized symbol in the last lines of the story:

> "Anyhow, it was a great day," Terry said. "She's been a bonny war."
> "She's been a bonny war," I said, and took another swig at the bottle.
> (477)

The men assign this incongruously "bonny" glow to the war itself, which can be seen as "good" in part because it helpfully masks problems at home. Mick is depressed when his batman departs, suspecting that the war may be over before his servant's three-month leave ends: "But if blokes like Bandy were getting out of it alive, going home and all, then the chances were you would yourself. And then what the hell would you do?" (465). He hints that underlying economic and social problems—unemployment, tedious jobs, or lack of purpose—make war more attractive than peace. Yet rather than examine the "real conditions of existence," which deny him (in New Zealand) and the peasants (in Italy) power and excitement, Mick focuses on an "imaginary" world (Althusser 162), where women take center stage. Although few women fight, declare wars, or run large businesses in peacetime, Mick's ideology spotlights them as if they were the main players. The soldiers fancifully see women in the starring roles: either entirely sexualized beings, to be alternately guarded or dragged through the streets, or nonhuman symbols, the bonny war itself.

Whereas Davin's Mick congenially agrees to escort the endangered whores of the story but leaves them ciphers, William Manchester in *Goodbye, Darkness* invokes an image of Whore with real rancor. This rancor extends to all women, although he also idealizes them. Three-quarters of the way into his memoir, almost as an afterthought, he cites protecting women as one of the causes for fighting the war, begging the question whether American men were rushing to the Pacific to help women (324). American women seem well out of danger, except for the remote and exaggerated scenario that the Japanese might invade California. Were American men protecting Pacific women? Manchester hazards a guess that 77,000 civilians, including women, died in the battle for Okinawa (447); both sides considered these losses acceptable.[5] When Manchester discovers an

Okinawan girl sprawled on a beach, murdered (and apparently raped) by an American, the author admits that he was "deeply troubled" (408). The sight disturbs him so much because this incident conflicts with his conception of his countrymen and their protective purpose; her messy corpse also summons up all the other civilian deaths, usually repressed.

Women do not really figure in the strategic calculations, and if the war mows them down instead of saving them, history glosses over that outcome. In his other references to women, Manchester sees myths more than people. His depiction veers between the two poles of the old Victorian angel–whore dichotomy. Idealizing his mother, he also imagines her asexual; like the nineteenth-century angel in the house, she "wouldn't have understood" his desire to lose his own "virginity" before being shipped overseas (176). Nor could she comprehend war. Within the context of praise for his mother, he explains that General MacArthur gave Japanese women the vote after the war to counteract "samurai militarism" (175). At this point, Manchester seems to agree with MacArthur's Victorian assignment to women of an essentialized peaceableness.

Nevertheless, Manchester simultaneously holds the exact opposite opinion. Even his mild mother descended from "Confederate Valkyries" (176). Instead of fostering peace, women as battlefield hyenas incite the fighters. In the most shocking example of the hold on his imagination by this myth of the valkyrie, much stronger than the briefly invoked angel, he personifies the war itself as a woman, whom he calls the "Whore of Death" (88). After the men of his squad have all been killed, he hallucinates her in a vision as graphic as anything in the book. Imagining the apparition in "a cashmere twin-sweater set, a Peter Pan collar, a string of pearls, a plaid skirt," he has patched her together from a semiotic grab bag: a merchandiser's notion of expensive innocence, combined with a biblical figure of viciousness—both Mount Holyoke college girl and Whore of Babylon (88).

By this allusion to Chapter 17 of the Book of Revelation, Manchester identifies the college girl's entire being with sexuality, which he condemns. Actually, his own sexuality, not anyone else's, has solicited his attention; after discovering his lone survival, he finds himself intensely aroused. Exhilaration at being alive, plus horror at the violent deaths of his companions, might push him to take refuge in bodily delight. Yet why is this moment of potential sanctuary expressed only as hatred? One reason is that his Christian training has labeled sexuality bad; after all, his father taught him that masturbation would render him both brain-damaged and impure (42). Perhaps because he resents his liability to the charge of wrongdoing when he just wants comfort after the slaughter, his arousal turns to hostility; he tells us it's the first and only time in his life he understood the urge to rape. He needs an external temptress to seduce him, to deny his own sexuality and not get in trouble with the fathers. If he conjures her up, he can assure any accusers: she made me do it.

Furthermore, guilt at this moment may derive not only from his own sexuality but from the randomness of survival. Angered that so many of his buddies have died, he could hate the Japanese, yet because their soldiers are lying dead and rotting everywhere too, they seem as much victims as his own comrades, and he feels "unable to purge my shock by loathing the enemy" (430). He could also direct rage against his own government, for wasting men. This last target of reproach, however, seems inadmissible. Just as Frederic Manning's Pritchard in World War I learned to redirect ire from his officer to his distant wife as he mourns the death of a "chum" (16), here too Manchester shifts his revulsion at men's killing onto Woman.

Deflecting any possibility of fulminating against his government for calling him to fight, Manchester also avoids chastising himself, for answering that call. Although all these American and Japanese soldiers are male, suddenly, when he realizes most clearly the destructiveness of the men, Woman surges up in his mind as an alternative to upbraiding themselves. She is a convenient culprit, precisely because she is absent and cannot protest. She is also available to be the villain because he has already been trained to blame her for his sexuality. Once that mechanism is in place for dealing with resentment and guilt in one area, he can activate it to exculpate himself in another. He can placate any potential new accusers: I'm not really participating in all this killing because, again, she made me do it, this Whore of Death.

Ironically, though a man may go to war in part to prove that he is active and women, passive, as soon as the sickening carnage of battle is borne in upon him, he can deny agency. And though a man may claim to fight to protect weak, sweet Woman, here when it suits him, he construes her not as sweet but vicious, not as defenseless but all-powerful, victimizing his passive self.

Chapter 4

The Vietnam War: Out from Under Momma's Apron

(a) I Fight to Prove I'm Not My Sister (but I Suspect I Am)

By the time of the American war in Vietnam, the need to fight to prove oneself a man pressed even more acutely than in earlier wars of the century. In World War I, Vera Brittain's fiancé hurried to the front because "effeminate" men whom he "despised" had unexpectedly joined up, and he didn't want to be left behind as the new nominee for effeminacy (126). In World War II, American GIs teased, "Whatsa matter, bud—got lace on your drawers?" or "Christ, he's acting like an old maid" (Stouffer 2: 132). By Vietnam, however, in addition to peers conveying the cultural norm, drill instructors (DIs) systematically instilled fear of womanliness, in a self-conscious manipulation. One of the voices in the oral history *Nam* recalls his DI sneering, "All right, ladies. You look like shit" (M. Baker 22). Philip Caputo remembers a DI needling marines, "Square those pieces away SQUARE 'EM AWAY GIRLS" (9), while the infantry sergeant in Tim O'Brien's nonfiction *If I Die in a Combat Zone* ridicules a man who lodges a complaint, "You're a pussy, huh?" (54). Women are the lowest of the low, and military men are taught not only to look down on them but also to worry that they themselves might stand revealed as permanent "ladies."

That such fears did motivate Americans to fight in Vietnam can be seen in Caputo's *A Rumor of War* (1977) and O'Brien's "On the Rainy River" (1990). Minorities faced added pressure to prove manhood, since they still suffered the stigma of "boy" or subhuman "savage" from slavery and conquest, as reflected in Yusef Komunyakaa's *Dien Cai*

Dau (1988) and Sherman Alexie's *The Lone Ranger and Tonto Fistfight in Heaven* (1993). Long after the war, with some benefit from the women's liberation movement, a few veterans began to question the gender assignments that pushed them to battle, yet neither O'Brien's "Sweetheart of the Song Tra Bong" (1990) nor John Mulligan's *Shopping Cart Soldiers* (1997) go far enough in their revisions to modify significantly those gender definitions that contribute to war.

In his memoir *A Rumor of War*, Caputo frankly admits that he joined the marines and went to Vietnam to prove "manhood" and gain admittance to a "tough, masculine world" (6, 33). This elusive manhood seems to pose three hurdles: be a brave hero, perform "I-and-I" ("intercourse and intoxication"), and shed blood (37). These tests generate a number of ironies. Either Caputo's precepts do not match up with facts in Vietnam, or, as we will see, the requirements mutually contradict each other. Although the older, more knowledgeable Caputo can mock his younger, deluded self and point out how little the Vietnam War provided appropriate opportunities to fulfill these tests, he never permits himself more fundamental questions, about the need to meet such muddled prescriptions for manhood in the first place.

In a simplified world of "good guys" versus "bad guys," a brave hero presumably defends the "right," but the young Caputo paints a veneer of public service over a very personal daydream, unconcerned with moral rightness. Vaguely stirred by President Kennedy's "missionary idealism," Caputo in his twenties knows nothing about communism or Vietnamese nationalism (xiv). Instead, he pursues a fantasy derived from American myths of cowboys versus Indians and cops versus robbers. Caputo is not alone in identifying Vietnam with the Wild West (Hellmann 49). His fellow soldiers regularly refer to Viet Cong–controlled territory as "Indian country" or give such orders as "Saddle up, Second" (102, 49). But were the Indians the "bad guys"? The young recruit has no idea why Native Americans fought Europeans, any more than he sees the parallel situation of Vietnamese trying to expel the French, the Japanese, the French again, and then the Americans. Moreover, Caputo is not really sure if he sides with the cowboy or the Indian. As a child, he hoarded arrowheads and himself played the Indian (5). Similarly blurring his other mythic pair, he presumably signs up to be the "cop," but he admits that he needs the skills of a "burglar, bank robber, and Mafia assassin" (34).

For the young Caputo, to be cast as cowboy/cop or Indian/robber does not really matter, as long as he can star in the show. He covets

John Wayne's movie role as good cop against World War II enemies, but here the older Caputo can detect contradictions (6). The face on a marine recruiting poster attracts his younger self because it is "athletic, slightly cruel-looking . . . a cross between an All-American halfback and a Nazi tank commander" (6). Is the marine fighting the Nazi or becoming the Nazi? Caputo acknowledges that the corps relies on the "psychology of the mob, of the Bund rally" and that marine indoctrination sessions also "seemed to borrow from Communist brainwashing techniques" (12). The new marine wants to fight evil, but he has no training what that is. The "good" side simply means "my" side, and the hero means "me," the person who might win "little pieces of ribbon" and the all-important words of praise from older men (33). "Be a hero" as the prerequisite for "be a man" turns out either to have no content, or to supply a content remarkably similar to the conformity, prejudice, and coercion of a "bad guy."

On a less grandiose scale, the American in Vietnam can take time off from heroism and engage in "intercourse and intoxication" to bolster his credentials for manhood (37). However, when Caputo drinks at a bar only because an Australian officer dares him, his acquiescence sounds more childish than manly, and his cowardice about appearing one jot different from the other carousers clashes with the masculine ideal of bravery. When he becomes so befuddled that he doesn't remember leaving with the Chinese bargirl in whose bed he wakes up, he passively misses the active agency that men supposedly demonstrate (136). Yet if he can portray his younger self as slightly clownish, the older Caputo still does not question the macho reputation of these antics. Caught in the Apollo Syndrome, which assumes that heterosexual intercourse will ensure and advertise his future fighting ability, Caputo revealingly speaks of "whoring and drinking" as "soldierly duties," rather than personal desires (62). The aim of these socially imposed "duties" is to impress observing fellow soldiers, who add a nick beside the yardstick of prescribed masculinity.

As Caputo and his companions engage in "I-and-I" for status and a false sense of invulnerability, they shed blood as a rite of passage, to move into manhood from the rank of "infants" (a word that is, he remarks, embarrassingly like "infantry") (120). Although he records widespread "disappointment and depression" after the first kill, the older Caputo never modifies his fundamentally ritualistic approach to this "sacrament of war" (120). To be marked by blood, in a "baptism of fire," is designed not to obtain larger public goals but to strengthen private bonds, almost to paint identifying group colors, in an elite band of brothers (120).

Caputo's religious language recalls ancient initiations, but original rites for the shedding of first blood would have belonged to girls, not men, to acknowledge the onset of menstruation. Ancient men seem to have imitated these ceremonies, to appropriate some of their power (Ehrenreich 106). However, girls' blood naturally sloughs off when unneeded, whereas boys' blood in rites must be shed violently, by older men. Initiators mutilated boys in circumcision or the much more drastic subincision: in effect, to trace an imaginary vagina on the penis and create a super-person, man and woman in one (Campbell, *Primitive Mythology* 103). Sacralized war, as well as sacred initiation rites, seems to try to compete with and outdo women's natural shedding of blood, as men compare wars to "labor pains," which will supposedly deliver a new society (Huston 133). Ironically, though Caputo and his companions go to war to prove manhood—a difference from and superiority to women—the roots of their sacrament betray a kind of envy of women. Unfortunately, men's jealous imitation of women's blood-flow leads to deaths, not births, and it hurts others as much as it proves an initiate's own stoicism in pain.

Whereas Caputo eagerly enlisted in the marines, fiction-writer Tim O'Brien was drafted into the army, but the need to prove manhood through fighting finally determines O'Brien's presence in Vietnam as much as Caputo's. The story "On the Rainy River," loosely based on O'Brien's own dilemma as a young man, depicts the long summer during which a fictionalized "Tim" debates his options once his draft notice arrives. The last two sentences of the story—"I was a coward. I went to the war"—beautifully upset conventional expectations (*Carried* 63). Whereas a reader might think that "coward" will be followed by "*didn't* go to the war," the ending instead proclaims fighting itself as the failure of nerve. This Tim is not a coward when it comes to blood and guts. More cleareyed about the physical facts of war than the young Caputo at his cowboy games, Tim broods over induction as he works in a stinking, gory meatpacking plant, maneuvering a heavy "gun" to spray "blood clots from the necks of dead pigs" (46). Horrified by this tacit preview of the war, Tim would still rather face the meat-grinder of Vietnam than something more frightening at home. What could be scarier than killing, suffering, dying?

It's a little word, a tiny taunt, which O'Brien lets us hear in a vivid scene. Just as he concretizes the possibility of becoming dead meat by having his character handle meat, he literalizes Tim's choice of answering Uncle Sam's call or escaping to Canada by moving him to the Rainy River between Minnesota and Ontario and seating him in a boat straddling the boundary. Unable to decide between war and exile, Tim imagines people on both banks—parents, cheerleaders, local Chamber of Commerce, even Plato—rooting him on or urging him back. This fantastic posse of social influences all start screaming, "Traitor! . . . Turncoat! Pussy!" (61); at the same time, the regulars at the Gobbler Café murmur about "the young O'Brien kid, how the damned sissy had taken off for Canada" (48). Now, being called a "traitor" hurts, but it's clear that "sissy" or "pussy," in the final, strongest position of the taunts, clinches society's pressure. Even when the twenty-one-year-old Tim, unlike the young Caputo, has already suspected that the United States might be wrongly interfering in a Vietnamese fight for independence (44), the only word so powerful that he would rather give up his principles or even die than face it is "woman," or one of its derogatory surrogates.

If becoming a man through war compels whites such as O'Brien and Caputo, the need may push minority Americans even more urgently: "blacks and Asians, as well as Latinos, joined the armed forces during the Vietnam war in hopes of gaining the respect of their cultural community, of escaping a life of poverty, or of proving their mettle to themselves and to 'the Man' " (DeRose 38). In slave days, Boss Man laid down the law and the labels; during the Vietnam War, commanders still echoed his old command, "C'mere, boy," driving several black officers either to cynical withdrawal or to political action (W. Terry 153, 201). Yet the slang term "the Man" oddly seems to grant white males a monopoly on manhood itself. Even when some minority soldiers uncomfortably realized that they may have been helping to "oppress a colored people [Vietnamese]" (DeRose 45), resentment focused on the indignity of a supposedly feminized position. That is, taken in by propaganda for a war that they later came to doubt in the field, the disillusioned soldiers felt "seduced and abandoned by the Man" (qtd. in DeRose 45).

In a poem that addresses an Amerasian son the speaker may have left behind in Vietnam, black veteran Yusef Komunyakaa strikingly condenses the image of a traditionally masculine, African warrior, who fights with a shield, and a modern American soldier, who pursues his masculine "I-and-I" during "nights I held your mother / against me like a half-broken / shield" (58). Komunyakaa acknowledges the sadness of the "broken" prostitutes, "these voices / wounded by their beauty & war" (29), and he may also allude to the "broken" quality of the Americans' technological weapons, supposedly superior to primitive shields or punji sticks but still inadequate to victory (29). In the brothels of "Tu Do Street," the offduty soldiers not only search for a desperate comfort but they also seek each other, through the women: "There's more than a nation / inside us, as black and white / soldiers touch the same lovers / minutes apart, tasting / each other's breath" (29). Like Pat Barker's British character Billy Prior, feeling somehow reconciled to World War I German soldiers because they too have enjoyed sex with the same French teenager (*Ghost* 248), Komunyakaa's black troops manage only this virtual meeting with their white comrades, within the bodies of Asian women. This sharing must substitute for a less mediated dialogue, where whites would, face to face, at last recognize the black soldiers as men.

Komunyakaa further complicates the ironies of being close yet still far away from either the prostitutes or the white clients. The speaker reminds us, "Back in the bush at Dak To / & Khe Sanh, we fought / the brothers of these women / we now run to hold in our arms" (29). The men at the brothels taste "each other's breath, / without knowing these rooms / run into each other like tunnels / leading to the underworld" (29). Here the poet condenses a sexual tunneling into bodies with the building of a vast, literal network of tunnels, by which the National Liberation Front provisioned itself and defeated the Americans. Yet along with this frightening image of tunnels—Asians sending Americans to hell, their own underworld—Komunyakaa perhaps also invokes a potentially positive, underlying connectedness of black, white, and yellow, a honeycombed unity forced underground by prejudice and war.

Like Komunyakaa, Sherman Alexie sees how ironically ethnic groups may hate but also envy each other, as they claim to see oppositions but also duplicate one another. In *The Lone Ranger and Tonto Fistfight in Heaven*, a linked collection of stories like O'Brien's *The Things They Carried*, a character watches coverage of the Vietnam War on TV from the Spokane Indian Reservation: "The white people always want to fight someone and they always get the dark-skinned people to do the fighting . . . and Seymour said every single gook he killed looked exactly like someone he knew on the reservation" (120–21). American Indians enlisted for the Vietnam War out of proportion to their numbers in the general population for several reasons. Because the U.S. government still praised (and stereotyped) Indians as "natural fighters," envying their supposedly innate bravery and close-to-nature stealth, they were "heavily recruited" (Holm 59, 62). Poverty and an ingrained ideal of "warriorhood" also drove Native Americans to enlist (Holm 61). Once in Vietnam, these young men experienced many conflicts. Just as Alexie's Seymour notices that "gooks" look like his friends and relatives at home, Native Americans who engaged in forcibly resettling Vietnamese villagers had the uncomfortable feeling of turning into the whites who had forced earlier generations of Indians to reservations (Holm 65).

Alexie's central character, Victor, too young to have fought in Vietnam, enviously complains to his father, "my generation of Indian boys ain't ever had no real war to fight. The first Indians had Custer to fight. My great-grandfather had World War I, my grandfather had World War II, you had Vietnam. All I have is video games" (28). Here Alexie skillfully shows Victor floundering in a number of contradictions. For one thing, Victor tries to revive the legendary image of Indian warrior, but the more evenly matched contest with arrows has disappeared in the mass destructiveness of bombs. Victor confusedly calls the warriors against Custer the "first Indians," when someone else might more accurately call them almost the last (traditional) Native Americans. Actually, the "Indian" whom Victor recognizes is not an untouched Spokane but part of a Hollywood myth, a Tonto. In fact, the helpful "Indian companion" started appearing in Westerns after Native Americans' heavy enlistment in World War II (Holm 56). Although Victor half wants to slug the Lone Ranger, he also keeps tuning him in. For if the young man only exists as a component of "cowboy and Indian," he cannot afford ever to win and erase Custer, or he would be erased too. Hence, he needs new oppressors and new enemies, *any* enemy—like the Viet Cong.

When Victor's father listens to his son's nostalgia for the Vietnam War, he grumbles, ". . . why the hell would you want to fight a war for this country? It's been trying to kill Indians since the very beginning. Indians are pretty much born soldiers anyway. Don't need a uniform to prove it" (29). The father can point out the irony of fighting alongside the whites who have long been eradicating Indians and, as Caputo showed, still invoking that genocide by naming areas controlled by the Viet Cong "Indian country" (*Rumor* 102). Yet Victor's father is entangled in his own unacknowledged paradoxes. Although the father protested the Vietnam conflict, he went to prison not for Conscientious Objection, but for beating up a National Guard private with a rifle butt. When Victor scans the old "Pulitzer Prize winning photo" of his father arrested in bell-bottoms and "red peace symbols splashed across his face like war paint," with a caption reading "PEACEFUL GATHERING TURNS INTO NATIVE UPRISING," he resents the editor's assumption that Indians will always be violent (25). Yet father and son buy into that assumption themselves. If Victor is a "born soldier" (29), he may, no matter what his father says about not needing uniforms, more easily sign up to fight in any new foreign adventures, confusedly seeking acceptance as a manly Indian warrior in the garb of a soldier-cowboy, both the Lone Ranger and Tonto consenting to unjust wars for the cause of their own manliness.

Elsewhere in his novel, Alexie tries to include women in his fighter ideal for Indians by claiming that "Norma was a warrior in every sense of the word," but we don't see her in literal combat (167). One author who does imagine a woman warrior is Tim O'Brien in "Sweetheart of the Song Tra Bong." This story implicitly asks, *what if* women fought in Vietnam: would they have behaved any differently than the men? O'Brien promisingly hints, no, they wouldn't, granting an equality of potential to women and men—for good or for bad. However, in the end the story disappointingly eclipses its hypothetical female soldier under the language of myth. Whereas O'Brien's male characters who "joined the zoo" still remain recognizably human within the crazy slaughter, Mary Anne Bell, after she too has turned into "one more animal," disappears into outworn iconography for inhuman, devouring goddesses (*Carried* 117).

When seventeen-year-old Mary Anne shows up in Vietnam in a pink sweater, lives with her boyfriend, Mark, in his hooch, and wears a fetching swim-top to toss a volleyball, the story plays out a blatant fantasy. Although an often forgotten 50,000 American women did serve in Vietnam, as nurses, entertainers, Red Cross volunteers, and the occasional journalist (Vartanian 192), Mary Anne arrives untrained, solely to cuddle her beau. O'Brien puts this unlikely tale in the mouth of Alpha Company's raconteur, Rat Kiley, known for exaggeration. Rat likes to "rev up the facts," not to deceive, but to convey an already incredible, hyperbolic reality, and to make his audience feel, through his fictional spin on the facts, the "burn" of a "truth" they might otherwise miss (101).

When one of those truths concerns the gender assumptions of the time, Rat anachronistically borrows language more characteristic of the late 1980s when the story was written, while his buddies keep to the vocabulary of the early 1960s. For example, when Mary Anne insists on visiting a dangerous village, the soldiers judge that she has "D-cup guts, trainer-bra brains" (108). Even when they praise her courage, they reduce all her faculties to breast-size, still her primary attribute. Despite these low expectations, Mary Anne does exercise her brains after all, learning to perform medical procedures as competently as her boyfriend, then swiftly picking up military tasks from nearby "Greenies" (112). When she goes on ambush with these Green Berets and starts to enjoy the endorphin-adrenaline rush of the kill (123), Mark and his buddies are surprised, but Rat dismisses their prejudices: "You got these blinders on about women. How gentle and peaceful they are. All that crap about how if we had a pussy for president there wouldn't be no more wars. Pure garbage. You got to get rid of that sexist attitude" (117). The story relies on the implied example of Margaret Thatcher's truculence in the Falklands War, which Rat could not yet know, but he keeps the old term "pussy"—in the process, undermining the dignity of his proposal for equality.

Still, despite his residual disparagement of women as all sex, Rat does seriously consider that a woman might make a president as vigorous—or as belligerent—as any man, and he also firmly believes that a woman would develop as a soldier along lines parallel to her male counterparts. If Mary Anne arrived innocent, Rat guides his buddies to ask, did their own platoon reach Vietnam any less naive? In fact, other stories in *The Things They Carried* bear out this notion of similarities between Mary Anne and the men. She might greet Vietnam giggling, like a child, but Mitchell Sanders, in "How to Tell a True War Story," brings a childish yo-yo (79). Rat neatly sums up the transformation that overtakes young Americans in Vietnam: "What happened to her, Rat said, was what happened to all of them. You come over clean and you get dirty" (123).

Nevertheless, if Rat intends to show that women and men can equally perform soldierly assignments and then equally get warped by them, there is something qualitatively different about Mary Anne's addiction to the kill. When she dances before a moldering leopard head, chants to a stack of bones labeled "assemble your own gook," and dons a "necklace of human tongues" (119–20), Mary Anne suddenly evokes old, skull-necklaced goddesses such as Hindu Kali or Aztec Coatlicue, who wears a belt from which dangle "either serpents or shorn penises" (Walker 172). Mary Anne's mythic aspect persists even though her grisly attire of body parts may be realistic; frequent references in the literature of the Vietnam War suggest that an American soldier here and there did "build his own gook" (Herr 35) or ornament himself with severed Vietnamese ears (Vaughn 174; Heinemann 7; W. Terry 26, 100, 251). Norman Bowker in O'Brien's title story "The Things They Carried" packs a rubbery thumb, which Mitchell Sanders sliced from a Viet Cong corpse (13). Yet Mitchell, by joking about TV shows even as he cuts off the thumb, stays in a realm of familiar reality (14), whereas Mary Anne passes into unreal myth.

One way O'Brien turns Mary Anne mythic and abstract is by associating her with the stereotype that women are somehow more physical than men. Mary Anne explains her new love for ambush as getting in touch with her body: "I want to *eat* this place. Vietnam. I want to swallow the whole country—the dirt, the death—I just want to eat it and have it there inside me . . . . When I'm out there at night, I feel close to my own body" (121). Regressing to Aristotle's influential notion that women are mired entirely in matter, whereas only men have souls (Lerner 207), Mary Anne hurtles even further into the past to merge with the goddess Kali. Mary Anne's obsession with swallowing makes her all mouth and vagina, as a fanged Kali is frequently pictured squatting on the corpse of Shiva, gnawing his intestines above his still erect penis (Campbell, *Mythic Image* 351; Walker 488). In a religious context, Kali's imagery teaches that although natural death might *look* frightening, a person need not fear dying, because the earth is just reabsorbing matter into itself, as it prepares to reincarnate each soul. Western observers, however, generally miss that assurance of rebirth, seeing only a demon. In the context of the Vietnam War, Mary Anne acquires Kali's fangs, but none of her power to regenerate humans.

In the course of O'Brien's story, Mary Anne travels from one myth to another: from innocent sweetheart, unconsciously sexy in a pink sweater, to devouring goddess, red in tooth and claw, with no human identity in either case. Stuck in the Virgin Mary/Eve dichotomy, Mary Anne has changed little since William Manchester's World War II hallucination of a sweatered Mt. Holyoke girl who can metamorphose into a Whore of Death (88). Once Mary Anne has blended with Kali or Coatlicue, the message of the story shifts too. Whereas Rat had been arguing that it's the essence of war to make anyone, male or female, chew up other people, the ending reverts to saying that it's the essence of women to devour men. This resurgence of stereotypes illustrates how hard it is to resist ingrained gender training, when even an author as perceptive and questioning as O'Brien cannot quite pull off his attempted revisions.

Like "Sweetheart of the Song Tra Bong," John Mulligan's *Shopping Cart Soldiers* bravely tries to reconfigure 1960s' gender divisions through fantasy. Nevertheless, the novel, like O'Brien's story, falls short of any real changes, by again reverting to the virgin/whore dichotomy and reducing women to abstractions. In Mulligan's case, women only symbolize supposedly feminine aspects of the Vietnam veteran and primary character, Finn MacDonald, rather than existing as characters in their own right.

Making the I-narrator a young, Asian woman, Mulligan invites us to expect a point of view different from the Americans', but as soon as she reveals herself as Finn's "soul," we are pulled back exclusively to the problems of Western soldiers (10). She explains that the traumatized Finn kicked her out of his psyche after a particularly brutal series of events in Vietnam, including decapitating a sixteen-year-old Viet

Cong soldier, to prevent her from attacking. Finn judges that "there is something wrong with being sensitive to the madness going on all around him," for he assumes that pity and awareness of craziness are not "manly" (6). As a consequence, he expels that part of himself which feels emotion, so that "she" must trail around after "an Empty" (19). This leftover Finn coldly "frags" American military police; then, his tour over, he haunts the streets of San Francisco as a homeless alcoholic, attached to his woman-soul by an umbilical cord now precariously wrapped around his waist (115).

Mulligan seems to be on the track of a central cultural problem, the false naming of compassion as womanly and therefore "wrong" for a man (6). However, by visualizing any "sensitive" response to the war as literally a woman's reaction, Mulligan only strengthens this association (6). Instead of calling the ability to care about others "human," Mulligan accepts that empathy is basically more natural to women, accessible only to men in a kind of Jungian feminine side. Mulligan then falls into a number of other stereotypes. The female narrator monopolizes all goodness and "spirit," whereas the male side of Finn possesses "the mind" (21)—no advance beyond the nineteenth-century "angel in the house" and her rougher, male relatives, who are still granted the sharper, controlling rationality (Christ 146). Mulligan's I-narrator also supplies all Finn's "creativity" and "love" (14), repeating a nineteenth-century fear that the arts might be feminizing (Clarke 25), as well as the Jungian assignment of "Eros" to women (Goldenberg 445). Moreover, as his exiled "soul" follows meekly after Finn, begging him to take "her" back into his psyche so she can help him, she duplicates a nineteenth-century wife or daughter, who has no existence beyond propping up her man.

If Mulligan vests all goodness in the female I-narrator, as if she were an icon of the Blessed Virgin, he reactivates the "whore" part of the old dichotomy in "Soldiergirl," the decapitated Viet Cong who now haunts Finn as the "bitch Grotesque" (68, 31). Not only does she torment him, but she also tries to seduce him (31), just as Manchester's Whore of Death seeks to arouse but then kill him (88). In a way, Finn tries to exonerate Soldiergirl by claiming that Redeyes, a male devil, has taken possession of her. However, this explanation only denies the Vietnamese woman the agency of her own revenge, sending her back into passivity. Eventually, Soldiergirl subsides into yet another stereotype, the all-forgiving woman (Chotirawe 212–13). Throughout *Shopping Cart Soldiers*, Finn projects his own, guilt-inducing deeds onto a female Other, either making Soldiergirl a death-dealing Eve or idealizing the all-good narrator (or the reformed, kinder Soldiergirl). In both cases, Finn, with no undercutting from the author, dehumanizes women.

At the same time, Mulligan does not provide men any way out of a hurtful training in manliness. This training, also drilled into the soldiers represented by Caputo, O'Brien, Komunyakaa, and Alexie, directs men to shed blood: not to defend a civilian community but to establish a ritual solidarity among themselves. It teaches men intoxication and intercourse: not primarily as pleasures but as performances, to convince other men of a blustery command or to reach out symbolically to each other through the bodies of whores. By reducing women to all sex or all kindly soul, such an indoctrination does not let men admit their own desires or claim their own compassion. Finally, this sad conception of gender elevates fighting—in the abstract, for no cause or even for a known bad cause—into the one irreplaceable "proof" that a man is not that lowly creature, "sissy" or "pussy."

(b) I Fight to Prove I'm Not Attracted to Men (but I Do Want to See Male Bodies)

Just as DIs in the Vietnam era explicitly needled recruits as "ladies," they also systematically ranted that the exhausted men in front of them must be "faggots." A daunting array of penalties—dishonorable discharge, civilian felony statutes, and church censure—backed this slur with real threat. Nevertheless, the taunt still gained its most explosive force from the continuing construction of homosexual to mean effeminate, for DIs insistently linked versions of these two adjectives as their most insulting epithets: "No goddamned bunch of little girl faggots who can't run seven miles as a unit are going to rest" (Michalowski 331). The effectiveness of the name-calling depended on a number of false but deeply embedded associations: of homosexual men with women, of women with weakness and cowardice.

This section briefly surveys the situation of homosexuals after World War II and then examines military pejoratives to expose their social constructedness, their contradictions, and their survival because of utility in intimidating all men. That is, as Tim O'Brien's memoir *If I Die in a Combat Zone* (1969) illustrates, societies construct homosexuality so as to control and coerce *everyone*. Oliver Stone's film *Platoon* (1986) and David Rabe's play *Streamers* (1976) show how imaginative works about the Vietnam War respond to this control tactic. When a single scene in *Platoon* offers one possible, very oblique reference to homoeroticism, the surrounding scenes seem to multiply standard markers for masculinity, as if to fend off from the characters any taint of femininity. Much more daringly, *Streamers* breaks down the false polarization between heterosexuality and homosexuality, undermining the "othering" on which the creation of scapegoats relies.

John Costello believes that World War II contributed to the gay liberation movement twenty years later by enabling homosexuals to forge a "collective identity" and by showing heterosexuals that the homosexual beside him was neither sick nor cowardly (119). John D'Emilio similarly argues that mobilization, which threw together people from the big cities and the small towns, allowed gays and lesbians to meet others like them and to understand, often for the first time, that their own feelings were not unique (472). According to the well-known survey by Alfred Kinsey, published in 1948, "one in ten American males between the ages of sixteen and fifty-five was more or less exclusively homosexual, three out of ten admitted to some adult sexual experience with other men, and one in five was bisexual" (Costello 103). While Jeffrey Weeks faults Kinsey for still norming and quantifying desires, the report upset expectations by showing that half the males in the survey group had engaged at some time in same-sex activities (Weeks, "Hocquengham" 694).

Unfortunately, the publicity from the Kinsey report, along with the increased visibility of a homosexual community, led to a backlash. In the 1950s, Senator Joseph McCarthy infamously hunted down "perverts" as well as "commies," President Eisenhower banned homosexuals from employment by the federal bureaucracy and government contractors, and the FBI opened letters, spied on bedrooms, and solicited men in restrooms to try to entrap people (D'Emilio 472). Yet D'Emilio finally characterizes the self-affirmation during the Stonewall riots of 1969 as a complex outgrowth of World War II: "The dangers involved in being gay rose even as the possibilities of being gay were enhanced. Gay liberation was a response to this contradiction" (472).

Despite these beginnings of gay resistance, legal barriers and prejudice remained formidable throughout the Vietnam War years. In civilian life, forty-nine out of fifty states had laws that could mete out jail terms of five to twenty years for "unnatural" sex (Shilts 65, 170). The military services could impose less than honorable discharges for homosexual orientation, let alone acts (Shilts 163); though an expelled man may already have won medals, dismissal severely limited his chances of getting a job (Shilts 198, 164). However, as manpower needs increased during the war, the military more fitfully observed this code, and a sizeable gay subculture was able to grow up overseas, if not on stateside bases (Shilts 149). In and out of the service, Randy Shilts finds two groups of homosexuals during the Vietnam War years: those who accepted social dictates about sexuality as "*truth*" versus those who recognized them as arbitrary "*rules*" (41). The first group internalized scorn and repressed desires, whereas the second, knowing the rules to be unjust, sought willing partners, felt no shame, but prudently hid their lives.

Although Shilts says that military indoctrination against homosexuality became less formal during training for Vietnam, extemporized taunting by DIs seems to me more pervasive. Authorities may have dropped the 1948 lurid lecture which warned homosexuals would commit "fiendish and horrible sex crimes," kidnap small children, and mutilate victims (Shilts 134), but DIs were now peppering training sessions with the words "faggot" and "queer," as a means of controlling all men. In fact, though official doctrine claims to be rooting out homosexuality as inappropriate to the military, trainers keep inviting it back in, as a topic. In the oral history *Nam*, a soldier recalls trying to answer a baffling instructor: " 'You like me, don't you, boy?' 'Yessir.' 'You're queer for me.' 'Nossir.' 'You don't like me?' 'Yessir. Nossir'" (M. Baker 21). This routine might be comic if it weren't so insidious. The point is to put the recruit always in the wrong, no matter what he does. As another veteran summarizes, when a man can do fifty pushups, the DI demands a hundred; when a trainee can run two miles, the DI asks for five (Michalowski 330). Why should the trainer scream "faggot" precisely at the point when the recruit inevitably fails?

Most recruits want to be accepted by big-daddy trainer and the band of brothers; the taunt "fag" can *only* work to exclude men from this homosocial bond if they learn to define homosexual as womanly. An episode from Tim O'Brien's memoir *If I Die in a Combat Zone* clearly shows this mechanism of exclusion manipulating the behavior of even the most reflective soldiers. During basic training, O'Brien's friend Erik makes an appointment with the drill sergeant to protest the Vietnam War, but instead of dealing with Erik's arguments, Blyton simply deflects them, with two little words. Distracting Erik with "coward," then knocking him out with "pansy," Blyton easily shuts up his adversary (43). Shortly afterward, the sergeant has the opportunity to deliver a new round of epithets, as he discovers Erik and Tim cleaning rifles by themselves, talking about politics and poetry:

> Out behind them barracks hiding from everyone and making some love, huh? . . . You're a pussy, huh? You afraid to be in a war, a goddamn pussy, a goddamn lezzie? You know what we do with pussies,

huh? We fuck 'em. In the army we just fuck 'em and straighten 'em out . . . . Maybe I'll just stick you two puss in the same bunk tonight, let you get plenty of pussy so tomorrow you can't piss. (54)

A poet despite himself, Blyton relishes word plays from "lezzie" to "pussy" to "piss," and he surrealistically morphs his scapegoat from an imagined gay man to a lesbian. Among his colorful invective, Blyton buries some interesting contradictions, which we will examine in a moment, but the most immediate point is that "pansy" works as a jibe because it boils down to "pussy." No one wants to resemble a *woman*.

Blyton's tirade seems to be effective, for eventually he corrupts Erik and Tim to his point of view. When the sergeant slaps on extra guard duty just for sitting together, at first they think that they have outsmarted him, for the privacy allows them to continue talking. Soon, however, they tire of trudging, and when they catch another young man making an unauthorized phone call, they report him. Gradually it dawns on them that Blyton had "won a big victory that night" (56). While O'Brien highlights their transformation into petty tyrants, just like Blyton, their sergeant has won in another sense too. For he has shifted not only Erik, at the time, but also O'Brien, in this retrospective memoir, from questioning the war, by making them question themselves instead.

To call any man "pussy" must make him ask, for a second, "*Do I have any womanly traits?*" The answer for everyone has to be "of course," because, as the previous chapters have shown, the diverse feelings that our culture names womanly—kindness, fear—are just human. Because Erik and Tim have learned to call these reactions feminine, they begin to worry that maybe they went to Fort Lewis "afraid to admit we are not Achilles, that we are not brave, not heroes" (45). O'Brien might have asked: *was* the quintessentially masculine Achilles such a good role model? In the *Iliad*, the Greek warrior lets scores of men on his own side die as he nurses an insult from his commander. During his initial quarrel with Agamemnon, Achilles also tellingly reveals that the Trojans never did him any harm, never stole his cattle or horses (Homer 63). He is willing to slaughter hundreds of these basically unoffending "enemies" for Agamemnon's family "honor," but really, one suspects, for the loot, concubines, and, especially, reputation as manly fighter, which he is constantly advertising. Although the West has called Achilles "hero" for centuries, his goals look (with less of an epic spin) like piracy, rape, and private image-building. More self-aware than Achilles, O'Brien does glimpse that a fear of "society's censure" about "manhood" motivates him and Erik (*If I Die* 45), but the chapter never resumes Erik's arguments against the war, so important does masculinity still seem to them, even though this construction of masculinity means fighting for fighting's sake.

If O'Brien hadn't been distracted by Achilles and manhood, he might have returned not only to question the war but also to examine the contradictions in his sergeant's surreal tirade. Despite Blyton's vehement scorn against homosexuals, he pictures the army and himself—"we"—engaging in sex with men: "In the army we just fuck 'em and straighten 'em out" (54). Now, under the military statutes against sodomy (Shilts 69), Blyton could certainly be prosecuted, since those laws do not distinguish between penetrator and penetrated. Because Blyton does distinguish, he bypasses the Christian condemnation of homosexuality as nonprocreative pleasure and harks back to other traditions. In some ways, he repeats the classical Greek view that an adult man had every right to penetrate male teens (who understood that they must not suggest any switching of roles) during a period of physical and intellectual mentoring. Blyton proposes to be the teacher, pounding a little sense into these neophytes. However, he still differs a great deal from his classical forebears, of course, in that the Greeks imagined some sentiment and caring animating the penetrator, whereas Blyton intends to punish his boys. Here he echoes another tradition, found in some ancient cultures, that a conqueror or superior could humiliate a male by anal rape, since symbolically the act was thought to turn the man into a woman (Trexler 21, 65).[1]

Blyton also exposes another contradiction in military thinking. Whereas the government through its statutes against gays is supposedly affirming that heterosexual relationships are good and homosexual ones are bad, actually Blyton believes in no relationships. All sex is punishment, not partnership, and he disdains a woman as much as a foe: "You know what we do with pussies" (*If I Die* 54). Like the god in Ovid's tale of Daphne, Blyton in his modern Apollo Syndrome could probably muster surface flattery toward ladies, but he really equates intercourse with conquest. If Daphne refuses Apollo's advances, the god will punish her and get back to crowning Rome's warriors with laurel leaves, just as Blyton wants to dominate and humiliate women, along with humiliating men.

This hostility to women clearly surfaces in another example of Vietnam trainers' ranting, this time directed toward marines addressed as "women": "Unless you women get with the program, straighten out the queers, and grow some balls of your own, you best give your soul to God 'cause your ass is mine and so is your mother's on visiting day" (Michalowski 331). Like Blyton, this DI has portrayed himself in sexual intercourse with his men. Although he would prosecute consenting sodomy, he can boast of anal rape. Then he claims that he'll rape the men's mothers. Again, the DI as supposed role model for recruits is not validating heterosexual relationships but teaching that all sex pits a tormenting master against an inferior slave.

Moreover, this marine instructor is not just railing inventively in a world of words but instigating real, frightening actions. Leading up to this speech, he isolates one private, Green, who cannot complete a grueling run, and makes him the scapegoat for the exhaustion that the other men are also feeling. The DI arbitrarily brands Green a "good-for-nothing queer," then forces the other trainees to do extra exercises: "As long as there are faggots in this outfit who can't hack it, you're all going to suffer" (Michalowski 331). When the DI finally eggs them on to "straighten out the queers," the marine who is recounting the incident admits—now in horror at his own deeds—that sixty men beat Private Green almost to death (332).

The DI's intention to coerce soldiers supersedes even the tactic of inviting them to join the band of brothers. Keeping in reserve the possibility that everyone will always be too weak to join him, the DI perhaps calculates that his always frustrated boys will be more murderous when thrust into battle. Maybe they will take out their resentment, not against the person who actually riled them—their own instructor—but against some other schmuck, presumably the enemy, whose own DI maybe goaded him in similar ways. It doesn't really matter what the enemy stands for. This DI has just illustrated that he can turn his charges into killers, of *anybody*: the other side, their own side, communist, capitalist, Vietnamese, American, somebody named Ho, somebody named Green.

If the mere word "queer" unleashes this extreme violence against Green, it's no wonder that a man would hide sexual feeling toward another man, or that a movie director concerned with a mainstream audience might only indirectly refer to homoeroticism among characters. In Oliver Stone's film *Platoon*, Sergeant Elias dances toward the young, newly arrived soldier Chris at a dreamlike, drug-blurred party in Vietnam; when Elias holds out a rifle, asks Chris to put his mouth on it, and offers to blow marijuana through the barrel, the imagery sounds like dream-code for "blow job." If so, there's no way of telling if Elias participates in a gay subculture, with separate hooches for men dancing (Shilts 80), or if the sergeant is one of the many wartime heterosexuals who practiced what was called in World War II "emergency" or "deprivation" homosexuality (Costello 102). The labels seem arbitrary and irrelevant, not so important as the bit of physical comfort that Elias may be kindly willing to exchange during an otherwise hellish tour of duty.

However, in American culture, even kindness can damn a man. Elias has already strayed into a realm that the nineteenth century called feminine, simply by his characterization as the "good sergeant." Stone neatly quarantines all the evil of the war in the person of Sergeant Barnes, who kills civilians. The director then makes Elias, though fighting what many in the audience regard as an unjust war, represent not only a decent man in a bad situation, but also a Christ figure, simply because he tries to restrain Barnes's rampages. After Barnes murders a civilian woman, he brags that Elias will never be able to bring charges, because Elias is weak, "like those water-walkers . . . like those politicians in Washington trying to fight this war with one hand tied around their balls" (Stone, video). Ironically, whereas the Christian clergy traditionally cautioned against "self-abuse," Barnes, the real abuser of others, here groups "those water-walkers," Christ and followers, with masturbators, in the process conflating two separate myths. The first goes something like this: "Politicians have tied our hands, so that's why we're losing"—despite the seven million tons of bombs dropped on Indochina, more than twice the explosives used against Europe and Asia in all of World War II (Zinn 469). In his second myth, Barnes accuses Elias and the politicians of fondling themselves, so that's why we're losing. In a continuing Antony Syndrome, Barnes assumes that enjoyment of the senses imposes womanliness and weakness.

If Stone does not agree with Barnes's ramblings, he still apparently worries about such charges. After the director lets Elias at the party venture into this second supposedly feminine arena, pleasure as well as goodness, the film seems anxious to erase any imputation of effeminacy. Stone's imagery of two men communing through a phallic rifle, like Wilfred Owen's World War I lines about men's hearts twining as "hard wire" with hard "stakes" (Owen 101), reinforces the notion that male camaraderie, physical or emotional, *only* escapes femininity in the context of weaponry and fighting. To further drive home this point, Elias must fistfight Barnes. The unedifying spectacle of two U.S. noncoms brawling seems designed solely to reestablish Elias's masculinity. American military culture has not advanced beyond the boarding school that John Dos Passos depicted in *The 42nd Parallel*, where the boys, all equally reluctant but resigned, fistfight each other—then eventually sign up for World War I—to deflect that most horrible of insults, "girlboy" (104).

Much bolder than Stone, David Rabe represents homosexuality openly in his play *Streamers*, where seven men in a barracks wait to be shipped off to Vietnam. Richie frankly reveals that he is interested in men, but his buddies keep denying this information obtusely, "Do you even know what you're sayin', Richie? Do you even know what it means to be a fag?" (19). Do they? Roger and Billy's desire to hide facts that might unsettle their learned gender assignments—as well as remind one of oneself—fits into a larger theme of "hide-and-go-seek" in the play (62). For the characters cannot face a number of important truths: that they might die in their war, that they don't know why their country is fighting (especially in Vietnam, but also in the Korean War remembered by the two older sergeants), that some of them are gay, and, even more upsetting to them, that all the men, not just Richie, display some characteristic, emotional or physical, which their culture has named homosexual or unmanly, terms now inextricably linked.

Rabe's soldiers have grown up in the American 1950s and 1960s with social expectations that urge a man to drink, fight, experience no fear, feel no homoeroticism, and deny tenderness. Rabe, however, satirizes all these requirements. The old sergeants Rooney and Cokes demonstrate "how men are men jumpin' outa planes," but their drunken routine of the "Screamin' goddamn Eagles" and their lunges off footlockers reveal that drinking and aggressiveness may really be childish—as well as murderous and suicidal (25). Billy thinks that Rooney can go to Vietnam to "Make a man outa him," but Roger suspects that the "Disneyland" confusion of Vietnam may turn him instead into a powerless "Mickey Mouse" (9). Carlyle recognizes even more clearly that war may not mold men: "They gonna be bustin' balls, man—kickin' and stompin' " (16). He knows the war could turn him into a corpse, no longer a man at all.

All the characters in *Streamers* share Carlyle's dread of dying in Vietnam, but they cannot acknowledge it, because their society labels fear unmanly. A person may perhaps overcome fear through a strong enough belief in a cause, but these men cannot ascertain a cause or, worse, have an inkling but do not fully support the official rationale. When Billy explains that Ho Chi Minh is like Hitler, Roger counters that some people think President Johnson is Hitler, pursuing imperialist policies (21). Carlyle protests, "It ain't our war," meaning that blacks have little share in running the United States, or that the Vietnamese conflict should remain local (16). He wonders why everybody is "just sittin' and takin' it" (16). Rabe shows, however, that with no national consensus on rightness, a country can keep a war going as long as propaganda invokes manliness.

One of the most volatile definitions of masculinity for Rabe's characters is that a man is not supposed to want sexual contact with other men. Yet the enormous irony of this play about soldiers trying to deny and expel homosexuality, which they think will brand them unmanly, is that virtually all the characters could love other men, emotionally and probably physically. Cokes and Rooney come on stage arm in arm, obviously devoted to each other. Although Rooney repeats a rote scorn for "you pussies," the sergeants' own togetherness, "almost kissing," makes them an old married couple (29, 24). Their affection constantly seeks out physical expression. Billy announces Rooney's arrival with the chant "Hut who hee whor," a variant of "Hut-Two-Three-Four" (23). Rabe's earlier play *The Basic Training of Pavlo Hummel* (1971) skews this march into "HUT HOO HEE HAW," as if to ask, who's the butt of this bad joke of a war (61)? By contrast, Billy's version of the chant seems to ask, "Who's the he-whore," the male attracted to men. The sergeant's presence as answer to that question suggests that it is not only Richie but also Rooney who might desire men. In fact, it could be any of them.

For Carlyle too displays both emotional and physical longing for men. His early interaction with Roger implies a need for affection. As the only other black soldier in the vicinity, Roger sometimes looks out for him but also keeps his distance, in case Carlyle should get him into trouble. When Roger refuses a trip to town, Carlyle reveals hurt under his sarcasm: "That's sad, man; make me cry in my heart," because "You ain't gonna make it with me, man" (16). Carlyle is conducting a kind of courtship, and when he feels rejected, he tries to be stoical: "Okay, okay. Got to be one man one more time" (16). To "be one man" means to buck up, be brave, but also, unfortunately, be alone. His need for comfort from men extends in a continuum from emotional to physical, with no clear break between the two, just as the other men's willingness to offer Carlyle blankets when he sleeps on their floor draws no line between heterosexual and homosexual generosity (33–34).

Carlyle is also the character who most openly seeks out a male partner for oral sex, apparently without altering his self-image as a macho man who can look down on Richie. Randy Shilts reports, "For thousands of gay soldiers in Vietnam, overtures from heterosexual colleagues were the most confusing experiences of their service careers" (43). Usually the suitors were careful to cast themselves as penetrating, not penetrated, or sucked, not sucking, yet the pleasure need not always be so one-sided: "In the 101st, for example, there were two soldiers who jerked each other off every night in a jeep behind the barracks. It raised few eyebrows. They were not queer . . . . They both had wives at home" (Shilts 44). Although the sexual behavior of the men called heterosexual and of those called homosexual differs little in this setting, the labels remain unchanged and strictly ranked.

As Rooney, Cokes, and Carlyle all reach out toward a solacing homoeroticism, so too do the rest of the men. Although Martin may only feign a suicide attempt, hoping for dismissal, one possible motive for real self-hurt is the strain of an attraction to Richie, which could expose him to others' sneers (7). Even Roger, who seems to be the most "straight" character, recommends playing basketball because a "Little bumpin' into people" is comforting (36). He certainly understands loving friendships with men, to the extent that Richie envies Roger his closeness with Billy: "I never had that kind of friend ever. Not even when I was little" (22).

Billy especially seems to be drawn to men but cannot admit it. When Rooney is "almost kissing" Cokes and splashing whiskey on Roger's chest, Billy jokes, "Who do I follow for my turn?" (24). The stage directions specify that he moves into the sergeants' proximity "almost seeming to want to be a part of the intimacy" (29). Because Billy gravitates toward touch, pushes Richie away so angrily, yet talks so obsessively about "fag stuff" (22), he seems to protest too much. Although neither Robert Altman in his film based on *Streamers* nor critic John Clum in his study *Acting Gay* sees this possibility (222), to me the real center of the play is Billy's unadmitted homosexuality and the tragedies that follow when society won't allow him to live out and love that life.

The first tragedy is that once Billy hides his affections, he becomes an easier tool of war. *Streamers* illustrates this transformation in an interesting series of apparent non sequiturs. Roger is telling the others that as a child he saw a neighborhood bully beat up a "faggot" who, Roger claims, paused as the attacker was "bouncin' him off the walls" and "gave his ass this little twitch, man, like he thought he was gonna turn me on" (20). Although (or perhaps because) Roger recognizes at some level a kinship, using the same phrase "little fella" within a few lines for both the "screamin' goddamn faggot" and then himself, he seems more upset by the man's flirtation (if such it was) than by the beating (19–20). Billy, who is sitting up attentively, "staring at Roger," is learning or relearning from this anecdote that he himself cannot possibly be homosexual, because such a label invites attack: either literal bashing or the hurtfulness of Roger's slurs (20).

Billy reacts to this lesson in the dangers of being gay by asking abruptly, "How long you think we got?"—how long until they are shipped out to Vietnam (20). His question only apparently changes the topic. The unstated connection implies that Billy fears getting bombed, as he fears getting bounced off walls. Ironically, however, if he fears the war, he also needs the war, to prove that he doesn't "deserve" the same treatment as the street victim. As Randy Shilts speculates, many repressed homosexuals went to Vietnam to "prove I was a man," and, in that era of instilled shame, some even hoped they would prove they weren't homosexual (32, 34). Yet Billy's solution to persecution is hardly a smart move; if he needs to be bombed so as not to be bounced, he may end up smashed in either case. To drown out any voices imputing unmanliness to him, Billy uses the din of war, whose vague cause he need not analyze further, because it has already become his own cause, acceptance by peers. Nevertheless, if Billy feels pressured to establish masculinity (because his culture links homosexual with womanly), the important point is that he shares this goal with all the men of his culture.

Because Billy does not admit any homoerotic desires, he loudly disapproves the oral sex that Carlyle and Richie are planning, but, at the same time, he insists on witnessing that very encounter. Roger storms out of the barracks, but Billy stays and even turns on the lights, shouting, "I don't run, don't hide" (51). His cry is ironic, as he seems to be hiding his own interest at that moment. Ostensibly, he holds his ground because "it ain't gonna be done in my house," but his obstinacy makes it seem as if he wants to be present for the sexual exchange himself: "Jealous, Billy?" (50).

This scene turns violent not because the sexuality is somehow inherently dangerous, but because Billy's trained denial of this possibility of human sharing already kills off a part of his humanity: "I am not human as you are. I put you down" (53). His violence against himself and his passion leads him to try to blot out mirror images of himself in others, those aspects that he fears would marginalize him, as they have excluded others. Hence, Billy hurts Richie by calling him "you gay little piece of shit-cake," and he wounds Carlyle, another outsider, by labeling him "SAMBO" (53). The racial slur provokes Carlyle to stab Billy. When Sergeant Rooney tries to apprehend the assailant with a broken bottle, Carlyle, partly in self-defense, confusedly stabs him too.

As Cokes searches for Rooney, not knowing he is dead, Cokes recalls an experience from the Korean War which suggests that when a society denies pleasure, including a homoeroticism that may belong to both gays and straights, then that society is able to co-opt the energy of sexuality into violence. When a North Korean soldier in a spider hole wounded Cokes—"shot me in the ass"—Cokes dropped a grenade into the hole and sat on the lid, all the while aware of "him bouncin' and yellin' under me. Bouncin' and yellin' under the lid" (27). As the old sergeant on the stage now sits on the footlocker remembering, he embodies what each of the characters has been doing all along: keeping the lid on both a desire to touch and an urge to be gentle. Any "shooting in the ass" might hint an unacceptable anal sex—so repress that glimpse. Any recognition of the Korean soldier as a human being with an equal right to live might subvert the demonizing fictions of war—so clamp the lid on that impulse too. What could have been a description of lovemaking—"bouncin' and yellin' under me," crying out in pleasure—becomes an account of fear and death, because none of the characters know how to let out love, whether passion or compassion.

Rabe delivers a second powerful image of the displacement of repressed sexuality into violence, through Cokes's story of O'Flannigan, a jokester who detaches a parachute too soon and so slams "into the ground like a knife" (26). Cokes explains that both O'Flannigan and the trapped Korean are "singin' it," the song "Beautiful Streamer," which Cokes and Rooney make up to the tune of Stephen Foster's "Beautiful Dreamer" (65, 26). The first lines, "Beautiful Streamer, / Open for me," beg the parachute to unfurl or the American enemy to open the lid of the spider hole (28). At the same time, however, the song evocatively suggests the call to a lover: to open his body, to open his heart. Continuing this impression that the sergeants are singing a love song, Cokes describes O'Flannigan's parachute as phallic: straight up like an icicle, like a tulip, but "All twisted and never gonna open" (26). What's twisted is a homophobia that fears touch between men to such an extent that the military police even order Roger away from holding the dying Billy in his arms (57).

Rabe's characters hide or evade a whole range of topics: that men do want to hold each other, that they don't really know why the Vietnam war is being fought, that they don't want to die, that they don't invariably want to kill. They mask the fact that they could, instead, even love that enemy, because compassion might be construed as feminine or passion labeled effeminate. Putting the lid on all these evasions is equivalent to throwing a grenade: figuratively deadening lives and literally killing people, in private brawls or public wars. For Rabe, wars become more likely if men need to prove manliness by blotting out so-called womanly compassion in violence, by projecting their own traits onto "queers," "pussies," and "gooks" (13, 29, 24), and by displacing the energy of prohibited sexuality into the travestied substitutes of mechanical explosions.

(c) I Fight to Prove I'm Not Emotional
(but I Do Love My Comrades)

During the war in Vietnam, American culture at home still assigns the "softer" emotions to women. In popular TV sitcoms, Mary Tyler Moore or Lucille Ball regularly dissolves in tears, a role not assigned to male actors. Yet men in Vietnam clearly experience the same emotions that their society has named womanly, from tears to hysteria to love, as seen in works by Philip Caputo, William Broyles, and Robert Olen Butler. Nevertheless, the open expression of these feelings, at least as depicted in literature, encounters more barriers in Vietnam than in earlier wars of the century. Standard operating procedures inhibit camaraderie, ever stricter gender rules may cause men to stifle caring, and when soldiers do give tenderness, they often hedge the account or the acts of kindness themselves with contradictory unkindness, simply because they have been taught to consider hurtfulness masculine. As a final, serious problem, illustrated in Donald Bodey's novel *F.N.G.*, military authorities may co-opt camaraderie, manipulating soldiers who have lost faith in any other cause to fight for each other. While everyone admires saving a pal, the glow obscures the questions about the bad causes endangering the pals in the first place.

As we saw in section (a), Philip Caputo went to Vietnam to prove "manhood" by passing three tests: be a brave hero, engage in "intercourse and intoxication," and shed blood ritualistically (6, 37). Implicitly, Caputo's candidate for manhood must pass a fourth test: reveal no feelings. Yet this requirement, like the other three, generates contradictions, for his cohorts do demonstrate the same feelings that their society has called feminine. During the central, "ugly" incident when he loses control of himself and his men and they burn a village for no military purpose (288), the frustration and misplaced revenge of a rampage duplicate the hysteria that the corps expects so disdainfully only of women.

In another ironic display of the emotion they have belittled, Caputo and his buddies exhibit positive tenderness as well as negative tantrums. Even when Caputo grows disenchanted with America's adventure in Vietnam, he manages to salvage out of his tainted military experience a valuable camaraderie. Just as Remarque prized the World War I bond between comrades as "nearer than lovers" (212) and Manchester longed to reforge the ties of World War II marine training like those of a "broken marriage" (148), Caputo effuses over "the intimacy of life in infantry battalions," using the same hyperbolic terms: "the communion between men is as profound as any between lovers" (xvii). When

Corporal Parker visits Pfc. Esposito, about to be evacuated to the states, Parker's eyes look "damp," his voice is "cracking," and Caputo feels as if he is "listening in on the conversation of two lovers who are about to be separated" (97). Whereas recruits destined for Vietnam hate to be called "ladies," with women's supposedly greater emotionalism, here Caputo elevates a fully emotional tie, tears and all, into the most "profound" experience of a serviceman's life (xvii).

Caputo not only observes this fondness in others but confesses to it himself. When he mourns a dead buddy, Levy, he remembers "your gestures, the words you spoke, and the way you looked," all "the small things that made us love you" (213). The word "love" seems able to sneak into the dialogue only when he addresses a corpse. Similarly, in the film *Apocalypse Now* (1979), once Chief is dead, Lance gently paints camouflage on his face, kisses him tenderly, and holds his head against his chest for a long time, before letting him sink to a watery grave. Here, in representations of the Vietnam War, Coppola and Caputo take the same route as Manchester, who in portraying World War II can try on the word "love" and kiss his comrade Lefty on the mouth only after his death (236). Sassoon too, in World War I, can most safely name "love" for a subaltern after the man's death. Sassoon is then allowed to throw himself on an empty plot of ground and embrace a ghost: "I knew him crushed to earth in scentless flowers, / And lifted in the rapture of dark pines" (33). In all three wars, only danger licenses the intensity of emotion that might otherwise risk suspicion as "faggoty," to use the term that plagues James Jones's characters in *The Thin Red Line* (324), and only death certifies that no further incriminating touch can take place.

Another Vietnam writer who touts camaraderie as a supreme value is William Broyles, Jr. In his much-quoted *Esquire* essay "Why Men Love War" (1984), Broyles finds a lot to praise in bloodshed. He indulgently endorses this chance for men to play "games" and carry out a "love of destruction" (57, 61). Nevertheless, his nostalgia fastens most strongly on "comradeship," what Broyles calls the "enduring emotion of war, when everything else has faded" (57). He then explains two versions of this comradeship.

On a workaday level, Broyles claims that comrades willingly pitched in for "the group," in a "love" that ignored differences of "race," "personality," "education," "possessions," and "advantage" (57). Although he may be right that suspicions among races and classes dimmed in combat, other Vietnam veterans believe that tension reasserted itself whenever the shooting stopped: "There were two wars going on—one out in the boonies against the V.C., another in the rear between blacks and whites. I felt safer in the boonies" (qtd. in Shay 60). Whites brought prejudice, and blacks resented real inequities. Minorities were less likely to afford college (and a deferment), secure a better-paying job elsewhere, or pull family strings for the National Guard, so that blacks suffered combat deaths disproportionate to their numbers in the population (Shilts 64–65; Hsiao 23). Unusually honest about such discord, Oliver Stone's *Platoon* does not hush up friction between black and white soldiers, and the film's scuffle between white sergeants reflects other internal rivalries, in a fundamentally hierarchical institution. In a less melodramatic key, such competition already chipped away at camaraderie in Manning's *The Middle Parts of Fortune*, from World War I; a similar jostling for status by rank, race, or class still keeps soldiers in Vietnam from perfectly enacting Broyles's "brotherly love" (57).

In Broyles's second, more exotic version of camaraderie, he remembers prostitutes who "specialized in group affairs, passed among several men or even whole squads, in communion almost, a sharing more than sexual" (65). Although the prostitutes are female, eroticism flickers among the men too, and only male communion counts. He also claims to detect (and seems to approve) a look of "beatific contentment" on the face of a colonel loading the dead bodies of North Vietnamese regulars, all "naked and covered with grease and mud so they could penetrate the barbed wire" (62). These two scenes, where men can view male nakedness or ejaculate with other men, record an "ecstasy," which Broyles attributes to "some subconscious appreciation of this obscene linkage of sex and excrement and death" (62). Regarding such a link as natural, Broyles misses the role of training, perceptively brought out by James Jones in *The Thin Red Line* (see the discussion in section (b), chapter 3). Once a society brands nonprocreative sex "obscene" and requires suffering as punishment for "fallen nature," participants may need to seek out hellish destruction to achieve any sex at all.

As Broyles's essay reduces women to an accessory object facilitating a sacred, erotic ceremony among fellow soldiers, Robert Olen Butler's novel *On Distant Ground* (1985) further explores how longing for communion among men can encompass even the enemy, while still exploiting women as go-betweens. Although Butler's central character David has sexual relationships with a Vietnamese woman, Suong, and later an American, Jennifer, both female partners rouse only tepid sentiment, compared to his deep concern for Tuyen, a male North Vietnamese prisoner whom David helped escape. Returning to Vietnam immediately before the fall of Saigon to look for his son,

Khai, he hears that Suong may have spent the preceding year in prison, for protesting the corruption of South Vietnamese President Thieu. However, in striking contrast to the long pages that David devotes to Tuyen's incarceration, pitying every deprivation and admiring the aloofness he imagines, he now skips over Suong's ordeal in a few lines. He eagerly seizes the excuse of inquiring about her fate to seek out Tuyen, now an official with the Communist victors.

Constantly drawn to cool detachment and irony, David finally learns the hurtfulness of detachment only when Tuyen hurts *him*, by coolly refusing to acknowledge the American's earlier help. Yet David tries to mend his own lifelong aloofness not by showing more considerateness to the women or refusing to use them further. In fact, the book forgets the women, as Suong's death in prison conveniently frees David to take his son, and he puts his new knowledge about the value of attachment into effect by returning to embrace Tuyen. Although this empathy admirably tries to reconcile former enemies, the bond also suggests that if a society prohibits intimacy to men in peacetime, they may need to clinch with enemies to achieve a substitute embrace in the fight, recalling World War II poet Keith Douglas's indirect love in "How to Kill" (section (b), chapter 3). Former enemies may then touchingly forgive each other, as, elsewhere, comrades may use a buddy's imminent or recent death to authorize a final enfolding.

Even within these helpful smokescreens, however, Vietnam writers attest that friendships among soldiers encountered real impediments, perhaps greater than in earlier wars of this century. Whereas World War II units trained together, stayed together for the duration, and (if they survived) went home on the same boat, with time to talk and decompress, Vietnam soldiers arrived and left singly, tossed back to the states in a day by plane (Shay 198). The twelve- or thirteen-month tour of duty prevented the kind of ties that World War II fostered, as each man in Vietnam reached the end of his rotation on a private schedule. Furthermore, grunts long in the field might look down on a newly arrived officer, and perpetual transients forged less unit loyalty (Stewart 148).

Even when men did find a comrade, they faced other obstacles, specific to Vietnam operating procedures, which interfered with the expression of strong friendship. Jonathan Shay, a psychiatrist who works with Vietnam vets still suffering post-traumatic stress disorder (some quarter of a million in 1994), argues in *Achilles in Vietnam* that soldiers needed to cry at the death of buddies and to feel part of communal mourning. Instead, medics gave survivors pills, treating grief as sickness, and told mourners that tears would brand a "weakling" (Shay 63). Meanwhile, helicopters whisked away the dead for handling by strangers. By contrast, Shay points out, ancient Greek and Trojan warriors in the *Iliad* wept publicly, burned their own dead, and mourned in set rituals. Once at home, American vets wanted to confide to families the grief and love that they were still feeling for a lost comrade, but a cultural view of compassion as "maternal" inhibited them (Shay 49).

Because of this American stigma around nurturance, as if it were exclusively feminine, soldiers may keep their feelings to themselves. When they do try to tell emotion, they often grope for words or notably hedge caring with gratuitous expressions of violence. Recounting his first experience under fire, one soldier interviewed in *Nam* claims that when someone asked, "Where's the new guy," this concern moved him so profoundly that he will never forget it, because he is "amazed" that anyone could be so "generous? Caring is too big a word somehow" (M. Baker 36). Does he really mean too "big" a word or too womanly? Another interviewee ventures to admit caring, but he soon retreats. Reporting that he discovered among soldiers a fund of "tenderness which society only assumes of women," he complains that he could not locate this "sensitivity" once he returned home: "Then you come back to the Land of the Big PX and it's business as usual. Men are being male in traditional ways, stepping on each other's toes on the way up the ladder" (M. Baker 295). Suddenly, however, the speaker insists that civilians fail to listen not because of greed and competitiveness but because they "are not willing to deal with the same amount of necessary ruthlessness or compassion on a daily basis" (M. Baker 296). *Necessary* ruthlessness? The word "ruthless" goes beyond any kind of austere discipline required of oneself, to imply instead an abuse of others—although the veteran has just confessed that he finds stepping on people's toes stupid. He seems to need the word "ruthlessness" because he thinks it's masculine, to counterbalance the imputed feminine content of "tenderness" and "compassion." Suddenly panicked by his society's gender divisions, he backs out of the human caring, equally available to men and women, which he came so close to accepting.

Like these two veterans in *Nam*, Caputo defuses caring among men with testimonials of violence. Although he speaks forthrightly about Corporal Parker's catch in the throat for a hurt friend, or about his own "love" for dead Lieutenant Levy, Caputo blusters that *of course* the "tenderness" of such camaraderie "would have been impossible if the war had been significantly less brutal" (xvii, 213). Whereas *danger* might draw people together, does *brutality*? As a matter of fact, the two examples of brutality that Caputo acknowledges in his memoir—burning the homes of 200 people and killing prisoners—do not enhance solidarity at all; the men slink apart in shame when they can look back on what they did. Caputo needs the word "brutal" not because it really describes his experience of tenderness, but because it implies heartlessness, and he apparently worries that the examples of Parker and Levy display too much *heart*—still foolishly pinned exclusively on women.

These accounts demonstrate what Michel Foucault calls the "rules of formation" governing "discursive groups that are not arbitrary, and yet remain invisible" (*Archaeology* 38). The often invisible rules assigning nurturance to women and destruction to men cause Vietnam writers to suggest men's caring only tentatively, then neutralize the imputed femininity by adding words such as "ruthless" and "brutal." But as Foucault also argues, discourses are not superadded "signs" referring to preexistent "contents," but rather "practices that systematically form the objects of which they speak" (*Archaeology* 49). Although seeming to discover preexisting male aggressiveness, the discourse available to men in Vietnam instead forms and perpetuates masculine brutalities.

One of the most important problems besetting camaraderie in Vietnam is that when men do achieve strong ties, military authorities may co-opt them. In Donald Bodey's *F.N.G.* (1985), two striking scenes of bonding—from Commanding Officer to men, and from buddy to buddy—do comfort a squad, but the bonds also serve to deflect protest away from the war. The novel plots a series of mutinies, from verbal to violent. (See Moser 44–51 on soldier protests such as "combat refusal" and "fragging.") Usually, Bodey's mutineers resent specific combat strategies, but occasionally the men may doubt larger goals as well. Although the characters often muddle their reasons, Bodey separates from his creations and tacitly allows the reader to conclude that the war was unjust. However, when he shows camaraderie buying off protests, he seems as distracted as his characters, for the book validates the war again precisely because it provides an opportunity for tender emotion between men.

The one open, conscious challenge to authority in Bodey's novel occurs when a squad leader, Pops, dares to question orders that resulted in the death of a popular lieutenant, "Eltee" Williams. Omitting the respectful word "sir," Pops lounges insolently: "He has undone his pants and is standing there talking to the CO with his dick out, rubbing one finger all around the jungle rot on his balls. I notice the CO has rot too, on his neck" (137). Finally Pops ventures to put the squad's resentment into words: "I think somebody fucked up back here" (137). The Commanding Officer, however, skillfully contains this incipient unrest in two ways, by claiming empathy and by turning the men's mourning for Eltee into a quasi-erotic ceremony. In a rare show of commiseration, he puts his hand on Pops's hand and insists, "Listen, I *know* how you feel":

> The way he says it, the way he looks around at all of us with a tiny little frown, the way he gives Pops's ball-handling wrist an additional shake . . . something makes me think he *does* know how Pops feels, and probably how I feel even if I don't. I feel something in my throat. Prophet spits, Callme spits, Peacock spits. The CO turns to leave and spits. I spit. (137)

The location of this paragraph at the end of a chapter lends it solemnity and signals that something important has occurred. When the CO professes to understand his men, even the insubordinate Pops, he succeeds in convincing the I-narrator that he does know "how I feel" better than Gabe knows himself. Drawn away from Pops's anger and subsumed back into the official group, Gabe is no longer "F.N.G.," the "fucking new guy" of the title, but fully "G.I.," government issued, in attitude as well as clothes. The men respond to the CO's unexpected empathy with emotion of their own: "I feel something in my throat" (137). Nobody actually cries in front of the CO, although elsewhere in the book men do secretly weep (216). Here, spitting relieves the lump in the throat, a manly substitute for unacceptable public grieving.

If the spitting drains off emotional pressure that might otherwise have erupted into embarrassing tears, the saliva may also double for semen, as the scene enacts a carefully controlled, purely symbolic bonding ceremony. The strong repetition of words and actions in Bodey's account—"spit" five times, "the way" three times, "feel" or "feels" three times—announces a kind of ritual. When the CO places his hand on Pops's "ball-handling wrist" (137), he eerily echoes ancient puberty rites, in which an older man holds the penis of a youth while another male marks it with cuts of circumcision or subincision (Campbell, *Primitive Mythology* 92–103). The representatives of the two generations in Vietnam, as much as their traditional counterparts, still share genital pain: mutilation or jungle rot. Pops and the CO wear an in-group insignia of scabs, although the latter's mark has been discreetly displaced upward, to his neck. Serving as a kind of high priest who passes down the mores of the tribe, the CO evokes a traditional initiation, where a young man at puberty absorbs the semen of an older initiator. This institutionalized, temporary homosexuality is supposed to counter any femininity that is said to have contaminated the boy through his birth or his childhood with his mother (Rubin 181; Conway-Long 67). In Bodey's scene, oral sex occurs symbolically, with spitting replacing ejaculating.

The traditional rites behind this scene may seem to celebrate a natural passage, since the youth is now able to inseminate a woman and help create life. However, an initiate is actually learning very specific cultural attitudes toward sex. He learns to associate his genitals first with pain, which prepares him for the further role of enduring pain in battle and for the elevation of destruction to a position more valued than life-giving capabilities. Whether or not Bodey is consciously drawing on popularized anthropology, he certainly understands the dynamics of a ritualized, sexualized solidarity across generations. In its ancient or modern versions, patriarchy flatters men by making them feel close to the already socially empowered father and superior to disempowered women, the disdained "ladies" to whom DIs threateningly compare new recruits. Nevertheless, such a system of male privilege actually keeps younger men in line as oppressively as it limits women, for the men learn to accept symbolic substitutes for sex and submit to the deaths of expendable Eltees.

Once the modern initiate learns to see the pains of battle as the continuation of a solidarity ritual, he need not seek further reasons for his war. He may, in fact, suppress a nagging suspicion of purposelessness, for fear that he might lose the means to that concord. Betraying some doubt, Pops mutters, "this [war] ain't ours," hinting that the United States has no legitimate interest in Vietnam (58). Gabe, feeling sorry even for the enemy, thinks of Viet Cong soldiers on patrol as "poor fuckers" (208), and Prophet, although able to imagine revenge against "Charlie [Viet Cong]," finally concludes, "there ain't no sense to any of this, man" (103). Yet it is left to Gabe's mother to refer in a letter to talk about "the war being wrong" (101).[2] Only she can get away with such explicitness, precisely because she is not socially required to keep up a macho image before buddies, who gain acceptance for tenderness only in the context of inflicting and enduring suffering.

Nevertheless, if the soldiers cannot allow themselves consciously to formulate the explosive thought that their war might be wrong, Gabe does adopt this viewpoint unconsciously. He seriously mutinies, yet Bodey defuses the implications of protest by having Gabe neither plan nor remember his deeds. After Callme steps on a mine, stripping his legs to the bone, Gabe competently calls in a medevac helicopter, but he blanks out everything else, to wake up in a hospital tent reserved for "battle fatigue" (246). Gradually he learns that during the period now covered by amnesia, he marched his men at gunpoint back to the landing zone, where he wildly challenged the CO. One of these coerced soldiers recounts Gabe's actions: "You said you were gonna make goddamn sure Callme didn't die and you pointed your rifle right in my face," screaming, "ChieufuckingHoi you whole goddamn army" (268, 260). The Americans used the Vietnamese phrase *Chieu Hoi*—literally, "with open arms"—to mean "surrender" (166, 260) and broadcast this advice to the enemy from helicopters (W. Terry 83). Although Gabe now judges that he must have been ill to advise *Americans* to surrender—"*Flipped out? Christ, I guess*"—he has demonstrated, of course, a method to his madness (268). Here Bodey seems to allow readers to wonder if Gabe might be right (in sentiment, if not in tactics), in that the best way to keep the Callmes of the army from dying would be for the United States to greet North Vietnam with "open arms" at the bargaining table and withdraw from an unjust war. Yet Gabe at the time does not know or claim that he is right, nor does Bodey in retrospect seem to take a definite stand.

Instead of rationally proposing a U.S. "opening of arms," which might expose the men to a charge of cowardice, linked to the irrationally effective taunt of unmanliness, the best these doubting soldiers can do is "open arms" to each other, providing help as each one in turn frays to the breaking point. Peacock, for example, usually one of the steadiest, panics during incoming artillery and takes the safety off his rifle, against standing orders. To prevent him from endangering himself and others, Gabe kicks the rifle out of Peacock's hand and wrestles him down, but then turns the harsh discipline into comfort: "I use the hand that a minute ago had him by the throat to wipe the sweat off my forehead; then I trace the outline of the tattoo on his chest and finally rub him as though I was in The World and on top of a girl. Without opening his eyes, he stops my hand and holds it" (207). When Callme walks in, Peacock explains, "your squad leader just saved my life" (207). Callme is gracious enough to recall a difficult river crossing where Gabe rescued him too: "I've seen a lot of that over here. I've seen more lives get saved than I've seen get took, and my black ass is one of them." He adds, "You guys go on holding hands. I'm gonna go fight the war with these Effengees in the next hole" (208). Gabe caresses Peacock, and Callme approves.

When Gabe says that he lies on Peacock "as though I was in The World and on top of a girl," he becomes aware of the potential sexuality of the scene, even as he assures us of heterosexuality (207). But if the camaraderie stops short of consummation, it shows a dynamic by which physical solace, ostensibly time-out from war, can be manipulated to refuel war. Groups such as the military services that loudly ban sex between men typically multiply the number of nongenital behaviors (the touch of a hand), which supposedly signal homosexuality. When South Vietnamese ARVN troops routinely held hands, culture-bound Americans were shocked, interpreting this Asian expression of friendship as proof that their allies were "perverts" (Baritz 22–23). So when Peacock grasps Gabe's hand, even this small gesture might potentially embarrass them. Significantly, although Callme does not condemn them, the characters seem to need countermeasures to cancel out any contamination from the "feminine" pose. Like Caputo and the veterans from *Nam*, sandbagging accounts of tenderness with the words "brutal" and "ruthless," Brodey neatly brackets the men's caress with two examples of supposedly masculine violence. Gabe begins the contact by wrestling with Peacock, and Callme closes it by ostentatiously announcing his return to a foxhole to "fight the war" (208). Once a society defines homosexuality as effeminacy and masculinity as violence, any homoeroticism, any touch at all, provokes the need to re-prove masculinity by more fighting.

Yet it is fighting that causes soldiers to crack and need comfort in the first place. This vicious circle co-opts Bodey's characters into perpetuating a governmental lie, when Callme insists that more lives are saved than "get took" in Vietnam (208). Although he and the reader might see only a few deaths—four Viet Cong and two Americans, in the course of the whole novel—eventually the toll would be 58,000 Americans and more than three million Vietnamese (Turner 8). The physical and emotional closeness among Gabe, Peacock, and Callme, like the symbolically erotic and sentimental content of the spitting and cock-handling session between the CO and the squad, diverts crucial attention from the costs of the war. The military services can permit and actually encourage eroticized tenderness, but only to the extent that it blocks protest.[3]

Closeness among comrades can keep men in the field amid doubts about the whole war and about individual illegal and shameful actions within it. In the collection of memoirs *Vietnam Voices*, Michael Clodfelter confesses that "the body count itch" pushed his platoon to kill a randomly chosen old man, unarmed and unoffending (Fussell, *Norton* 686). Although this murder motivated his later antiwar activities and will, he says, haunt him for the rest of his life, he tries to exonerate his failure to intervene in time or to report the deed later; after all, a soldier needs to be relying on the "good will" of other men, rather than "sinking into a morass of fear and isolation" (689). Even when he recognizes that he owed a bigger "loyalty to truth and justice and conscience," he still feels nostalgia for "the strange but special loyalties of war" (689–90). Comrades corroborate the fiction that they all feel no fear (because that would be womanly), and they provide the alibi (protection, not caring) for strong emotional ties, which in peacetime might also be mislabeled womanly.

While some commanders benefit unconsciously from closeness among soldiers, others manipulate loyalties purposely. In a perceptive but chilling study, published in 1991, N. Kinzer Stewart examines "why men stand and fight or break and run" (145). He lists a number of factors, including "charismatic leadership," but then asserts that the "most important" motivator is a "unity or sense of belonging," summed up in the word "buddy" (145). As a former member of the U.S. Army Research Institute for the Behavioral and Social Sciences, Stewart points to "scientific" evidence from World War II, the Korean War, and the Vietnam War to demonstrate a link between the "cohesion" of a small group of soldiers and "high performance in battle" (145, 147). He then exhorts statesmen and officers to increase military effectiveness by fostering "ties of friendship" (149).

Unfortunately, Stewart's discussion occurs in a vacuum about the causes of the wars he mentions. He assumes that the United States will always fight on the side of right; no need to lay out any arguments. When he comes to the Vietnam War, he does not examine whether that war should have been fought in the first place, but only how it could have been waged more efficiently. If individual rotation hindered group cohesion, then keep men together for the duration. When Stewart looks for guidance from World War II, he can learn either from American or German examples; the radically opposed political philosophies of the two sides do not matter. Citing Samuel Stouffer's famous study of American soldiers, Stewart finds that "affection" and "machismo," not ideological conviction, motivated GIs to fight well (148). Turning to a study of German soldiers (146), Stewart notes that they too refused to give up because of closeness to buddies and "the gratification of certain personality needs, e.g., manliness" (Shils and Janowitz 143).

These remarkably similar, dual goals—watching out for buddies and looking like a man—for Germans or Allies in World War II or Americans in the Vietnam War provide almost the entire motivation for fighting. Yet Stewart never questions if murderous and suicidal fighting indeed makes a man. And if manly troops can also bond as buddies, Stewart advises military planners to make their side invincible—in whatever cause—by appropriating soldiers' most valuable reward, camaraderie.

(d) I Fight to Protect My Sister (but I Hate My Sister—So as Not To Be Her).

In World Wars I and II, the notion that men fight to protect women clashed with the reality that wars hurt women. The ideology of male saviors also belied some underlying resentment against women. As we saw in chapter 2, D. H. Lawrence's fictional soldier Henry Grenfel contradicts all his supposed concern for Banford and March when he finally kills one of the women; Lawrence further describes the murder in terms that make it sound like a simultaneous rape. A similar conjunction of sexuality with violence briefly appears in William Manchester's memoir of World War II, *Goodbye, Darkness* (chapter 3). The sole survivor of his squad, Manchester hallucinates a vicious and all-powerful "Whore of Death," whose seductions he avenges by imagining that he could rape her (88–90). He has, of course, raped someone only in his head, and Lawrence confines Henry's murder to a fiction on a page. By the Vietnam War, however, a surprising number of soldiers acted out these violent and sexual fantasies in reality and, setting themselves apart from similar offenders in earlier wars, went on to talk about the rapes and tortures in print.

In *Echoes of Combat*, Fred Turner estimates that one in ten American combat soldiers in Vietnam committed "abusive violence," which he defines as "torturing prisoners, raping civilians, or mutilating a corpse," and one in three saw others participate (29). Uncontrolled violence serving no military purpose is likely to break out in any war, but, by many accounts, the Vietnam conflict sparked an unusual incidence of gratuitous hurting, including attacks against women. In "The Misogyny of the Vietnam War," Jacqueline Lawson chronicles an array of assaults, and the voices in the oral histories *Nam* and *Bloods* detail the mistreatment of women in a chillingly matter-of-fact retrospective. Annoyed at being punished with extra guard duty for smoking dope, one group of soldiers took potshots at a woman, "obviously not an enemy agent . . . just harvesting something," until they killed her (M. Baker 108). On hearing of the My Lai court martial for massacring 400 civilians, mostly women and children (Zinn 469), one vet wondered who would be next: "A lot of us wiped out whole villages" (W. Terry 255–56, 261). A group of GIs gang-raped a South Vietnamese girl, then shot her and her father, simply because someone had given these victims canned pears better than their own rations (M. Baker 191).

This low flashpoint at which frustration burned others eventually scorched the soldiers' own sense of a livable world. According to psychiatrist Jonathan Shay, a feeling of "betrayal of 'what's right,' " by superiors or oneself, joined with unexpressed grief for comrades as the two most powerful causes of post-traumatic stress disorder (3). An officer casually told a soldier who had been ordered to fire on "enemy" boats (actually unarmed "fishermen and kids"), " 'Don't worry about it. Everything's fucking fine' . . . . A lot of medals came down from it" (qtd. in Shay 3–4). Another man, swept into a group rape, admits, "I was hoping for some kind of reprimand," but when no one exacted punishment (or offered expiation), he never recovered his sense of an ordered universe (qtd. in Turner 30). Brought up to expect that "America's power was the measure of its moral rectitude," many soldiers discovered that neither they nor their country could claim moral behavior even remotely (Turner 30).

One speaker from *Nam* hints at several reasons why men may have singled out women in cases of abusive violence: "I'm jumping behind a dike in a rice paddy. I'm firing. All of a sudden this broad peeks her head up with a big smile on it. Something told me that she had to pay. I capped her" (M. Baker 69). The soldier is really blaming his own restless companions for seeking out this fight, but he transfers his resentment to a more available target. Like Manning's World War I character Pritchard, who rechanneled his anger from the war to women (16), some Vietnam soldiers made women "pay" for the threats from male enemies or their own companions and government. Moreover, this speaker from *Nam* may have been targeting traits assigned to women that he also recognizes in himself. If he assumes that women always sit out wars, but then finds himself, at least at moments, wishing that he could leave the danger zone too, he may punish the woman for somehow infecting him with her "weakness." The sight of a woman not fighting may incense a man, for he has had to shoulder that burden alone. But the sight of a woman who is fighting (North Vietnamese, for example) may also enrage him, for her presence loses him his one perquisite of war, the flattery of masculine uniqueness and superiority over all women.

Three works of imaginative literature about the Vietnam War illustrate the devastating effects, on both women and men, of the social requirement placed on men to prove that they are not "womanly." Tom Mayer's short story "Kafka for President" (1971), Larry Heinemann's novel *Paco's Story* (1979), and Emily Mann's play *Still Life* (1980) expose the deep conflict between an ideology of helping women and a reality of hurting them. Whereas main characters in all three works believe in strict differences between men and women, the works as a whole undermine these assumptions, to show fundamental similarities between the sexes. The inability to admit such similarities fuels the violence.

Tom Mayer's "Kafka for President" plays on the gap between the image that the Pentagon wanted to project—that the U.S. was protecting South Vietnamese civilians—and the reality—that the United States was invading and destroying their land. Bender, a free-lance reporter (like Mayer himself), arrives in Vietnam just as marine units are teaming up with South Vietnamese Popular Forces (PF) to provide "security." A marine Public Information Officer welcomes Bender because he thinks the publicity will further the picture of the United States as savior-warrior:

> From his point of view it was a perfect story, one that couldn't be told often enough. Instead of zippo-ing villages Marines were protecting them, instead of killing civilians or creating refugees they were helping, providing security from the marauding Cong, medicines, no squatting prisoners, no crying mothers, only Christian brotherhood and American social work. A story to which not even the most militant Vietnik could take objection. (41)

As a matter of fact, if Bender's eventual report can be imagined to resemble Mayer's own story, the contents contradict the Information Officer's planned propaganda at every point. The marines and the PF are still "creating refugees," herding entire villages to relocate against their will. The corpsman Lowenstein does hand out medicines, but he also dispenses a string of racist slurs that cancel any "Christian brotherhood." And in the center of the story, a PF sergeant, approved and aided by Americans, tortures two women, Viet Cong suspects. If the Information Officer wishes to erase disturbing pictures of "squatting prisoners" and "crying mothers," the portrait of women vomiting for hours as their interrogators force them to swallow soap hardly improves the PR effect.

As a very subjective first-person narrator, Bender focuses on the loss suffered by Greer, "a giant Negro," who had been living with one of the suspects and now watches the torture session with anxiety, but no protest (43). Eventually, her confession reveals that she has inventoried U.S. weaponry for the Viet Cong and (in the interpreter's translation) that "Betty Lou fucky VC" (60). Finally led out of the interrogation hut, she spits at Greer. As a stoic marine who must repress emotion, Greer has no words, certainly no crying, to express his bewilderment. Nevertheless, Bender reads Greer's strong emotion from his look, that of a "hurt animal," and, in the last paragraph, from his diving into the river and staying underwater "until I was holding my own breath and the bank threatened to interfere with my line of sight" (60, 63). The reporter sympathizes primarily with Greer, who, at least in Bender's romantic "line of sight," may even contemplate suicide over what both men regard as Betty Lou's perfidy.

Nevertheless, if Bender ignores the possible story of a fighter who defends her country, to tell instead the tale of a fine, upstanding marine betrayed by his lover, Mayer separates from his narrator enough to insinuate a more evenhanded appraisal. For if Betty Lou has deceived the marines, they have already dehumanized her. The very phrase that Lowenstein uses to condemn Betty Lou for spitting at Greer, "Fucking slope cunt," almost exactly duplicates his supposedly praising introduction, "Prime slope cunt . . . Greer's giving it to her" (62, 44). Depriving the Vietnamese woman of her own name, deemed unpronounceable, the men further reduce her to meat, whose status value ("prime") accrues from one body part only.

Lowenstein's terminology radically separates men and women, into consumer and consumed. Yet the experience of women and men in Vietnam may not diverge so much as this discourse claims. If Lowenstein uses racist slurs such as "slope" for Betty Lou, a few lines later he talks about Greer as the "big coon" (45). And if the men can feel superior to a feminine piece of meat, the war reduces soldiers to meat. The story explicitly underlines this similarity of dead animals and dead men. As the marines are bringing in one of the suspects, along with the corpse of a PF, other PFs extravagantly fish from the sampans by throwing grenades in the water. The story equates the dead fish and the PF by showing that both are fragile before powerful technology, and by noting that the blood-crusted poncho wrapping the corpse "smelled of fish" (57). Yet if the men glimpse that they too can be meat, they try to hide their mortality by projecting the butcher shop language exclusively onto women.

In fact, the language keeps scrambling to foist off onto women not only the men's own vulnerability to death but also their fear. Bender observes the school of fish hit by a grenade: "One fish swam crazily along the top of the water, its head out like a girl who doesn't want to get her hair wet, and a PF dove in after it" (57). The imagery tries to locate human fear only in girls, who are said to be so afraid to swim that they could not dip their heads underwater and so frivolous that they would not ruin a hairdo. When the next paragraph describes the suspect with her "head up," the echo of "head out" demotes her to the timidity of a girl, despite her resolve (57).

Nevertheless, Mayer's story, consciously or unconsciously, keeps unsettling such polarized gender definitions. Against the soldiers' expectations, Betty Lou and her co-conspirator have carried out military operations, just as men do. Although the women finally divulge information, Bender has to admit that after their ordeal, they "both looked resigned, but sullen and determined and not scared" (62).[4] Any glimpse that women, like men, can plan operations and (at least for some moments) suppress fear is so inadmissible that the language foregrounds analogies of a panicky girl who doesn't want to get her hair wet. Yet beyond this overt metaphorizing, the actions of the story give a different message. The ending, for example, when Bender sees Greer dive into the river and stay down an alarmingly long time, quietly corrects the dichotomizing into strong men and weak girl/fish. When Greer dives, he comes up gasping for breath, as the grenade-stunned fish was gasping. Although Bender elevates Greer into a "black god," his swimming puts him on a par with the puny fish (62). The fish, PF, and Greer are all vulnerable to death; Greer might easily drown and turn into dead meat in a minute or two more. And Greer is also vulnerable to emotion—that supposedly girlish domain—as he undergoes intense rejection and loneliness.

"Kafka for President" gives, then, a conflicting message, as the characters strictly polarize the sexes but the story itself equates them. Larry Heinemann's *Paco's Story* deepens both sides of this contradictory message. As part of its separation of the sexes, the novel not only presents women as very different from men but also registers strong animosity against women. The veteran Paco, carrying a cane and living on painkillers and antidepressants, tries to reintegrate into American life, but his less than airbrushed look and manner deny him jobs and comfort from an indifferent public. Although male barbers and storeowners repeatedly disdain Paco—"Them Vietnam boys sure do think you owe them something, don't they"—Heinemann compresses all Paco's resentment into the portrait of one cruel young woman (85). After a World War II vet finally hires Paco to wash dishes, a neighbor, Cathy, leaves the shades up so that Paco can see her undressing, and she parades her lover Marty-boy to make Paco jealous. Although at first she tries to seduce Paco, she changes her mind; in a long sequence at the end, Paco reads her diary, in which she scorns him as "the gimp" (148). Because the book spends so much time depicting Cathy's heartless teasing and mocking, she blots out the other insensitive citizens, as if only women are really merciless.

Discovering that the townsfolk do not appreciate Vietnam vets, Paco complains, "Imagine breaking your balls for these people!" (66). At the time of his service, he somehow thought that he was fighting to protect the lives of Americans on American soil, and, astoundingly, he still believes (perhaps needs to believe) that the war aimed to save

U.S. civilians: men, women, and children. The fact that Vietnamese women and children did not always come under that shield weighs on Paco's conscience, although he approaches this guilt indirectly. As a kind of alter ego for Paco, a fellow vet and drifter named Jesse rants against "snappy-looking little girlies from some rinky-dink college" who brush him off, for he suspects they might be thinking, "Killed all them mothers and babies. Raped all them women, di'n'cha'—*I only got two hands, lady!*" (156). Jesse articulates one of the accusations that Paco fears most, and though the drifter protests that no man could have perpetrated all that damage with only two hands, Paco does finally dredge up a horrific memory of a time when his two hands helped gang-rape, then kill, a teenage Viet Cong fighter. She had just shot two Americans, but Paco discerns that the revenge against her exceeds retaliation against male counterparts. Significantly, Paco describes the American soldiers "watching one another while they ground the girl into the rubble," indicating that the key motive, for most of them, is not lust or even revenge but image: someone able to take revenge in a supposedly manly mode of sexual dominance (180).

Just as Cathy's antics occupy the largest portion of Paco's post-Vietnam reception in Texas, this gang rape makes up one of the longest recreations of the war in Vietnam (174–85). Although Paco recognizes the rape as "evil," he seems to be trying to lessen its heinousness by juxtaposing the evidence of Cathy's manipulativeness, as if her multiple boyfriends might cancel out the multiple rapists. Perhaps these two women absorb all Paco's hatred of the war because his society has made *him* feel womanly. That is, toward the end of the book, he hears someone at a softball game deriding the batter, "SWING, you gimp! Aw, COME ON, you swing like a girl!" (187). Already identifying himself as a "gimp," Paco has learned to equate cripples with females and to consider both invalids: in-valid, less than human. Once society separates and puts down women, Paco has to punish women for supposedly originating the range of traits—vulnerable flesh, susceptibility to peer pressure, possible cruelty—that equally inhabit him and all humans.

In Emily Mann's *Still Life*, a marine veteran, Mark, is having as hard a time fitting back into American life as Paco does. Similarly unable to communicate, Mark sits on the stage locked into a static "still life" with his wife, Cheryl, and lover, Nadine, all three talking past each other to the audience. Based on interviews with real people, the play carries the documentary flavor of oral history, yet Mann adds an important dimension of art. She rearranges the speakers' tangy, colloquial utterances into apparent non sequiturs, which produce two effects. The surprising juxtapositions bring out contradictions in an individual speaker's testimony, and the careful mosaic also exposes unexpected parallels among characters, especially highlighting similarities between the sexes.

Just as Paco tries to maintain his image of himself defending the American home front, so too does Cheryl grasp the same comforting ideological construct: "And war's the only time man really goes out and protects woman" (244). In fact, Mark horrifyingly gives evidence that the marines he knew in Vietnam were hurting, not protecting women. He gradually reveals that his buddy R.J. refused to take prisoners and shot "this 'person' " in the face, that this North Vietnamese fighter was a woman, and that the South Vietnamese soldiers (and probably R.J.) raped her dead or still dying body all night (232, 240–41). As Mark knows all too well, some soldiers in Vietnam inflicted gratuitous violence on women, and at home too, he does not safeguard his wife but beats her.

Mark's and R.J.'s mix of violence with sex combines the old Apollo and Antony Syndromes, which have for many years haunted American culture simultaneously, despite their contradictions. Taught by the Apollo Syndrome that an ambiguous sexual "aggression" against women will ensure fighting ability, the two men use coercive sex to patch up a shaky confidence. However, indoctrinated at the same time by the Antony Syndrome, which holds that women's sexuality will contaminate a man's fighting powers, they radically push away the women whom they have sought out. When R.J. takes that revulsion to the point of shooting the woman, he only extrapolates from the aggression by which many of his peers at home maintain dominance, distance, punishment, and self-punishment.

Nadine tries to make sense of such sexual violence by attributing it to the repressions of Catholicism: "Take an infant and start him out on the whole world with / THOU SHALT NOT / and you're perpetually in a state of guilt / or a state of revolt" (240). If the church calls sexuality a part of fallen nature, then any erotic thought puts a person in sin. Anger at being made to feel guilty just for existing produces hostility. But if Nadine accurately diagnoses some of the causes of frustration, she unhelpfully prescribes the solution, by declaring complacently: "So you send these guys out there / all their lives they've been listening / to nuns and priests / and they start learning to kill . . . . Sure Mark felt great. I understand that. / His senses were finally alive" (241). He may feel alive, but he has left the bodies of others literally dead. And, in the end, Mark doesn't garner more life either. While he is heightening his senses on ambush, he is deadening his heart and his mind.

Moreover, if this license is supposed to unbind the bodies of repressed men, the out-of-control marines finally deny their physical senses too. Mark and R.J. both displace sex into violence: "getting off on having all that power every day . . . . It's like the best dope you've ever had, / the best sex you've ever had" (230–31). These lines echo nonfiction accounts: "A gun is power. To some people carrying a gun constantly was like having a permanent hard on. It was a pure sexual trip every time you got to pull the trigger" (M. Baker 187). In a study of the language of pilots in oral histories, Stanley Rosenberg finds that airmen from the Vietnam War are much more likely than their World War II counterparts to identify with machines, technology, and air combat itself as objects of erotic interest (56, 59). Paradoxically, the war-makers' implied promise that finally a man will have a right to enjoy his body actually counsels a man to do without his body after all. Who needs testicles and penis, if a metal trigger will do just as well?

All this violence, devastating to victim and unsatisfactory to victimizer in the long run, derives not only from skewed, guilt-ridden attitudes toward sexual desire but from warped gender definitions. Mark, like Philip Caputo, went to war mainly to prove manhood: "My biggest question to myself all my life was // How I would act under combat? / That would be who I was as a man" (220). However, once he is humping the boonies, Mark learns to distrust the equation of manhood with war: "The point is, / you don't *need* to go through it. // I would break both my son's legs / before I let him go through it" (221). Ironically, Mark is so imbued with the lesson linking manhood with force that he can word his new protest against war only by repeating the same violent terms.

The play prods us to ask whether Mark's training in Vietnam spilled over into domestic abuse, or whether attitudes already played out in America's households helped stoke its wars. The answer seems to be "both." Philip K. Jason believes that soldiers' language games produced lingering effects at home: "The metaphor of fucking the enemy, of course, turns the enemy into women, and vice versa" (126). Jonathan Shay finds that for many traumatized vets,

> sex is as sure a trigger of intrusive recollection and emotion from Vietnam as the sound of explosions or the smell of a corpse. Sex and anger are so intertwined that they [the vets he sees] often cannot conceive of tender, uncoerced sex that is free of rage. When successful treatment reduces their rage, they sometimes report that they have to completely relearn (or learn for the first time) the pleasures of sex with intimacy and playfulness. (135)

Shay's striking phrase "learn for the first time" turns the argument from the effects of war back to the effects of cultural attitudes imprinted in childhood. These attitudes, toward women as "conquests" and toward a man's intimate body as weapon, confuse battlefield and bedroom, harming both sexes. Mann's Cheryl cautions the audience not to interpret Mark's abuse solely as war trauma: "He blames it all on the war . . . but I want to tell you . . . don't let him" (221, ellipses in original). Long before the Vietnam War and continuing after it, American society teaches boys that they need to develop whatever violent potential may reside in a child, to prove "who I was as a man" (220).

Mann's play skillfully undermines trained gender dichotomies, however, by means of juxtaposed lines, which bring out unexpected parallels between male and female characters. When Mark announces at one point, "I want to tell you what a marine is," Nadine and Cheryl instead tell us the life of a mother of small children; it turns out that both the men and the women have led slogging existences on the edge of exhaustion (226–27). If Mark fears for his buddies, Nadine worries about her daughters getting mugged or raped or even nuked (260). To bring out other common experiences, Mann interlards the catalogue of Mark's grisly war photographs with Nadine's account of a harrowing caesarian birth complicated by a tracheotomy (224–25). Both Nadine and Mark know pain, both have come close to dying at a young age, and neither can talk about their ordeals to those around them. The parallels suggest that these alienated characters could perhaps understand each other's lives, if they could ever turn to one another instead of the audience. And if they did mutually listen, they might grasp that the sexes are not so far apart as their society has led them to believe.

One of the most important parallels between the sexes brought out by Mann's incongruous juxtapositions is that both men and women are capable of violence, no matter what the characters' society assumes about essentially peaceable women and essentially aggressive men. If Mark abuses Cheryl, Nadine has beaten her alcoholic husband. Even when Mark finally confesses his worst guilt, that in Vietnam he killed three children in front of their parents, we cannot quarantine him in a uniquely "masculine" excess. For Cheryl tells us that her "crazy" sister-in-law, Marge, has also shot one of her children, in full view of another child (230). Mann does not make one child-killer worse than the other. Nor does she allow us to label either one monstrous, to separate them from ourselves. Instead, Marge "snapped" as a result of abuse from her husband; as Cheryl insists, "IT TAKES TWO"

(230–31). Marge and Cheryl's brother had to collaborate to produce such a tragedy, just as Mark and American society conspired to devastate the land and the people they were supposedly protecting. The extreme destruction in Indochina derived mainly from official military force but also from unofficial, abusive violence by individual soldiers.[5]

The male characters of "Kafka for President," *Paco's Story,* and *Still Life* illustrate, against their own expectations, that they resemble the women they know in a number of ways: in their ability to carry out military operations, suffer, summon occasional bravery, break down, or inflict cruelty. However, a society which forbids a man to admit that commonality and makes him try to prove difference pushes him to hurt women, whose presence reminds him of his prohibited identity with her. And a society that separates and hierarchizes the sexes also leaves men, in their supposed godhead, isolated and aching.

Conclusion

Why did the taunt "sissy" work so effectively in the twentieth century to propel men to war? Men don't want to be compared to their sisters because they don't want to be demoted to women's still inferior status and, to be blunt, because they are afraid they would have no more orgasms. If a society can convince a man that not fighting—for whatever reason—means that he is unmanly, and that "unmanly" means "unmanned," literally emasculated, then that society possesses leverage, no matter how irrational. Modern Britain and America have pushed men to war (1) by artificially polarizing gender definitions and keeping women secondary and (2) by devaluing pleasure and miseducating people about sex. While these topics may appear to stray far from an M16, a strategic plan, and a nuclear button, the rhetoric of both popular and literary sources reveals over and over that social constructions of gender and sexuality have fueled consent to war.

Artificially Polarizing Gender Definitions

Societies that widely separate gender definitions typically fashion a series of binaries: masculine/feminine, hard/soft, cold/caring, courageous/cowardly, active/passive, fighting/peacemaking. Such lists elevate the terms classed as masculine, devalue the traits construed as feminine, and arbitrarily equate all the terms on one side of the great divide: caring *is* feminine *is* inferior. As Carol Cohn emphasizes, polarized gender discourse not only "shapes how we experience and understand ourselves as men and women," but also "interweaves with other discourses," so that a whole set of ideas becomes unsayable, once the available vocabulary is deemed womanly and hence lesser ("Wars, Wimps" 228–29). Since polarized gender discourse mires peace itself in a supposedly feminine softness (Ashworth and Swatuk 74, 82), promoters of peace must constantly take apart these artificial binaries.

Conventional wisdom calls men hard and women soft. If a society bars women from exercise (as classical Greece forbade wives the gymnasium and Victorian England swathed ladies in hoops and stays), the muscles of nonservant women might indeed grow soft. However, whenever women perform manual labor or sports, their bodies harden, while sedentary men soften up. On average, men possess larger bones and more extensive musculature, but in technological warfare, the importance of personal strength diminishes. Even in more primitive guerrilla warfare, enormous, hard muscles may be superfluous. When a Vietnam veteran in Ronald Cross's story "The Heavenly Blue Answer" discovers a movie advertisement picturing "this ridiculous stud with muscles popping out all over him" (Rambo?), the vet corrects the movie's bland assurance that a muscled man "punches out [Viet] Cong" (148). Instead, the less pumped up enemy did more effective punching: "it was the little ones you worried about . . . who could scurry into cracks in the walls like cockroaches" (148). While some American GIs were still mocking Vietnamese soldiers as girlish because of their small stature (M. Terry 72), the Viet Cong gained the upper hand by traveling light, sniping, and fading back into the jungle.

Besides referring to muscles, the artificial soft/hard pair in gender discourse also evokes breasts and phallus. Actually, men have soft body parts too. In fact, anatomy exposes men's tender genitals more than women's, and masculine toughness may in part be a reflex of denial, to camouflage that vulnerability. The rhetoric of war confuses bulging, hard muscles with the hard metal of the armory and then falsely promises that the muscles and the metal together will guarantee the hard penis. In "The Heavenly Blue Answer," the veteran who disdains the movie ad with its "ridiculous stud" also scorns the actor's "fancy gun with a big knobby head on it, from which was spraying— you guess. Talk about phallic" (Cross 148). This iconography and the language games that go along with it distribute hardness from iron muscles to erect guns to toughened hearts, tricking the recruit into expecting invulnerability to death and a permanent hard-on through war. However, war is more likely to mutilate his body (including genitals) and turn him into a soft, decaying corpse at a young age.

In addition to polarizing hard and soft, gender discourse in the twentieth-century West, as in the nineteenth, labels compassion, caring, and grieving womanly. Actually, the literature of World War I, World War II, and the Vietnam War constantly insists that men do feel all these emotions for other human beings, including each other, but are allowed their most open expression of tenderness only under the extreme conditions of war. Ted Allenby, a marine interviewed by Studs Terkel in his book on World War II, vividly articulates the contrast between peacetime and wartime rules for caring among men. When a buddy who had mistakenly thought Allenby dead caught sight of him on a ship leaving the battle zone, "He grabbed hold of me, hugged me, and couldn't let go. He was crying uncontrollably. He was a human being rehumanized" after "the mess that was Iwo Jima" (178–79). Allenby comments perceptively, "It was a joyful moment for him. It has to do with the very deep emotions that men can have for each other, gay or not. Unfortunately, in our society, men aren't supposed to show that kind of affection except under such stress as this. If Barrett and I were to have done the same thing in the street in San Diego—Oh, a couple of queers" (Terkel 179). Only the setting of war licenses the expression of intense affection. Yet that fleeting unbending must be paid for by other terrible costs: in physical wounds, mental scars, and death.[1]

According to the often "invisible" rules of discursive formation (Foucault, *Archaeology* 38), if war writers want to talk about men's mutual love, they must counter the socially assigned femininity of that term by linking caring to aggression. This rule stays in place and even intensifies during the century. Saying "love" with "comrade" in World Wars I and II dictated the word "fighter"; by the Vietnam War, saying "love" with "comrade" mandates additional, gratuitous violence on the same page: not just "fighter," but "ruthless" and "brutal" fighter (see section (c), chapter 4). Because discourses "systematically form the objects of which they speak" (Foucault, *Archaeology* 49), the reiterated association of masculinity with hurting other people must contribute to what many observers have characterized as the increasingly random ferocity of wars throughout the twentieth century (Glenn Gray 132).

Western gender discourse has further associated masculinity with bravery, and then defined bravery in terms of stoically bearing physical pain (an oddly passive ideal, considering the opprobrium placed on passivity), rather than the emotional courage of opening oneself to caring or the moral courage of standing with a minority against a push for war. Courage may also be erroneously defined as fearlessness, assumed of "real men" but not of women. However, any commentator on war brave enough to be honest will tell you that everybody feels fear. Michael Adams claims that terror caused at least half of the combat troops in World War II to lose control of their bowels at some point (*Best War* 104). World War II authorities, abandoning the earlier, official explanation for shell-shock, finally concluded, "it is not just the weak soldiers, or the sensitive ones, or the highly imaginative or cowardly ones, who will break down. Inevitably, all will break down if in combat long enough. 'Long enough' is now defined by physicians and psychiatrists as between 200 and 240 days" (Fussell, *Wartime* 281). It's not that a *womanly* fear contrasts with a *manly* courage, but that a *human* fear, which both men and women may temporarily manage—given a good enough cause—flips over into a human horror, which eventually breaks down everyone. Moreover, "breakdown" may take two forms: either an inability to continue fighting (paralysis or raving) or a capacity to keep fighting only when numbed. The more frequently soldiers switch on this enabling numbness, however, the more likely it is that they cannot switch it off, so that they return to civilian life emotional cripples, as Wilfred Owen in World War I and James Jones in World War II flatly predicted.

But what cause would be "good enough" to suppress fear, which is, after all, a natural, biological defense mechanism to prevent people from jumping off cliffs? Surely only immediate, real danger to oneself or a larger community may justify trying to ignore fear. However, even when "physicians and psychiatrists" in mid-century, from their safe offices, magnanimously grant soldiers permission to feel terror after two hundred days, the U.S. *Officer's Guide* still advises that a man "smothers his fear" not for a defensive, community-wide goal, but rather "to retain the good opinion of his friends and associates" (qtd. in Fussell, *Wartime* 274). This "good opinion" invariably stamps a masculinity quotient. The induced need to keep earning an always rescindable manliness pushed men of the twentieth century to forget causes, costs, risks, and alternatives to their wars and to inhibit natural fear to such an extent that millions did go over the cliffs.

In addition to the dangerous notion of tireless masculine bravery in the abstract, another gendered myth of war is that it provides men an opportunity for autonomous action, which is supposed to be a masculine preserve. Even after Samuel Hynes admits in *Soldiers' Tale* that twentieth-century, mechanized battle pins men down more than it lets them act and imposes "randomness and anonymity" more than it nourishes individual deeds, his study still focuses on the relatively few areas allowing one-to-one confrontations, such as World War I aerial dogfights, or rare personal initiative, such as World War II commando action outside the chain of command (56). For the vast majority of soldiers, however, war permits no active initiative, only docile obedience to a superior's orders. As Simone Weil shrewdly detects, looking back on the *Iliad* from 1939, "Battles aren't won or lost between men who think, plan, resolve and do, but between men flayed of such faculties, changed, sunk to the level either of inert matter, nothing but passivity, or of blind forces, nothing but momentum. There you have the real secret of war" (245, my translation). War reduces men to passive pawns, whether moved along frantically or locked into boredom or death.)

As societies have wrongly expected men to be active in war, they have also called men exclusively active in sex. This misperception may seem to have nothing to do with war, but it actually goes to the heart of the taunt "sissy." The false notion of women as the "passive" partner reinforces an odd, recurrent myth that women do not really have any sexuality. When the Victorian middle class assigned "respectable" women "passionlessness" as an essential trait (Showalter 21), this presumed asexuality contradicted the medieval Christian accusation that women desired sexual contact more lustily and uncontrollably than men. The two opposite stereotypes persisted side by side in the familiar Angel/Whore dichotomy. Moreover, when twentieth-century doctors investigated sex "scientifically," they often just added an ignorant new version of passionlessness. Sigmund Freud advised women to face the "fact of castration," their inescapable "deficiency" ("Female" 5: 261). He infamously proclaimed that to mature into true womanhood, girls must "renounce" the clitoris, "in favour of a new zone—the vagina" ("Female" 5: 262).

While venturesome women no doubt did not need Freud to tell them what they were feeling, a chorus of misinformed voices setting up false expectations can instill self-doubt and even prevent self-discovery. Generations of wives must have judged themselves inadequate if they (like most women) did not respond to intercourse alone, and considerate husbands must have wondered why "they" could not satisfy their wives. Basic female anatomy and physiology, which do let women desire, initiate, and experience pleasure as actively as any man, are still apparently not widely understood. Although the women's liberation movement in the early 1970s did openly discuss women's sexuality, both America and Great Britain seem to be regressing. In 1989, a majority of respondents "flunked" a Kinsey Institute "sexual literacy test" in America (Eisler 324), and in 1998, only five out of fifteen standard sex-education books for students in Great Britain even mentioned the clitoris (Jaggi 25).

Obviously, this poor training blights individual sex lives, yet ignorance exacts another terrible social cost. Calling a man who doubts the justice of a given war a "sissy" implies, subliminally, that he has turned into a woman—that creature whom Freud arrogantly declared castrated. Not fighting, for any reason, fuels an irrational fear of duplicating her supposed sexual "deficiency," as long as significant numbers of men are taught that only they have access to active sex.

Artificially Linking Sex to Gender

As the persistent ignorance concerning women's sexuality shows, mis-education about the body can contribute to war. Attitudes toward sex feed wars in several other ways. Although America and Great Britain might appear to pursue pleasure frenetically, the two countries still predominantly value power, money, and status through sex, rather than joy and awe at sex, whether alone or with equal others. In the case of solitary sex, the twentieth century kept alive nineteenth-century strictures against "self-abuse" as both sinful and "effeminate" (Kimmel, *Manhood* 46). Magnus Hirschfeld, a radical in seeking to decriminalize homosexuality after World War I, remained a conservative in regarding "self-pollution" as "evil" (74, 77). In World War II, even when each British barracks cot might transform itself into a "wanking pit" (Fussell, *Wartime* 256), attitudes still sit uneasily with practice. Norman Mailer's American infantryman Brown in *The Naked and the Dead* knows that he and many others are "beating our meat for company," but he nevertheless considers himself "disgusting" (120). If a person learns to recoil from and condemn his own body and its basic delight, why should he guard it or value and preserve others' bodies?

By the Vietnam War, this deep-seated fear of sensuality is still unexpectedly widespread. In his study *Echoes of Combat*, Fred Turner interviews a Vietnam veteran whose rhetoric reviles masturbation as the worst sin. A former helicopter crew chief who grew ashamed of torching South Vietnamese homes, rounding up the occupants against their will, and herding them to relocation camps, the interviewee finally condemns the Americans' policy by asking, "Who gave this country the right to masturbate with other people?" (qtd. in Turner 146). The interviewer then unquestioningly adopts and expands this odd metaphor:

> Traditionally, initiation ceremonies celebrate a young man's passage into sexual maturity, his right to take a female partner and start a family. Vietnam, however, presented young men not with images of the military penetration of a foreign country and the successful procreation of American myths, but with the specter of violent national onanism. (146–47)

This paragraph contains a number of dubious assumptions about the war. Would reproducing "American myths" in Asia, even nonviolently, be a worthy goal? Is military "penetration" really analogous to sexual penetration? Is onanism, which remains private and hurts no one, a suitable comparison for violence against others? Both Turner and the veteran make masturbation symbolize the root of all evil.

In an especially chilling example of reproving pleasure in and of itself, novelist John Mulligan uses an image of a woman's sexual "delight" as a sign for all the "terrors" of the Vietnam War (109). In *Shopping Cart Soldiers*, an allegorical character named Redeyes explains the goals of a demon:

> Mix it up, that's my motto. Husband against wife. Son against daughter. The sky against the earth. Dark against light. I like to massage the earth, caress it with my firm, cold hands until it moves, until it squeals with delight and belches forth rivers of lava or creaks and groans in great rippling chasms underneath the skin, deep in the bellies of cities. That's what we do, me and my ilk. We create terrors of every kind. We alone create Vietnams in the minds of men. (109)

This demon is not raping the Earth, personified as a woman; rapists don't take time to caress, and victims don't "squeal with delight." Instead, the text equates a woman's pleasurable orgasm with the convulsions of war, putting her and her body at fault for somehow generating the chaos in Vietnam.

In case anyone should think that attitudes have improved since the Vietnam War, Dr. Joycelyn Elders, the U.S. Surgeon General, was fired in 1994, after only one year on the job, solely for recommending the "Dreaded 'M' Word" (Elders and Kilgore 130). In her defense, she later wrote that masturbation "cultivates in us a humble elegance—an awareness that we are part of a larger natural system, the passions and rhythms of which live on in us . . . . Far from evil, masturbation just may render heavenly contentment in those who dare" (133).

If solitary or mutual manual stimulation evokes such horror, intercourse does not fare much better, unless procreative. Although the easy availability of sex during military training or leaves may seem to extol pleasure, war literature often shows this license promoting power and display, not joy and respect. In a survival of the Antony Syndrome, which holds that sex with women feminizes a man and hinders his ability to fight, military authorities in James Jones's *The Thin Red Line* distrust Lt. Bell's sensual love for his wife as if it were a virus, which, unchecked, would spread to other soldiers and hamper the war effort. If Bell adds tender emotion to his enjoyment of sex with one partner, he has, in the eyes of some of his fellow military men in this World War II book, strayed unacceptably into womanish behavior on two counts: sensuality and tenderness (section (a), chapter 3).

Another example of the Antony Syndrome appears in Stanley Kubrick's 1963 film *Dr. Strangelove*. Fearing that contact with women will contaminate his pure "essence" and leach his war-making powers, a general insists that he and all American men must learn to retain "precious bodily fluids." When he launches a nuclear missile, his subordinate surrealistically rides it, symbolically pursuing the ecstatic release that the general has prohibited physically. Although Kubrick's film makes it too easy to dismiss sexual displacement as a personal insanity, the satire hints at a more widespread fear that valuing life and sensuality will somehow be effeminizing.

When a society damns pleasure but then contradictorily provides bar girls, sex may instill guilt, which in turn feeds hostility and violence. Perhaps the most telling example of this process occurs in Manchester's vision of a Whore of Death in his memoir *Goodbye, Darkness*. After he alone of his squad survives a World War II battle, his exhilaration at being alive arouses him, and he hallucinates a Mt. Holyoke college girl to seduce him. Yet instead of being grateful to her for helping him celebrate his survival, he feels intense hatred and imagines sex only as rape. Because he has been trained to regard masturbation as wrong, he conjures up a visionary woman as an external temptress to blame for his own arousal. Then, because he also feels guilty for the carnage he sees on all sides, and because the social tracks have already been laid down to hold her solely responsible for sex, he attributes all the killing to her as well, vilifying her as Whore of Death (see section (d), chapter 3).

In a depressing continuity with this World War II example, John Mulligan's character Finn in the novel *Shopping Cart Soldiers* obsesses after the Vietnam War over a vision of "the bitch Grotesque," who simultaneously excites him and attempts to kill him (31). Caught up in random violence against both humans and animals, Finn desperately tries to foist off his own guilt onto her. He regrets both the killing and his ordinary sexual desire, since he has learned to place both "murder" and "sex" (pleasure, in and of itself) in the same list of "evil" (108). Like Manchester hallucinating his Whore of Death, Finn only imagines this "bitch Grotesque" in his head, but the disturbing level of violence against real women in Vietnam also betrays the same two guilts projected outward (see section (d), chapter 4). That is, the soldiers feel burdened by the often random killing and shamed by a supposedly feminine need for sensual and emotional comfort.

In addition to generating violence against female sex partners, another consequence of condemning pleasure and recommending power to men is that their guilt may turn into hostility against themselves. Pat Barker in her trilogy from the 1990s and James Jones in *The Thin Red Line* shrewdly locate contributors to the two world wars in a cultural disapproval of sexuality. Among the most insightful and original authors in this study, Barker and Jones indict war as a huge sadomasochistic machine. War conditions hold out the lure of extra opportunities for trysts, and then war provides the punishment thought necessary for sex. Underlining that any nonprocreative sex qualifies as transgressive in his still puritan culture, Jones shows that the men worry equally over sex with women, sex with other men, or masturbation. Barker makes the same point about a generally condemned "fallen nature" through Billy Prior's omnisexuality. For Jones, once the Christian West has insistently associated sex with chastisement, then chastisement in turn may evoke sex, so that suffering itself becomes perversely desirable (see discussion, section (b), chapter 3). For Barker, if men are made to feel tainted solely because they are sexual beings, they may defiantly grab thrills but then also accept pain and death, unconsciously believing that they deserve them (see section (b), chapter 2). Jones and Barker predict that under this regime, men may acquiesce more readily to the wounds of war.

Within the many forms of ignorance about sexuality that contribute to war, misunderstandings of homosexuality work especially virulently. The military establishment postulates a completely separate category for homosexuals, who supposedly have nothing in common with its "few good men." Yet homosexuals have always served in the armed forces, many with distinction (Shilts 3, 227), and the literature of war allows the reader to draw no clear dividing line between the experiences of men who identify themselves as heterosexuals or those who identify themselves as homosexuals. Even their respective descriptions of male bonding overlap, in three ways. First, the affections of both groups may equally take on a strong romantic tinge, as veterans repeatedly praise camaraderie in terms usually reserved for male–female pairs. Remarque in World War I defends comrades as "nearer than lovers (212), Manchester in World War II remembers leaving boot camp as breaking up a "marriage" (148), and Caputo in the Vietnam War insists that the "communion between men is as profound as any between lovers" (xvii). Second, for men of any sexual orientation, the intensity of this bond may possess a physical component. Manning's soldiers enjoy wrestling naked in their common baths, Manchester kisses his dead friend Lefty on the mouth, and Bodey's character Gabe calms a pal by lying on top of him and caressing him. Whether such instances of comforting touch stop short of genital contact might seem to distinguish homosexual from heterosexual, but even here, in this third area, experiences blur.

The very existence of the World War II sociological term "deprivation homosexuality" suggests that genital sharing between men is not so unthinkable for nominally heterosexual men as strict divisions would imply (Adams, *Best War* 84; Costello 102). Alfred Kinsey's well-known study of men's sexuality after World War II records that "fifty per cent acknowledged erotic responses to their own sex" and "over one-third had had a postadolescent homosexual experience that resulted in orgasm" (D'Emilio and Freedman 291). Adding those who would not admit impulses to researchers might make an even heftier total. Similarly, Randy Shilts reports that one of the most "confusing experiences" for gays in Vietnam was to have straights seek them out for sex (43). Steven Zeeland, in his provocative study *Crossing the Line between "Straight" and "Gay" in the U.S. Navy*, finds that men who name themselves according to these two polarized sexual identities may nevertheless engage in identical sexual behaviors. At the same time, the participants give widely varying interpretations of those behaviors, depending on their ways of negotiating a multiplicity of conflicting sex and gender codes (7–13). Zeeland boldly concludes that, "homosexual expression is a natural possibility for men who identify themselves as heterosexual, and that the unavailability of women is often not so much a cause of, but an excuse for, sexual feelings for other males" (9).

If clear boundaries between sexualities break down, why then does the military try so hard to incise them? Carol Cohn finds that the military's "official heterosexuality" in combination with a ban on homosexuality actually preserves both homoeroticism and emotional closeness among servicemen, letting them "transcend the limitations on male relationships that most men live under in civilian life" ("Gays" 145). Drawing on the work of Allan Bérubé, Cohn points out that the ruse lets the very same behaviors show up in two separate camps, one called "queer" and the other "simply what men do in the military" ("Gay" 142). It is important to add that, despite the horror of homosexuality that military authorities profess, they rely for recruitment on a very useful concept of homosexuality, construed as effeminate. This constructed effeminacy includes all the words shunted into a feminine camp in the list of discursive binaries: passivity, cowardice, caring. Since all men are likely to have felt lethargy, or fear, or kindness—and, perhaps, at least at moments, an erotic response to another man—all must worry that they have strayed into an inferior realm. The false label "feminine" for experiences that are more widely human opens men to manipulation, if their society also assigns a positive, masculinizing value to fighting for its own sake. Military services can more easily recruit (or prevent resistance to the draft) among self-identified heterosexuals and homosexuals alike, as long as all men can be made to fear some version of supposed effeminacy in themselves.

The taunt "little girl faggots," as used by Vietnam era Drill Instructors (Michalowski 331) or upperclassmen at military academies into the 1990s (Faludi 70), gains its coercive power to goad men to soldiering not only from its arbitrary association with "womanly" emotional traits but also from a constructed parallel to women's supposed passivity and asexuality. Just as modern society has fitfully doubted that Woman really has any sexuality, all the while contradictorily slurring this bodiless Angel as inescapably Whore, mainstream society has similarly fashioned Homosexual Man as undersexed "eunuch" (Norton 125), while simultaneously perpetuating an opposing stereotype of oversexed predator (Weeks, *Sex* 107). Drawing on the first half of this contradiction, the taunt "faggot" against a man who refuses to fight for any reason again threatens an end to all his sexual responses, in the same way that calling him "sissy" does.

Two examples, from World War II and the Vietnam War, illustrate that British and American societies have indeed instilled such a sexual threat as a way to keep men fighting. When a group of Oxford University undergraduates voted in 1933 never to fight for "King and Country," the student debaters provoked an outcry. *The Daily Express,* for example, ranted against "the woozy-minded Communists, the practical jokers, and the sexual indeterminates of Oxford" (qtd. in Pace A-20). By calling the students who wanted to seek world peace "sexual indeterminates" (code for homosexuals), the journalist not only omitted any substantive arguments about the impending war in favor of *ad hominem* attack, but also exposed that he himself might need a new war—any war—simply to advertise heterosexuality. Whereas the Apollo Syndrome usually assumes that heterosex promises well for a future fight, here it operates in reverse, as if fighting guarantees heterosexuality. All other complex points that the journalist may have brought to bear, pro and con, on the Oxford student vote—questions about the carnage of World War I in the past, Hitler's recent accession to power and the need to deal with that specific danger, or the misuse of emotional phrases such as "King and Country" to hide greed and imperial aims—all disappear completely under a discourse that connects war to sex and masculinity.

Sonya Rose corroborates that throughout World War II in Great Britain, conscientious objectors could be "publicly shamed by being labelled 'sissies,' 'pansies,' and other terms denoting effeminacy and hinting that their sexuality was suspect" (175). This atmosphere was then useful to pressure all young men out of uniform, who could be lampooned in cartoons as "lisping and fawning" on a conscientious objector (Rose 178).

Like the journalist covering the Oxford debate who focused on masculinity to the exclusion of all else, veteran Milton Bates in "Men, Women, and Vietnam" refuses to argue with former draft resisters but prefers to dismiss them all with gratuitous sexual slurs: "Some feigned homosexuality so as to be declared unfit for service, only to wonder later how much was pretense and how much truth" (33). Summing up his own decision to fight in the Vietnam War, he concludes, "There was finally no way to feel morally justified without also feeling sexually compromised" (33). "Compromised" seems to encode "homosexual" and "sissy," which still mean for him both inferior and incapable of sexual feeling. When a discourse manages to link two intrinsically unrelated areas—the morality of the war in Vietnam and Bates's orgasms—then that discourse chillingly makes him choose what he grants might be an immoral war, rather than join a protest that he wildly assumes will mean his own castration.

The present policy of "Don't ask, don't tell" in the American military does not undo this dangerous ideology eliding war-making with approved sexuality. For if a soldier reveals that he is gay, the armed forces can still discharge him as vaguely "unsuitable," a label that imputes cowardice and all the other clichés of womanliness (Shilts 16). While gay men know better than to equate "queer" with "castrated," men of any sexual orientation may seek out fighting for the sake of a personal stamp of masculinity, rather than for the sake of any larger community good.

During the first Gulf War, 33,000 American women and 1,000 British women saw military duty. In 1994, the U.S. Defense Department further revised its rules on "risk" to include even more "front-line roles" for women, excluding them only from infantry assignments in ground combat (Carter 34). Does women's greater participation in waging wars mean that fundamental changes are afoot in the view of military life as a test of masculinity?

If the 1997 Hollywood film *G.I. Jane* is any indication, the answer is no. Even as the film tries to erase the division "peaceful woman" versus "fighting man" by featuring a fighting woman, *G.I. Jane* only deepens every other polarization of gender, so that a look at this movie in some detail will serve to summarize the military usefulness of all the discursive binaries of masculinity and femininity and the social constructions of sexuality that we have been examining.

Ostensibly taking a feminist stance, director Ridley Scott sends Lt. O'Neil, played by a voluptuous Demi Moore, through the crucible of training with elite Navy SEALS. Facing not only the usual dunkings and drubbings of rescues at sea and harangues by superiors, O'Neil must also negotiate the misogyny of her fellow trainees, officials in Washington, and especially her immediate trainer, a Master Sergeant. Although she successfully completes the course, she, like the male candidates, is perfecting not so much skills as image, not so much competence for the public good as a private initiation for standing among peers. O'Neil too must prove herself a "man."

This transformation takes place during an exercise in the Florida swamps. Playing the part of an enemy interrogator, the Master Sergeant beats her, as he attempts to extract military secrets from her or her penned companions, who might take pity. He bends her over a table, cutting her belt with a knife and seeming to threaten rape. "Would that make me a better soldier?" she gasps out. "You it would," he replies, implying that somebody else—gays in the military?—would still not be good soldiers, even if he sodomized them. Instead of yielding, she launches (still bound) into martial arts foot jabs, kicking her tormentor's face and groin. When the Master Sergeant recovers and again begins hitting, the other trainees finally rebuke him by turning their backs, as the Master Sergeant limps over to the stockade to justify his violence: "Guys, I'm saving her life and yours. Her presence makes us all vulnerable. I don't want you learning that inconvenient fact under fire" (Scott, video). He claims to be uprooting a dangerous chivalry, but the degree of his violence seems to express his own resentment that a woman would encroach on male turf. Furthermore, he never questions whether the men might ever pity other males tortured, whether they might reveal some information in exchange for saving comrades, and whether the safety of greater numbers or a pure image of staunchness required silence in the first place.

O'Neil triumphs over her adversary, yet to do so, she has to deny part of her humanity. Dragging herself to her feet, she calls over to the Master Sergeant the punch line of the film: "Suck my dick." As he looks dazed and defeated, sagging against the stockade, the other men cheer. The scene consolidates camaraderie and convinces the Master Sergeant that she deserves to join the elite band of brothers. At the same time, however, O'Neil's verbal coup cancels the film's claim to any feminist message, either in the sense of seeking equality for women or in the larger sense of questioning patriarchal social structures that oppress both men and women. Most obviously, she has to deny her own body. Second, while she is required to conform biologically, she must also meet skewed social definitions of what it means to have a phallus. She has to fight and fight dirty (kicking head and genitals) in a purely exhibition bout, not for any public good. Even for men, the penis has never been sufficient proof of masculinity; only fighting clinches doubts. Third, her insult reinforces master–slave conceptions of sex. The punch line does not present oral sex as a generous gift from a skillful giver, who may in the future receive gifts in return, but as a humiliation, performed only under coercion. Since the giver must always have been conquered, pleasuring others supposedly betrays weakness. In such a worldview, no one willingly helps another, nor would anyone offer comfort out of a position of equal strength.

The end of the film does not reverse these assumptions when the Master Sergeant finally tries to protect O'Neil. According to the script, a U.S. nuclear-powered satellite has fallen out of orbit and landed in the Libyan desert. The SEALS try to sneak in and retrieve the power cells, before their weapons-grade plutonium finds its way into the unworthy hands of the Libyans. Never addressing the folly of America's introducing the dangerous material in the first place, the director instead demonizes the Libyans. As Libyan soldiers (rather understandably) fire on the U.S. forces now invading their country, the North African demons helpfully provide a marvelous filmic opportunity for exciting battle.

Into a firefight plagiarized from old cowboy and Indian movies, director Scott injects some oblique romance. As O'Neil and the Master Sergeant approach an outpost on foot, she mimes slitting the throat of the guard, but he preempts her and shoots the Libyan himself. He does so because he wants to make sure that she is safe (or, more cynically, because he still does not trust her to carry out her assignment). Bearing out his earlier warning, continued chivalry only endangers the group more, for his loud gunshot alerts many more Libyans. When the Master Sergeant is then wounded, is the audience supposed to savor the irony that O'Neil must now help rescue him? Or is the audience supposed to think better of the crusty Sergeant and forgive him his earlier brutal beating because, aw shucks, he likes her?

Possibly the Master Sergeant has resented O'Neil's presence all along because he fears just such emotion, what he might (inaccurately) call the woman in himself, actually a human caring for others. Moreover, her presence from the beginning seems to provoke a gratuitous homophobia (the belt-cutting scene), as if being attracted to her, then acknowledging her as a sailor, might encourage him to see the possibility of attraction to other sailors, including male. Yet the hint that the Master Sergeant thinks of gays while tormenting her not only reveals a preconception of homosexuality as sadomasochism, but perhaps also betrays a fear that he could experience polymorphous sexual desires himself. For him to stay in the military and for O'Neil to join the club, they must both deny parts of their own sexuality, harden their hearts (with only marginal softening), and seek out perpetual enemies to prove themselves, with no questions asked about historical causes of wars.

In the last quarter of the twentieth century, some writers about war propose androgyny as a way to close the gap between the sexes. However, if men try to explain their own peaceableness, fear, or compassion as a kind of matrilineal inheritance, this new amalgam of masculine and feminine defined in the old ways only reinforces polarization. Manchester, for example, accounts in 1979 for his placid childhood temperament and distaste for schoolyard scrapping by deciding that he had more "anima," a Jungian "feminine side," which also allowed him to be "sensitive, poetic, creative, warm"—implying that manly men are dense, prosaic, incapable of writing, cold (175). Donald Bodey in his Vietnam novel *F.N.G.* similarly ventures into androgynous terminology that does not reconcile the poles of gender as much as he thinks. An experienced grunt reassures a newly arrived soldier that all men feel afraid, since all possess a "clit" of fear; "if it gets rubbed, something happens" (145). Yet even as the older man makes it acceptable to have a womanly feature, he signals its inferiority; otherwise, why not draw his analogies to a glans of fear or a clitoral burst of courage? Finally, Mulligan in *Shopping Cart Soldiers* names Finn's compassion the "woman" in him; once trauma expels his woman-soul from his body, "she" must trail around after Finn, an "Empty" (11). In all three cases, labeling some of the men's traits a "feminine" component still erroneously teaches them that it is not quite natural to experience their own humanity.

If androgyny implies distinct masculine and feminine behavior, popular books and magazines seem to be scrambling to reinstate an even stricter polarization of gender definitions. A cover of *Time* from 1992 announces a story on biological sex differences but pictures a patently socialized scene; a boy bends his arm and admires his own biceps, while a girl looks over adoringly (Gorman). No one is born knowing these theatrical poses nor the gendered direction of the gazes. Similarly, an article from *Life Magazine* (March 1999) promises to prove that "body chemistry" pushes boys to belligerence, but offers as evidence a boy who chews his toast into the shape of a gun; because his parents never gave him guns, the author infers masculine genes—ignoring other socializing influences in peers, TV, toys, video games, and movies, which all insistently glamorize weaponry (Blum 44–45). The self-help book *Men Are from Mars, Women Are from Venus* (1992), with endless sequels and videos, proclaims that the sexes diverge so widely as to hail from "different planets" (John Gray 5). This bestselling author still assumes that all women will inherit Venus's natural allotment of "goodness, love, and caring" and will invariably rank relationships with people "more important than work," whereas men, from the martial planet Mars, inherently strive for "power" (John Gray 11, 16, 19).

Yet if power resides so inherently in men, why does it always seem so precarious? Men eye power worriedly, because they have been socially trained to be insecure—and therefore manipulable. This training goes on in our own backyards. A few years ago, one of my friends told me that her four-year-old son and his little buddy always greeted each other by screaming. The father of the other boy intervened and scolded them because—here he paused, giving my friend time to think—"Yes, because they're hurting our eardrums!" But, no, hurting others was not the main consideration. Instead, the father wanted the boys to be quiet because "you sound like a girl." Although he had just heard for himself that boys may scream as readily as girls, he still assigned the grating sound to girls only. By voicing his disgust in gendered terms, the father has warned the boys to look down on sisters, whom brothers should not resemble in any way. The boys have further begun to grasp that they possess furtive elements in themselves, which they must root out or hide, lest they be found out as too "feminine." All boys will be thus unstable, because all have human traits and potentials mislabeled "sissy." When the same friend's son at age six wrote in a "Dear Santa" list, "I want Spot to have kittens, a real life motor boat, small soldiers big battle, Whodunit, real tools, and a bathrobe," one wonders what big battle will be foisted off onto him and his peers—perhaps now a few female plebes too—as the one and only proof of manliness, or of women as "good" as war-primed men.

Epilogue

The Wars against Iraq: Red Alert on Girly Men

As the chapters on World War I, World War II, and the Vietnam War showed, all areas of induced gender fear in men either stayed at the same alarming pitch or worsened throughout the twentieth century. These trends continue in the rhetoric surrounding American soldiers in the two wars against Iraq: the Gulf War of 1991 and the war starting in March 2003.

Certainly a lot changed in the composition by sex of American troops arrayed against Iraq. During the Gulf War, some 33,000 American women flew combat aircraft and served in support units near front lines (Carter 34). By 1994, women could apply to ninety percent of military jobs, including combat by air and sea, though they were still excluded from combat with the army, marines, or special forces (Walters 21). In the second war, with no clear "front lines," women are "de facto in combat" (Walters 21). Nevertheless, little has changed in the construction of masculinity placed on men or, now, on women, who must prove themselves "as good as men" in exactly the same terms.[1]

The four gender fears that structured the chapters on twentieth-century wars still apply in the Iraq wars: (a) a general aversion to the label womanly; (b) fear of appearing homosexual, construed as womanly; (c) embarrassment at love, seen as feminine; and (d) resentment against idealized women, whom men are supposedly protecting. As we have seen, the reason these gendered fears work to propel men to war is that societies place the label *womanly* on widespread *human* traits, which men are sure to detect in themselves, rendering them insecure. The dynamic making this nervousness effective requires the military both to downgrade a "womanly" feeling and, paradoxically, to stoke it in men, making it more likely that a soldier will notice he has the proscribed feeling. Both sides of this tension seem to have intensified in military operations in Iraq.

In the wars against Iraq, the need to prove "I'm a man and not my sister" still dogs low-ranking soldiers and high government officials. Embedded reporter Evan Wright, allowed to accompany a platoon of marines during the invasion in 2003, records in *Generation Kill* that the most dreaded derision still labels a man with feminine terms: "Fucking pussy wimp" or "A scared little bitch" (57). Fear ceases to be a biological defense mechanism designed to protect all humans, as the marines' culture relegates "scared" to an exclusive realm for women and womanly men. The only way to display that a man has escaped such contagious womanliness is to fight.

Revealingly, this fighting does not have to accomplish any particular public goals for community good; instead, fighting tests *me* and *my manhood*. While it is true that many American grunts even in World War II distrusted their own government and rejected ostentatious patriotism (J. Jones, *Thin Red* 356; Featherstone 113), the degree of offhandedness about causes seems to have increased. In both Iraq wars, servicemen boast of knowing the motives are bad ones, as if awareness absolved the knower from acting on his revelation. In Anthony Swofford's *Jarhead*, his memoir of the first Gulf War, marines casually grumble that they came all the way to Saudi Arabia to defend not so much Kuwaiti freedom as Western oil-company profits, yet such suspicions spark no rebellions (11). When a friend sends Swofford antiwar articles tracing the war to oil, Swofford airily rebuts, "But we marines of STA [scout-sniper platoon] do not care about fuel, we care about living and shooting" (133). Although elsewhere Swofford can handily deflate myths of heroism, here he willfully obscures the real possibility that the platoon may be dying for that fuel, not living, just as he glosses over the fact that coalition "shooting" (or bombing from the air, against retreating troops) killed between 100,000 and 200,000 Iraqi soldiers.[2] Similarly nonchalant about causes in the second Iraq war, invading marines already suspect that an announced goal to "protect American freedom" belongs to a usual governmental "Big Lie" (Wright 6). Yet here too the reporter as well as the marines skips away from community goals to more important personal ones: "In a way, they almost expect to be lied to. If there's a question that hangs over their heads, it's the same one that has confronted every other generation sent into war: Can these young Americans fight?" (6). While Wright does not name why fighting—against *anyone*, even for bad reasons—should have rocketed to supreme importance, it's clear that the "living," which servicemen so desperately covet, is *living up to* a trained image of man, defined exclusively as warrior.

If aversion to taunts of "pussy" and "bitch" drives soldiers to fight wars, it also prods government officials to foment them. George Bush the Elder had to contend with a media-dubbed "Wimp Factor"; reporters or politicians who would calculate such a quotient automatically assume the masculinity of unleashing the first Gulf War (Ducat 7). The team surrounding his son, George W. Bush, reputedly goads each other to always more wars: "Anyone can go to Baghdad. Real men go to Tehran" (qtd. in Pariser). Commentator Richard Goldstein argues that a "mindset of manly belligerence was already in place when the planes struck" on September 11, 2001; he traces a "neo-macho hero," which he claims both the younger Bush and the rapper Eminem emulate, to a backlash against feminist gains in the 1980s (16). Although popular American heroes in the 1930s and 1940s also included soldiers, they were "reluctant warriors . . . with a secret decent streak" (18). Whereas stars of old gangster films acted as violently as today's "gansta" rappers sound, the new "bad boys" on the political or the entertainment circuit no longer target the "system" but aim solely for private "power" (18).

A few officials, of course, still try to project a "decent streak," but it has been allowed to fade. Scarcely a month after 9/11, a *New York Times* Sunday feature bids a cheerful goodbye to "past eras of touchy-feeliness (Alan Alda)" and eagerly welcomes "The Return of Manly Men" (Brown WK5). So ready is the author to praise not only male firefighters but also soldiers that one almost suspects a paid job to recruit, as the Bush administration later admitted paying journalists to advocate for policies on education or marriage (Hamburger and Wallsten A5). At any rate, *The New York Times* crows that men can once again flaunt "physical strength" as their primary virtue, since they can sign up for "wrestling hijackers, pulling people out of buildings and hunting down terrorists in Afghanistan caves" (qtd. in Brown WK5). Leaving out more sedentary and thoughtful tasks such as boning up on colonial history and its legitimate resentments, and omitting quieter operations that might include international cooperation, the feature article finally offers less a prescription for a new manhood and more a nostalgia for an old boyhood, where children can crawl in caves.

Just as twenty-first-century men still fear womanliness under the epithets "pussy" and "wimp," they also still feel threatened by a category of men specially constructed to mean womanly: "pussy faggot" or (for good measure) "pussy faggot leftie" (Wright 37). American men in both Iraq wars learn to police each other (and themselves) through the specter of homosexuality, tinged with scorn, at the same time that they receive continual doses of homoeroticism, tinged with pleasure. This combination continues to be highly useful to war-makers. If a society makes homosexuality seem feminine, it becomes undesirable. Let a man detect in himself traits associated—arbitrarily or not—with homosexuality, and he gets nervous. If the culture can also teach men that only fighting assures the desirable masculinity, then both straight and gay men will flock to war.

Although American service academies now officially frown on the Vietnam-era practice whereby Drill Instructors would ridicule recruits as "faggots" and "ladies," the same taunts still fly, with the links between homosexuality and womanliness carefully maintained (Burke 45). In *Jarhead*, Swofford bears out this finding, quoting a colorful DI, "Don't lie to me, you worthless cum receptacle" (45). However, at the same time that military life makes homosexuality loom as a threat, it also offers homoeroticism as a lure. Men take solace in frequent, affectionate, physical contact (masked as tackling each other), and they indulge in racy talk. During a slow point in the invasion, Wright records idle patter about feces: " 'It should be a little acid,' Person says, offering his own medical opinion. 'And burn a little when it comes out.' 'Maybe on your little bitch asshole from all the cock that's been stuffed up it,' Colbert snaps. Hearing this exchange, another Marine in the platoon says, 'Man, the Marines are so homoerotic. That's all we talk about. Have you guys ever realized how homoerotic this whole thing is?' " (82). Whether many marines would use the word "homoerotic," the innuendoes are ubiquitous enough to surface consciously.

Giving male–male sex the same double valence of threat and lure, Swofford describes a "field-fuck" during the first Gulf War. Called on to demonstrate the hated anti-chemical MOPP suits, the group instead sodomizes a marine named Kuehn, a rape supposedly enacted in front of two reporters and an officer. After Swofford defines "field-fuck" as a punishment against someone who has "been a jerk" or broken "the unspoken contracts of brotherhood and camaraderie" (20), he soon shifts the target of punishment from Kuehn to more elusive enemies:

> . . . we're fucking the press-pool colonel, and the sorry, worthless MOPP suits, and the goddamn gas masks and canteens with defective parts, and President Bush and Dick Cheney and the generals, and Saddam Hussein . . . we're fucking the world's televisions, and CNN; we're fucking the sand and the loneliness and the boredom and the potentially unfaithful wives and girlfriends . . . we're fucking ourselves for signing the contract . . . We take turns, and we go through the line a few times and Kuehn takes it all, like the thick, rough Texan he is, our emissary to the gallows, to the chambers, to death do us part. (21–22)

This list of perceived threats might qualify as "good writing" in the sense that it drives rhythmically and provokes thought. Nevertheless, the impassioned litany of menaces also distracts from the positive function of the sex in the scene: to forge communal bonds. Not only do the attackers draw together in their observed orgasms, but they even include Kuehn himself, presented as joking gamely, "I'm the prettiest girl any of you has ever had! I've seen the whores you've bought, you sick bastards!" (21). Rejected for a vague infraction against the "contracts of brotherhood," Kuehn instead enables brotherhood. Initially scorned, Kuehn emerges as a kind of noble scapegoat, graciously accepting all their resentments onto himself. As "an emissary to the gallows," to "death do us part," he is their partner in a marriage whose male–male sexuality is more valuable than anybody would care to admit.

No matter how precious, this male sexual sharing can *only* be enacted under the guise of punishment. This inability to accept attraction as good, mutual, or emotional still derives from two traditional sources: a Christian denigration of the body as fallen nature, and a Christian and classical isolation of both emotion and pleasure as part of a despised feminine realm. As the Catholic church condemned not only homosexuality but also any nonprocreative sex, dogma and symbol elevated sacrifice and pain as good and demoted pleasure as bad. The remnants of such attitudes resurface when the marines choose self-hurting over self-pleasuring. Yelling "I do push-ups until my knuckles bleed," a marine resembles some medieval flagellant, hoping to drive out the sins of the flesh (Wright 25).[3] And when these marines do occasionally masturbate, they call their actions "combat jacks," as if the word "combat," masculine-coded, will counter any feminine, sinful taint of delight (267).

If the marines deny the body pleasure (or pretend to), they also disdain goods that might pleasure the body. "They've chosen asceticism over consumption," Wright concludes, when he sees the men toss out sweaters or cold medicine (24). Yet this interpretation covers over a profound contradiction. The supposedly ascetic soldiers still require an extensive inventory of expensive toys: "I watch the artillery streak through the sky toward Nasiriyah. Marine howitzers have been pounding the city for about thirty-six hours now. Each 155mm projectile they fire weighs about 100 pounds," some 2,000 rounds of them (112–13). Forty years earlier during the Vietnam War, Philip Caputo tripped over the same contradiction when the acres of equipment—"an outdoor army surplus store"—cancelled out his claim that he went to war to escape "a land of salesmen and shopping centers" (41, 5). Neither Caputo nor the platoon that Wright observes need to dip into their own pockets, but they wildly dispense taxpayers' money even as they reject spending as sissified.

If the servicemen scorn goods but still voraciously consume munitions, the soldiers also pump up other businesses. Between 50,000 and 75,000 foreign civilians in Iraq in 2005 signed contracts to rebuild smashed infrastructure, guard convoys, and extract oil—making some observers rename President Bush's "coalition of the willing" the "coalition of the billing" (qtd. in Boot A10). Added to these sums, the payments from taxpayers to National Guard and Reserves beef up citizens' incomes without requiring employers to provide their own support to workers, including better pay, research for areas of sustainable development, and job training. Moreover, as supposedly self-denying soldiers become unwitting agents of a governmental indulgence, armchair theorists also insist that the "war on terror" can bring out "selflessness" in "rugged men," after "a decade of prosperity that made us soft" (Brown WK5). A century earlier, Theodore Roosevelt was relying on the same language to claim that "virile fighting qualities" would counter "effeminate and luxury-loving" behavior in men accustomed to economic well-being (Bederman 186). Yet just as Teddy Roosevelt used manliness to mask the economic and imperial interests the United States was trawling for in Cuba, the Philippines, and Hawai'i, so too does a revived ideology of manly and self-denying men hide new imperial interests and their selfish benefits for selected businesses.

This whole hypocrisy of the servicemen's "asceticism" comes to attention in the marine rallying cry, "Get some!" (Wright 2, 24). An apt slogan for the king of capitalist countries, "Get some" means get *stuff*—even if you have to kill and plunder for it. Accompanied by a fist pumping in air, "Get some" to celebrate ordnance exploding also means get "laid," in "whorehouses in Thailand and Australia" or America (Wright 2, 89). Not unexpectedly, getting women blurs with getting goods, since patriarchal culture traditionally demotes women to property. Yet the comparison "women are like possessions" can also work in the other direction in war, so that plundering and killing are described in terms of sex. For example, after nervous newcomers pour "wild, fairly indiscriminate fire" into an Iraqi city, a captain excuses his men's lack of discipline, "They all had to pop their cherries," as if this were their first sexual intercourse (qtd. in Wright 95). As military language insinuates to soldiers that fighting is as good as sex, gung-ho TV reporters similarly try to convince civilians that personified descriptions of American weaponry on the screen will vicariously thrill the viewer; "sizing up the body (e.g., what armour it has, look at those wings) and celebrating the potency of the weapon (how large the gun is, what a bomb burst it will make)" resemble the way "the human body is treated in adult movies and literature" (Rutherford 176). Such eroticized rhetoric taught to both soldiers and civilians offers sex as a lure for war, but in the end it devalues sex fundamentally, since it tells people that adrenaline and pyrotechnics will adequately substitute for orgasm.

Not only do twenty-first-century soldiers, like twentieth-century ones, experience a constantly titillated but only partly met desire for physical contact, but they also display the same need as their predecessors for a strong emotional bond with other men. For Anthony Swofford in 1991, war in the Kuwaiti desert forges two kinds of important bonds. First, the pains of war duplicate the childhood punishments that let him feel that the difficult training with a disciplinarian father was still on track. Because his father set "unattainable expectations," Swofford learned a sequence of "failure," then "punishment," then reconciliation (50). Although he needs to succeed to please his veteran father, in an odd way he also needs to fail. Once he has enlisted, he looks forward to the outbreak of war because "being a STA marine [scout-sniper] would increase the danger of my mission" (60). Danger swells the chances of suffering, which the father approves.

In addition to seeking out pain to achieve closeness with his father, Swofford requires suffering to bond with comrades. In a telling passage, he explains how in 1984, at age fourteen, he saw TV coverage of American marine quarters blown up in Lebanon (128). As "a boy falling in love with manhood," he watched while "jarheads, some in bloody skivvy shirts, carried their comrades from the rubble. The marines were all sizes and all colors, all dirty and exhausted and hurt, and they were men" (128). Strikingly, men are, by definition, *hurt* men; he can identify with them because he too has been hurt by his unsatisfactory family and lonely school life. But, unlike his isolated self, this military family discovered on TV uses their hurts to carry the wounded or be carried. Like other kids of his generation taught by combat vets or combat video games to be "tough," he needs war—any war—and its vast suffering to justify the touch and the mutual caring that have been labeled soft and feminine in any but violent settings. Already as a young teen, Swofford knows that "manhood had to do with war, and war with manhood"—not with Lebanon's situation or Palestine's or Israel's or Iraq's, but with his individual promotion to "man" and his bonding with other men (128).

In the second Iraq war too, this need for caring expression between men is so strong that a suspected lack of good reasons to attack does not seem to matter. In an interview from July 2004, an American Captain Clark, commanding units in Karmah and Fallujah, insists, "If I didn't believe in the mission, it would be like Columbus not believing in Copernicus," yet he does not spell out what the overall war aims are, nor does he pursue the hint that he, like Columbus, might really be a precursor to empire-making (Meek 17). When the reporter prods further, wondering if the men also believe in their "mission," Clark at first claims, "The majority, yes," but then immediately abandons the validity of any goal *except* camaraderie: "There are some that doubt. They never doubt their brothers—the greater political picture is pretty irrelevant. All that really matters is boots on the ground. It's not so much the mission, it's the brotherhood, the camaraderie, before anything else" (Meek 17). The men do not have to accomplish anything for Iraqi freedom or American safety, those two touted but debatable goals of the war, as long as they bond with their "brothers."

If such emphasis on camaraderie characterizes officers' explicit statements of purpose, it also colors enlisted men's rationales. In a newspaper report on the death in Fallujah of Lance Corporal Blake Maguoay, Corporal Catcher Cuts the Rope attends the burial, though he did not know the dead man personally: "He's a Marine . . . I'm proud of the Marines. We fight for each other. There's no hidden agendas with us" (Cole A2). Apparently, Cuts the Rope *has* heard of some unnamed and questionable agendas: Halliburton's vast profits and overlooked scandals? the money to be made by hordes of - non-Iraqi contractors for rebuilding (Boot A10)? Nevertheless, he dismisses any need to examine those agendas and denies any complicity with them. If the value of this unconditional giving among buddies is so great that it can excuse the corporate exploitation that has cost Cuts the Rope a leg and Maguoay his life, one wonders why that bonding is so rare in peacetime. Does capitalist competition just happen to blot out the coveted cooperation? Or is the suspicion against close male–male ties purposely kept at high pitch because that hysteria so usefully builds a supply of men starved for the brotherhood finally licensed by war?

Soldiers of the twenty-first century, then, prize emotional bonds with other men as deeply as their predecessors. At the same time, however, they still fear loving emotion, because they have been taught to regard it as womanly. To neutralize that constructed womanliness, men continue to approach emotional contacts through supposedly manly violence. Yet, as the rest of this book has shown, each war in the twentieth century further ratcheted up the *degree* of violence necessary for proving manliness. That is, World War I writers who admitted "love" for a comrade could remasculinize themselves with the word "fight," but by the time of Viet Nam War memoirs and oral histories, "fight" no longer sufficed. Instead, masculinity required even more violent words, such as "necessary ruthlessness" or "brutal" on the same page with "love" or "tenderness" (M. Baker 296; Caputo xvii). This intensification of violence and its increased randomness, all part of a never-finished masculine project, continue among American troops in Iraq.

Both Swofford in the first war against Iraq and Wright in the second testify to gratuitous harm beyond military need, as undisciplined soldiers shoot camels or civilians (Swofford 139). When nineteen-year-old Lance Corporal Trombley happens to machine-gun some shepherds, he rejoices as on hunting trips, "when I shoot a deer. I felt lucky, like I got the Easter egg" (Wright 279). Moreover, the rest of the team reassures him, "affectionately," that he is now "our little Whopper BK [Baby Killer]" (279). Whereas Wright presents Trombley as a terminal adolescent, monsterized by violent video games, the other men's nonchalance needs a different explanation. Trombley seems quintessentially self-absorbed, but the others almost self-consciously advertise a lack of caring—just blast those babies—as if to counter any femininity imputed to their own mutual caring. Meanwhile, Trombley's comparison of killing civilians to receiving an Easter egg contrasts Christian language with unchristian behavior, as well as his childishness with the manhood he thinks he is achieving.

If low-ranking soldiers may need to ratchet up violence to neutralize the supposed femininity of camaraderie, so too do men much higher up in the chain of command. A marine general active in both Afghanistan and Iraq boasted in February 2005, "It's a hell of a hoot" to kill people (Schrader A14). Lieutenant General John Mattis told a San Diego convention that "guys who slapped women around for five years because they didn't wear a veil . . . ain't got no manhood left anyway"; once he has dismissed other men's manhood, he builds his own by killing breezily: "So it's a hell of a lot of fun to shoot them" (Schrader A14). The newspaper report is titled "General Criticized," but the text reveals that Mattis's superior reproached him only for *revealing* his opinion, not for having it or acting on it.

General Mattis's calculatedly cool manhood finds mirrors in high civilian office. Alberto Gonzales was promoted to Attorney General and Donald Rumsfeld retained as Secretary of Defense despite the fact that they scoff at the Geneva Conventions against torture, calling them "obsolete" and soft on terror (Laverty 5). Manliness no longer means protecting the weak but torturing the randomly rounded up, a "harder," more manly position.

As men have to amplify violence to prove manliness, women moving into the military may also feel they have to display more offhand aggression to demonstrate that they are as "good" as (or as bad as) any man. The movie *G.I. Jane* modeled the process, when Demi Moore had to fight and fight dirty, in a purely exhibition bout, in order to claim the same "balls" as her peers (Scott). Following in Demi's footsteps, "torture chicks" in America's internment camps at Guantanamo torment detainees from Afghanistan (who have never been brought to trial) by combining unwanted sexual lures with the flouting of religious taboos. Reportedly, from December 2002 to June 2003, female interrogators wearing skimpy underwear would smear fake menstrual blood on a prisoner, making him unfit to pray (Dowd 4.17). Like Pfc. Lynndie England in the Abu Ghraib prison in Iraq, photographed holding a naked Iraqi on a leash and pointing leeringly at a naked prisoner's genitals (Breed A7), the women engaging in such tactics must still accept themselves as "unclean" lesser beings as well as sex objects, even as they try to duplicate the torture that supposedly hard men (not soft-hearted women) now admit into their repertoire.[4]

The contradictory twentieth-century military ideology that claims to protect precious womanhood but at the same time scorns women as the lowest of the low continues to confuse soldiers in the Iraq wars. The much hyped and falsified case of the injury and capture of Pfc. Jessica Lynch illustrates how imperative the desire remains to find a weak woman to save: so insistent that even as Iraqi medical personnel were trying fruitlessly to hand her over to American authorities, soldiers staged a dramatic rescue—against no defenders—at the hospital where she was quartered (Kampfner). Rumors of her "alleged mutilation and rape" proliferated, as if the more helpless the damsel and the greater her distress the better (Wright 109). At the same time, other, equally false rumors of her fierce resistance to capture (when she was already grievously wounded in the jeep crash) tried to cast Lynch as a mythical masculine soldier, all guns blazing. Her culture requires her to be both impossibly powerful and impossibly pitiful, just as the demands on men require them to protect sacred womanhood, even as their training simultaneously drills them to despise "bitches."

This misogyny continues to thrive not just to remove women from the competition but to keep men worried that somehow they themselves will be revealed as "ladies." To instill this worry, general human traits have to be mislabeled feminine. Michael Kimmel compares Al

Qaeda and paramilitary white supremacist organizations in the United States and finds in both violent groups the same confused mix of misogyny, idealization of women to be protected, resentment of women's success in the work force, and fear of so-called womanly traits in oneself. Both groups have recruited their members from lower-middle-class men, "downwardly mobile," whose good education or family status does not lead to promised prosperity (Kimmel, "Globalization" 427). Belittled by their fathers for failures that are more the result of global economic factors than personal incompetence, the potential recruits (in Muslim countries and America) may also be ridiculed for not measuring up to sisters who move into at least marginal independence through middle-class jobs.

Barred from an entitlement they believed settled by religion or nature, American white supremacists and Al Qaeda men want to "reassert domestic and public patriarchies," and they deploy the language of gender to demonize other men perceived as taking "their" jobs (Kimmel, "Globalization" 416). White supremacists tar black men as too feminine (lazy) and, contradictorily, as too masculine (unable to control sexual urges), and they illogically dismiss Jewish men as too feminine (weak) and too masculine (predatory) (420). The white groups leave only themselves as ideally masculine. Similarly, Mohammed Atta, who crashed the first plane into the World Trade Center on 9/11, learned to resent his professional sisters in Egypt, after his father reproached him that his engineering degree did not lead to equivalent success. As a child, Atta was already too "gentle" for his father, who told him to "Toughen up, boy," and, as an adult, this unsuccessful "man of the family," again derided by his father, inherited the underemployment that should have belonged to women only (428). A terrorist organization offered him a sheaf of gendered remedies: the warriorhood traditionally associated with men, the impugning of other men's masculinity (Jews' and Americans') to prop up his own, the idea of protecting women, and misogyny; in his short suicide note, Atta specifically forbid "unclean" women at his funeral (428–29). After 9/11, several white supremacist groups praised Atta and Al Qaeda: "Bill Roper of the National Alliance publicly wished his members had as much 'testicular fortitude' " (429).

Kimmel points out the gendered worries shared by Al Qaeda and paramilitary American hate groups; an even more unnerving parallel shows that American soldiers supposedly fighting a war against terror in Iraq also manage to combine these terrorist organizations' contradictory ideology: protecting women (Jessica Lynch), degrading women (the "bitches"), hatred of "lesser" men, and rooting out in themselves elements that have been mislabeled feminine. The Iraq wars abound in examples of soldiers trying to dig out or hide these supposedly womanly aspects of themselves. A corporal during the 2003 invasion loudly denounces a schoolgirl's letter praying for peace: " 'Hey, little tyke,' [he] shouts. 'What does this say on my shirt? "US Marine!" I wasn't born on some hippie-faggot commune. I'm a death-dealing killer. In my free time I do push-ups until my knuckles bleed. Then I sharpen my knife' " (Wright 25). The corporal steels himself to difficult tasks (which he fears are approaching) by insisting that others—females, homosexuals construed as womanly—must be less steeled than he. As we have seen throughout this work, "feminine" characteristics include everything from fear to love, kindness to delight in the body: none exclusively feminine at all. These potentials are instead *human*. Certainly humanity should, at last, be allowed to men too. Without it, they bleed themselves, and they bleed others, for the overriding purpose of proving themselves "men."

Notes

Introduction

1. In Germany's internal divisions, industrialization and urbanization pitted workers against entrepreneurs and new commercial interests against old landed ones. Meanwhile, a tentative women's movement and the most active homosexual rights movement in Europe had been quietly unsettling gender expectations. However, Germany, like England, preferred to project its domestic uncertainties onto foreign enemies, blaming "perfidiously commercialized Albion [England]," while ignoring its own growing commerce (Leed 59). Germany also took the evasive route of demonizing internal dissenters, to imagine monster women tearing up the world (Tatar 10).

2. During World War I, the Allies often suspended the democratic rights of free speech and free assembly for which they were supposedly fighting. English authorities could imprison a pacifist for six months for distributing the New Testament quotation "Love thy enemy" (Hynes, *War Imagined* 80–81). In the United States, vigilantes opened mail and stopped delivery of periodicals that carried antiwar articles, and the government used the Espionage Act of 1917 to prosecute some 2,000 cases, with up to 20 years in jail for discouraging enlistment (Zinn 356, 361–62).

3. See, for example, John Rae, *Conscience and Politics*; Blanche Wiesen Cook et al., *Reminiscences of War*; and Rachel Waltner Goossen, *Women against the Good War*.

4. Many enlistees, of course, were expressing not enthusiasm but a desire to choose their own branch of the service before the draft chose for them.

5. I confine myself to British and American writers in English (with a few from other countries where English is spoken). Two exceptions are Henri Barbusse's *Le Feu* (1917) and Erich Maria Remarque's *Im Westen Nichts Neues* (1928), because these two books significantly influenced the conventions of all subsequent World War I novels.

6. Good summaries of this position assuming women's natural peacefulness (and the objections to it) can be found in Ann Snitow, "Holding the Line at Greenham Common," and April Carter, "Should Women Be Soldiers or Pacifists?"

7. In World War I, British suffragists split over backing the war or not. As Susan Kent points out, those women who put the suffrage movement on hold to support the war often ironically reasserted the old anti-suffrage argument of separate spheres. That is, once convinced by recruitment language about German rapes, some women urged men to enlist to protect "weak" women (26). Nicoletta Gullace explains that women who gave men white feathers, a gesture now remembered as a "feminine betrayal," were at the time encouraged to shun men not in uniform and to exercise a "patriotic" duty, through women's reputed "sexual and moral power over men" ("White Feathers" 182, 191).

8. In the field of International Relations, several theorists have begun to remedy this neglect of gender. In *Violent Cartographies*, Michael Shapiro argues that modern wars are fueled as much by "ontological" as "strategic" goals; under "ontological" goals, he lists a sense of being "masculine," as well as a sense of being "cohesive," as part of "individual and collective identity drives" (52, 66). In *Manly States*, Charlotte Hooper finds four "archetypes of hegemonic masculinity" in the West; several of them intersect with militarism (64–65). In *Oh, Say, Can You See*, Kathy Ferguson and Phyllis Turnbull examine the ways in which the military in Hawai'i relies on gender constructs as a nonrational tool of persuasion.

9. Analyzing the masculine icons of American popular culture from the 1970s through the early 1990s, James Gibson still finds a Victorian ideal of restraint: a fear of overflowing the body's boundaries and a desperate need for control, of both self and others. In his provocative *Warrior Dreams* (1994), Gibson studies America's fascination with the figure of the lone warrior, as expressed in films, comics, techno-thrillers, gun magazines, conventions sponsored by the magazine *Soldier of Fortune*, paintball games, and theme-park restaging of battles. All these entertainments either omit women from the scene altogether or portray women as "dangerous temptresses who have to be mastered, avoided, or terminated" (12). Even as the male characters and audiences hypocritically sneak a secret titillation, the stories blame desire itself as evil and recommend rigid self-control as the highest good (76, 78).

Chapter 1   Background: Sexuality and War

1. A German translation of the complete work appeared first, in 1896, to good reviews. By contrast, the English edition of 1897 encountered many barriers. Symonds's family interfered with the inclusion of his essay "A Problem in Greek Ethics" (originally printed privately, in 1883), and the British courts declared the remaining work obscene in 1898. Ironically, the resulting scandal did publicize the basic tenets. Ellis was able to republish his portion of *Sexual Inversion* and the succeeding volumes of *Studies in the Psychology of Sex* in America, between 1905 and 1928 (Rowbotham and Weeks 153, 155, 191).

2. Ellis's and Symonds's divergent views of male homosexuals—as all somewhat feminine or all ultramasculine—are mirrored in the German homosexual rights movement. Whereas Magnus Hirschfeld's idea of an "intermediate sex" predominated, a competing group, the Committee of the Special, held that male homosexuals were *more* masculine than other men: meaning more athletic and more militaristic. Among this less prominent group, Hans Blüher pushed the ideal of "the soldierly, aggressive homosexual male" to an extreme of new imperialism (Plant 42).

3. Dr. Charlene Avallone reports still hearing this proverb in upstate New York in the 1950s.

4. Such limitations also shaped lesbians' self-concepts in the years surrounding World War I. When a lesbian ambulance driver in Radclyffe Hall's story "Miss Ogilvy Finds Herself" (1934) dreams of making love to a woman, the dreamer pictures herself as a caveman with a weapon, "useful for killing" (135). While Ogilvy may well wish to cudgel a few bigots in her society, she understands herself as a warrior not so much to claim her rage as to express what she accepts as the manliness of her sexuality.

5. Though shell-shocked, Winterbourne goads himself to plod on by calling himself "coward, poltroon, sissy" (Aldington, *Death of a Hero* 349). By contrast, the narrator believes that his friend is too hard on himself, since everyone breaks down after six months in the line. The narrator scathingly mocks their public school training to be "manly," which means to play sports, pretend to dislike Keats, ignore "smut" (i.e., any sexual desire), and above all "learn to kill things" (72–75). Nevertheless, when the narrator later concludes that Winterbourne died because he was "so horribly afraid of being afraid," he does not renew his questions about the gender training that makes the soldiers specifically afraid of being called a "sissy" (16, 349). Instead, he blames women and their "instincts" to be "predatory" for pushing his friend to sign up, as he tried to escape a jealous wife and mistress (17). The narrator even presents the two women as "Achilles against Hector," fighting over Winterbourne as over "the body of Patroclus" (19). Revealingly, this image puts off onto women the usually all-masculine warrior role; the men need that exclusive role to validate them in the larger society, but they nevertheless resent the burden of fighting.

6. Although Hall now hates women, in the end he turns his violence against himself, committing suicide shortly after his demobilization. In Germany, by contrast, postwar hostility against women played itself out in a whole cultural fixation on sex murders, as Maria Tatar argues in her excellent book *Lustmord*. Instead of facing up to the fact that young men dismembered each other in the war, Weimar Germany obsessively pictured the bloody dismemberment of sexualized women, through a surprisingly large number of paintings, novels, films, and extensive newspaper coverage of actual cases. Tatar attributes this fascination with rape-murder not only to soldiers' resentment that women did not have to fight, but also to traditional Christian attempts to foist off physicality

onto women only. Most tellingly, a newspaper article comes close to excusing the male serial killers, because all men want to soar toward "spirituality" but habitually have their "wings clipped" by women, who weigh them down with lowly, disgusting "earth and matter" (qtd. in Tatar 53). Incredibly, the newspaper seems to grant even these murderers a "striving for the divine" (qtd. in Tatar 53). If they kill prostitutes, the men are just cleaning up the cities, and if they kill mothers, didn't God himself single out Mother Eve for punishment?

7. Cynthia Enloe expands the concept of a "military–industrial complex" into present-day "military–bureaucratic–academic–industrial complexes," and she extends the nodes in it that foster militarized masculinities from the armed services proper to the research laboratory, the think-tank, the state house conference room, the defense factory floor, and the board room ("Beyond 'Rambo' " 88, 90).

8. Ovid's *Metamorphoses* continues to educate children to this day, through slightly bowdlerized versions such as *Bulfinch's Mythology*. The analogy to the tearing dog still appears.

9. Whereas most commentators influenced by Freud see a continuum between mastering a sexual partner and making war, Wilhelm Reich combines a Freudian emphasis on the importance of sexuality with pacifism and socialism. In *The Mass Psychology of Fascism* (1933), Reich argues that "the church's and reactionary science's denial of the pleasure function" can only further an "authoritarian society," because "the suppression of sexual gratification" is "intended to produce humility and general resignation in economic areas also" (128). Denouncing the repression of sexuality wherever he finds it, whether in German fascism, Russian communism, or the American bourgeoisie (129), Reich predicts that sexually stifled people will more likely seek "substitute gratifications," such as militarism, including "the erotically provocative effect of rhythmically executed goosestepping" (31–32).

10. If Antony's peers convey Elizabethan culture's standard assumptions about gender, elements of the play question at least some of these expectations. Enobarbus can cry and show devotion to Antony, even dying of a broken heart, as emotional as any woman. Cleopatra, redeeming her earlier retreat from a naval engagement, bravely and calmly deliberates her suicide, an act regarded as a manly Roman virtue. Yet Cleopatra and Enobarbus both have to die to prove their worth, and both return to a soldierly ideal, showing fealty to a defeated commander.

Chapter 2   World War I: No Half-Men at the Front

1. In *Orientalism*, Edward Said bitterly objects that Europeans imagined the "Orient" as "feminine," or "passive," "silent," and "supine" (138). Resenting the colonizers' proprietary gaze toward exoticized women,

Said especially rejects the accompanying view that feminized the colonized men. Yet Said scarcely questions the continuing appropriateness of these essentialized terms for Middle Eastern and Far Eastern women in relation to their own men. And while Said insists that Europeans always looked down on colonized subjects, he neglects instances when colonizers envied Asians or Africans. What the colonizers coveted, of course, turns out to be equally stereotyped notions of a greater sexual prowess, attunement to nature, spirituality, or inherent bravery supposedly belonging to various "natives."

2. When Barker creates characters named "Owen" and "Sassoon," she is not only fictionalizing real people but posing questions about sexuality that would not have been formulated in the same way in 1918. Yet by drawing on ideas of the theorist Michel Foucault (such as "panopticon" control), Barker's retrospective questions can yield new insights about the past, which must be tested against imaginative writings of the time, such as Manning's and Owen's, and documents, such as Ellis's and Symonds's. For homosexuality and Sassoon and Owen, see Das 65–66.

3. Despite the fact that Prior sleeps with both men and women, Barker never calls him "bisexual." She may omit the term in part because it would be anachronistic; Havelock Ellis, for example, uses the learned-sounding tag "psychosexual hermaphroditism" (76). However, she may also avoid labeling to provoke debate. In my seminars on the literature of war at the University of Hawai'i, 1996–1998, some students (using their modern vocabulary) decided that Prior is "really straight" but was "led astray" by an abusive Father Mackenzie. Other students declared that Prior is "really gay," pursuing Sarah only to negotiate the respectable social ladder. This argument does have historical justification; as Prior reminds his skeptical father, even Oscar Wilde married and had children (*Ghost* 84). A few students reproached Barker for not making Prior "simply" homosexual, accusing her of trying to placate a straight audience. However, Barker may be unsettling rather than placating her readers, making us question all categories. For "bisexual" would not be an accurate word for Prior if it again partitions him into a small, specific category. Instead, he represents *all* men—in two ways. Either he expresses the polymorphous urges that might belong to everyone, according to a "social construction theory" of sex, which speculates that sexualities develop to meet social shaping (Vance 43); or Prior stands in for all the men of his time, who must occasionally wonder if they match up with Ellis's extremely broad and shifting definitions of "inversion." To suggest Prior as everyman, I henceforth call him "omnisexual."

4. Ralph Waldo Emerson, for example, specifically used these concepts to distinguish women from men, pitying women their "tears, and gaieties, and faintings, and glooms, and devotion to trifles" (349).

Chapter 3   World War II: No Lace on His Drawers

1. The chance to prove manliness also enticed Japanese servicemen. In a collection of last letters home from kamikaze pilots, airmen frequently express gratitude for "this chance to die like a man" (Richler 570, 573). The pilots also picture themselves falling "like a blossom from a radiant cherry tree" (Richler 570, 575), drawing on Buddhist imagery for the evanescence of life. By contrast, no American or German man would likely compare himself to a flower, pretending that fragility belongs to women alone. Nevertheless, if these three combatant cultures label different traits feminine, all make their own version of "womanliness" inferior, and, significantly, all three keep men worrying if they might not be, somehow, women under the skin. The men require proofs of manhood, with the most convincing evidence said to reside in young death.

2. See the discussion by Santanu Das on "the dying kiss" in the literature of World War I and its predecessors. Das carefully places any homoerotic element within a whole range of emotions, such as reassurance and defiance of death. However, he claims that one story in *Great War Short Stories*, a popular anthology from 1930, "clears up" a Victorian confusion of "sexual difference" with "gender transgression" by putting the kiss between men in the context of wrestling and battle, thus discrediting the link between homoeroticism and effeminacy (68). Yet the story and the critic clear up one muddle only to restir another, by not questioning the Victorian assumption that masculinity resides essentially in fighting.

3. Titles of books published in the 1990s still equate airplanes with women: *The Lady: Boeing B-17 Flying Fortress* (Perkins) and *Red Ladies in Waiting: Soviet Aircraft in Storage* (Stapfer). Ostensibly complimentary, the metaphor praises the plane as a sleek, sexy, responsive companion, meanwhile reducing a female sexual partner to just another machine that a man rides. Alternatively, the metaphor may blame women for the destructiveness that the overwhelmingly male cadre of pilots, statesmen, and inventors brings about. None of this destruction, however, appears in the photographs, which focus entirely on stylish interiors and exteriors of airplanes and the dashing pilots propped against them.

4. Steve is not alone in highlighting dress. John Langellier's *The War in Europe* (*World War II*), published in 1995, forms part of a series called *G.I.: The Illustrated History of the American Soldier, His Uniform and His Equipment*, as if war presented one long fashion parade.

5. George Feifer estimates 150,000 civilian dead on Okinawa (xi). He also calculates "thousands" of rapes, by American as well as Japanese soldiers, and comments judiciously, "If a balance sheet between atrocities and generosities is ever drawn up, an outsider who has never suffered the pressures of combat will not be fit to do it. But ignoring the atrocities completely, as virtually every military account does, is too good to war and its phony legends" (496–97).

Chapter 4 The Vietnam War: Out from Under Momma's Apron

1. This same belief that sodomizing an enemy would transform him into a woman and therefore humiliate him appears in the picture language and rhetoric of the Falklands War. When British troops broadcast to the Argentine enemy images of vertical take-off fighters and marines in undershorts stitched out of two Union Jacks, one observer saw a message that "the Argentine forces and their effete supremo were going to be raped by the greater potency of the British," or as one British marine seconded, "We're going to go down there and 'dick' that lot" (qtd. in Foster 138).

2. Bodey never explains what "wrong" might mean. He might have mentioned the contradictions that the United States claimed to be waging the war to keep Vietnam free and democratic, yet blocked the elections called for in the 1954 Geneva Accords; as President Eisenhower blandly pointed out, "possibly 80 percent of the population would have voted for the Communist Ho Chi Minh" (qtd. in Stoessinger 88). America then set up as president the undemocratic Ngo Dinh Diem, who removed locally selected leaders, reinstalled hated landowners, forbid peaceful assembly, banned free speech, tortured or executed anyone who had opposed the French, and ordered Buddhists fired on for protesting his corrupt regime (Young 62, 95).

3. The kind of homoeroticism that underlies Bodey's ceremonies and Broyles's group sex continues to find outlet in many military hazing rituals. One navy recruit "just had a blast" in a "crossing the line ceremony," where tormentors beat recruits and poured urine on them: "I was on all fours, like a dog, and someone would be behind me actually hitting me with their dick like they were having sex with me . . . . I was laughing" (Zeeland 58). The assigned stances of administering or enduring punishment mask the possibility of giving or receiving pleasure. For a similar British military ritual in the Falklands War, see Foster 140. Because American and British popular cultures revere men fighting men and revile men loving men, both hazing and war itself cover over the extensive homoerotic release that goes on unadmitted among men of all sexual orientations.

4. For a nonfiction account of Americans and South Vietnamese torturing and killing a woman who won't inform, see Fussell, *Norton* 735–36. Significantly, a taunt of weakness (i.e., womanliness) keeps other American soldiers who want to protest the violence from speaking out.

5. For the extent of the military destruction, see Stoessinger 107 or Young 274.

Conclusion

1. In her perceptive *New Yorker* article on the Citadel, Susan Faludi finds that cadets value their experience at this macho U.S. military academy

because it allows them, paradoxically, to escape being "men," as defined in the larger society. Putting aside the masculine role of cold disciplinarian, the young men can share "tenderness," "dependency," and "nudity rituals," in a "true marriage" (79). However, because their society defines all these things as feminine, the cadets hide their intimacy and playfulness with misogyny, homophobia, and epidemics of sadistic violence (72, 79, 80).

Epilogue   The Wars against Iraq

1. Paul Higate and John Hopton ask whether an increased presence of women in the British armed services has caused "masculinist militarism" to abate, but their answer is "not really" (443). I have focused on American troops in this epilogue because they are the predominant military and because I have found more evidence of their gender attitudes.

2. For estimates of civilian casualties in the Gulf War, see Cohn, "Wars, Wimps" 243–44.

3. In fact, a view of the war as a welcome arena for the suffering Christian occurs high up in the ranks. Lt. Gen. William G. "Jerry" Boykin, deputy undersecretary of defense for intelligence, publicly preached that "radical Islamists" attack the United States "because we're a Christian nation . . . and the enemy is a guy named Satan" (qtd. in Cooper). Boykin believes, "We in the army of God . . . have been raised for such a time as this," i.e., readied for a war of simplified good and evil and for pain, certainly not for pleasure and cooperation (qtd. in Cooper).

4. Beyond these disgraced guards, more respected women in the military may similarly strive to attain manly toughness more than rectitude. Retired navy captain Lory Manning, director of the Center for Women in Uniform, says that no one wants to see casualties of either sex because "none of the deaths in Iraq is justified—because the war itself is not." Manning then sidesteps to the general case, "But if you are going to fight wars, women have to be there, and they have shown how tough they can be when they need to be" (Walters 21). Like men who glimpse that their war might be unjust, Manning quickly pushes past immorality to the all important masculine image, which both sexes now must prove and reprove.

Works Cited

Abelove, Henry, Michèle Barale, and David M. Halperin, eds. *The Lesbian and Gay Studies Reader*. New York: Routledge, 1993.

Adams, Michael C. C. *The Best War Ever: America and World War II*. Baltimore: Johns Hopkins UP, 1994.

———. *The Great Adventure: Male Desire and the Coming of World War I*. Bloomington: Indiana UP, 1990.

Aldington, Richard. "The Case of Lieutenant Hall." Tate 77–91.

———. *Death of a Hero*. New York: Covici-Friede, 1929.

Alexie, Sherman. *The Lone Ranger and Tonto Fistfight in Heaven*. New York: Harper Collins, 1993.

Althusser, Louis. "Ideology and Ideological State Apparatuses (Notes towards an Investigation)." *Lenin and Philosophy and Other Essays*. By Louis Althusser. New York: Monthly Review Press, 1971. 127–86.

Altman, Robert, dir. *Streamers*. Prod. Robert Altman and Nick J. Mileti. Perf. Mitchell Lichtenstein, Matthew Modine, and Michael Wright. Media Home Entertainment, 1984.

Anderegg, Michael, ed. *Inventing Vietnam: The War in Film and Television*. Philadelphia: Temple UP, 1991.

Ashworth, Lucian M., and Larry A. Swatuk. "Masculinity and the Fear of Emasculation in International Relations Theory." Zalewski and Parpart 73–92.

Baker, Mark, ed. *Nam*. New York: Berkley Books, 1981.

Baker, Russell. "The Flag." *The Penguin Book of Contemporary American Essays*. Ed. Maureen Howard. New York: Penguin, 1984. 44–49.

Baldwin, James. *Notes of a Native Son*. New York: Bantam, 1955.

Banghard-Jöst, Cristal. "In the Stocks." Klein 231–37.

Barbusse, Henri. *Under Fire: The Story of a Squad*. Trans. Fitzwater Wray. New York: Dutton, 1917.

Baritz, Loren. *Backfire: A History of How American Culture Led Us into Vietnam and Made Us Fight the Way We Did*. New York: Morrow, 1985.

Barker, A. L. "The Iconoclasts." Boston 241–64.

Barker, Pat. *The Eye in the Door*. New York: Plume-Penguin, 1993.

———. *The Ghost Road*. New York: Dutton-Penguin, 1995.

———. *Regeneration*. New York: Penguin, 1991.

Baron, Alexander. *From the City, from the Plough*. New York: Ives Washburn, 1949.

Barrie, J. M. "The New Word." Tate 225–40.

Bates, Milton J. "Men, Women, and Vietnam." *America Rediscovered*. Ed. Owen W. Gilman, Jr. and Lorrie Smith. New York: Garland, 1990. 27–63.

Bederman, Gail. *Manliness and Civilization: A Cultural History of Gender and Race in the United States, 1880–1917*. Chicago: U of Chicago P, 1995.

Berger, Maurice, Brian Wallis, and Simon Watson, eds. *Constructing Masculinity*. New York: Routledge, 1995.

Bérubé, Allan. *Coming Out Under Fire: The History of Gay Men and Women in World War II*. New York: Free, 1990.

Blum, Deborah. "What's the Difference between Boys and Girls." *Life* Mar. 1999: 44–57.

Bodey, Donald. *F.N.G.* New York: Viking-Penguin, 1985.

Boose, Lynda E. "Techno-Muscularity and the 'Boy Eternal': From the Quagmire to the Gulf." Cooke and Woollacott 67–106.

Boot, Max. "Freelance Gunslingers Fighting Iraq War." *The Honolulu Advertiser* 2 Apr. 2005: A10.

Boston, Anne, ed. *Wave Me Goodbye: Stories of the Second World War*. New York: Penguin, 1989.

Bourke, Joanna. *Dismembering the Male: Men's Bodies, Britain, and the Great War*. Chicago: U of Chicago P, 1996.

Braudy, Leo. *From Chivalry to Terrorism: War and the Changing Nature of Masculinity*. New York: Knopf, 2003.

Breed, Allen G. "Soldier Says Prison Abuse Statements Coerced." *The Honolulu Advertiser* 2 Dec. 2004: A7.

Brittain, Vera. *Testament of Youth: An Autobiographical Study of the Years 1900–1925*. 1933. New York: Penguin, 1978.

Brod, Harry, and Michael Kaufman, eds. *Theorizing Masculinities*. Thousand Oaks, Ca.: Sage, 1994.

Brooke, Rupert. "Peace." *Men Who March Away: Poems of the First World War*. Ed. I. M. Parsons. New York: Viking, 1965.

Brooks, Gwendolyn. *Selected Poems*. New York: Harper Collins, 1963.

Brown, Patricia Leigh. "Heavy Lifting Required: The Return of Manly Men." *The New York Times* 28 Oct. 2001: WK-5.

Broyles, William, Jr. "Why Men Love War." *Esquire* 102 (Nov. 1984): 55–65.

Burke, Carol. *Camp All-American, Hanoi Jane, and the High-and-Tight: Gender, Folklore, and Changing Military Culture*. Boston: Beacon, 2004.

Burrill, Mary P. *Aftermath*. Hatch and Shine 175–82.

"Bush Whacker." *In These Times* 24 (1 May 2000): 6.

Butler, Robert Olen. *On Distant Ground*. New York: Holt, 1985.

Butts, Mary. "Speed the Plough." Tate 45–51.

Campbell, Joseph. *The Masks of God: Primitive Mythology*. New York: Viking, 1959.

———. *The Mythic Image.* With M. J. Abadie. Princeton: Princeton UP, 1974.

Caputo, Philip. *A Rumor of War.* New York: Ballantine, 1977.

Carby, Hazel V. *Race Men.* Cambridge, Mass: Harvard UP, 1998.

Carter, April. "Should Women Be Soldiers or Pacifists?" Lorentzen and Turpin 33–37.

Chotirawe, Carina. "The Voiced and the Voiceless: Representations of Southeast Asian Women in Twentieth-Century Fiction in English." Diss. U of Hawai'i, 1995.

Christ, Carol. "Victorian Masculinity and the Angel in the House." *A Widening Sphere: Changing Roles of Victorian Women.* Ed. Martha Vicinus. London: Methuen, 1977. 146–62.

Clarke, Norma. "Strenuous Idleness: Thomas Carlyle and the Man of Letters as Hero." *Manful Assertions: Masculinities in Britain since 1800.* Ed. Michael Roper and John Tosh. London: Routledge, 1991. 25–43.

Clum, John M. *Acting Gay: Male Homosexuality in Modern Drama.* New York: Columbia UP, 1992.

Cohn, Carol. "Gays in the Military: Texts and Subtexts." Zalewski and Parpart 129–49.

———. "Wars, Wimps, and Women: Talking Gender and Thinking War." Cooke and Woollacott 227–46.

Cole, William. "A Hawai'i-Born Marine Is Buried." *The Honolulu Advertiser* 14 Dec. 2004: A1–2.

Conway-Long, Don. "Ethnographies and Masculinities." Brod and Kaufman 61–81.

Cook, Blanche Wiesen et al. *Reminiscences of War: Resisters in World War I.* New York: Garland, 1972.

Cooke, Miriam, and Angela Woollacott, eds. *Gendering War Talk.* Princeton: Princeton UP, 1993.

Cooper, Richard T. "General Casts War in Religious Terms." *Los Angeles Times* 16 Oct. 2003 <www.commondreams.org/headlines03/1016-01.htm>.

Cooperman, Stanley. *World War I and the American Novel.* Baltimore: Johns Hopkins UP, 1967.

Coppola, Francis Ford, dir. *Apocalypse Now.* Written by John Milius, Francis Ford Coppola, and Michael Herr. Omni Zoetrope/United Artists. 1979.

Costello, John. *Virtue under Fire: How World War II Changed Our Social and Sexual Attitudes.* New York: Fromm, 1985.

Cross, Ronald Anthony. "The Heavenly Blue Answer." Franklin 148–58.

Currey, Richard. *Fatal Light.* New York: Penguin, 1988.

Darwin, Charles. *The Descent of Man and Selection in Relation to Sex.* 2 vols. New York: Appleton, 1871.

Das, Santanu. "'Kiss Me, Hardy': Intimacy, Gender, and Gesture in World War I Trench Literature." *Men, Women and World War I.* Ed. Robert von Hallberg and Cassandra Laity. Special issue of *Modernism/Modernity* 9 (Jan. 2002): 51–74.

Davin, Dan. "Not Substantial Things." Jon Lewis 464–77.

D'Emilio, John. "Capitalism and Gay Identity." Abelove et al. 467–76.

D'Emilio, John, and Estelle B. Freedman. *Intimate Matters: A History of Sexuality in America*. New York: Harper, 1988.

DeRose, David J. "*Soldados Razos*: Issues of Race in Vietnam War Drama." *Vietnam Generation* 1.2 (Spring 1989): 38–55.

Dickerson, James. *North to Canada: Men and Women against the Vietnam War*. New York: Praeger, 1999.

Dos Passos, John. *The 42nd Parallel*. 1930. New York: Signet-New American, 1969.

Douglas, Keith. *The Complete Poems*. Ed. Desmond Graham. 3rd ed. New York: Oxford UP, 1998.

Douzou, Laurent. "Close Shave That Still Troubles France." Rev. of *La France "Virile": Des Femmes Tondues à la Libération*, by Fabrice Virgili. *Guardian Weekly* 2 Nov. 2000: 30.

Dowd, Maureen. "Torture Chicks Gone Wild." *New York Times* 30 Jan. 2005: 4–17.

Du Bois, W. E. B. *The Souls of Black Folk*. 1903. New York: Vintage-Random, 1990.

Ducat, Stephen J. *The Wimp Factor: Gender Gaps, Holy Wars, and the Politics of Anxious Masculinity*. Boston: Beacon, 2004.

Dunbar-Nelson, Alice. *Mine Eyes Have Seen*. Hatch and Shine 169–74.

Dworkin, Andrea. *Intercourse*. New York: Free Press, 1987.

Edelman, Lee. "Tearooms and Sympathy, or, The Epistemology of the Water Closet." Abelove et al. 553–74.

Ehrenreich, Barbara. *Blood Rites: Origins and History of the Passions of War*. New York: Holt, 1997.

Eisler, Riane. *Sacred Pleasure: Sex, Myth, and the Politics of the Body*. San Francisco: Harper, 1995.

Eksteins, Modris. *Rites of Spring: The Great War and the Birth of the Modern Age*. Boston: Houghton, 1989.

Elders, M. Joycelyn, and Barbara Kilgore. "The Dreaded 'M' Word." *Nerve: Literate Smut*. Ed. Genevieve Field and Rufus Griscom. New York: Broadway, 1998. 130–32.

Ellis, Havelock. *Sexual Inversion*. London: Wilson, 1897. Rpt. New York: Arno, 1975.

Emerson, Ralph Waldo. "Woman." 1855. *Miscellanies*. Boston: Houghton, 1883. 335–56.

Enloe, Cynthia. *Bananas, Beaches and Bases: Making Feminist Sense of International Politics*. London: Pandora, 1989.

———. "Beyond 'Rambo': Women and the Varieties of Militarized Masculinity." Isaksson 71–93.

———. *Does Khaki Become You? The Militarisation of Women's Lives*. Boston: South End, 1983.

———. "It Takes More Than Two: The Prostitute, the Soldier, the State, and the Entrepreneur." *The Morning After: Sexual Politics at the End of the Cold War*. Berkeley: U of California P, 1993. 142–60.

Epstein, Barbara. "Postwar Panics and the Crisis of Masculinity." *Marxism in the Postmodern Age*. Ed. Antonio Callari, Stephen Cullenberg, and Carole Biewener. New York: Guilford, 1995. 246–55.

Fairman, Elisabeth. *Doomed Youth: The Poetry and the Pity of the First World War*. New Haven: Yale Center for British Art, 1999.

Faludi, Susan. "The Naked Citadel." *The New Yorker* 70 (5 Sept. 1994): 62–81.

Faulkner, William. "All the Dead Pilots." Tate 29–44.

Featherstone, Simon. *War Poetry: An Introductory Reader*. London: Routledge, 1995.

Feifer, George. *Tennozan: The Battle of Okinawa and the Atomic Bomb*. New York: Ticknor, 1992.

Ferguson, Kathy E., and Phyllis Turnbull. *Oh, Say, Can You See?: The Semiotics of the Military in Hawai'i*. Minneapolis: U of Minnesota P, 1999.

Foster, Kevin. *Fighting Fictions: War, Narrative and National Identity*. London: Pluto, 1999.

Foucault, Michel. *The Archaeology of Knowledge*. 1969. Trans. A. M. Sheridan Smith. New York: Pantheon-Random, 1972.

———. *Discipline and Punish: The Birth of the Prison*. 1975. Trans. Alan Sheridan. New York: Pantheon, 1977.

———. *The Foucault Reader*. Ed. Paul Rabinow. New York: Pantheon, 1984.

———. *The History of Sexuality, Volume 1: An Introduction*. 1976. Trans. Robert Hurley. New York: Vintage-Random, 1978.

Franklin, H. Bruce, ed. *The Vietnam War in American Stories, Songs, and Poems*. Boston: St. Martin's, 1996.

Freedman, Lawrence, ed. *War*. New York: Oxford UP, 1994.

Freud, Sigmund. "Drei Abhandlungen Zur Sexualtheorie." *Gesammelte Werke*. Vol. 5. London: Imago, 1942. 27–145.

———. "Female Sexuality." 1931. *Collected Papers*. Ed. James Strachey. New York: Basic, 1959. 5: 252–72.

———. *Three Essays on the Theory of Sexuality*. Trans. and ed. James Strachey. New York: Basic, 1962.

———. "Warum Krieg?" *Gesammelte Werke*. Ed. Anna Freud et al. London: Imago, 1952. 16: 13–27.

———. "Why War?" *Collected Papers*. Ed. and trans. James Strachey. New York: Basic, 1959. 5: 273–87.

Fuller, Charles. *A Soldier's Play*. Hatch and Shine 364–93.

Fussell, Paul. *Doing Battle: The Making of a Skeptic*. Boston: Little, Brown, 1996.

———. *The Great War and Modern Memory*. New York: Oxford UP, 1975.

———, ed. *The Norton Book of Modern War*. New York: Norton, 1991.

———. *Wartime: Understanding and Behavior in the Second World War*. New York: Oxford UP, 1989.

Gallico, Paul. "Bombardier." Jon Lewis 448–63.

Gay, Peter. *The Cultivation of Hatred*. Vol. 3 of *The Bourgeois Experience: Victoria to Freud*. New York: Norton, 1993.

Gibson, James William. *Warrior Dreams: Violence and Manhood in Post-Vietnam America*. New York: Hill, 1994.

Gilbert, Sandra M. "Soldier's Heart: Literary Men, Literary Women, and the Great War." Higonnet et al. 197–226.

Gilbert, Sandra M., and Susan Gubar. "Charred Skirts and Deathmask: World War II and the Blitz on Women." *Letters from the Front*. Vol. 3 of *No Man's Land: The Place of the Woman Writer in the Twentieth Century*. New Haven: Yale UP, 1994. 211–65.

Goldenberg, Naomi R. "A Feminist Critique of Jung." *Signs* 2 (Winter 1976): 443–49.

Goldstein, Joshua S. *War and Gender: How Gender Shapes the War System and Vice Versa*. Cambridge: Cambridge UP, 2001.

Goldstein, Richard. "Neo-Macho Man: Pop Culture and Post-9/11 Politics." *The Nation* (24 Mar. 2003): 16–19.

Goossen, Rachel Waltner. *Women against the Good War: Conscientious Objection and Gender on the Home Front, 1941–1947*. Chapel Hill: U of North Carolina P, 1997.

Gorman, Christine. "Sizing Up the Sexes." *Time* 139.3 (20 Jan. 1992): 42–51.

Gramsci, Antonio. *Selections from the Prison Notebooks*. Ed. and trans. Quintin Hoare and Geoffrey Nowell Smith. New York: International, 1971.

Graves, Robert. *Good-bye to All That*. 1929. New York: Doubleday-Anchor, 1957.

———. *The Greek Myths*. 2 vols. Baltimore: Penguin, 1955.

Gray, J. Glenn. *The Warriors: Reflections on Men in Battle*. 1959. New York: Harper, 1967.

Gray, John. *Men Are from Mars, Women Are from Venus*. New York: Harper Collins, 1992.

Grayzel, Susan R. *Women's Identities at War: Gender, Motherhood, and Politics in Britain and France during the First World War*. Chapel Hill: U of North Carolina P, 1999.

Greenberg, David F. *The Construction of Homosexuality*. Chicago: U of Chicago P, 1988.

Griffin, Susan. *A Chorus of Stones: The Private Life of War*. New York: Doubleday-Anchor, 1992.

Gullace, Nicoletta F. *"The Blood of Our Sons": Men, Women, and the Renegotiation of British Citizenship during the Great War*. New York: Palgrave Macmillan, 2002.

———. "White Feathers and Wounded Men: Female Patriotism and the Memory of the Great War." *Journal of British Studies* 36 (Apr. 1997): 178–206.

Hall, Radclyffe. "Miss Ogilvy Finds Herself." 1934. Tate 125–40.

Hamburger, Tom, and Peter Wallsten. "Bush Aide Was Warned of Payment to Journalist." *The Honolulu Advertiser* 16 Apr. 2005: A5.

Harth, Erica. "In the Enemy's Camp?" *The Women's Review of Books* 16 (March 1999): 18.

Hatch, James V., and Ted Shine, eds. *Black Theatre USA: Plays by African*

Americans 1847 to Today. Rev. and exp. ed. New York: Free Press, 1974, 1996.

Heinemann, Larry. *Paco's Story.* New York: Penguin, 1979.

Heller, Joseph. *Catch-22.* New York: Dell, 1961.

Hellmann, John. *American Myth and the Legacy of Vietnam.* New York: Columbia UP, 1986.

Herr, Michael. *Dispatches.* New York: Avon, 1977.

Hibberd, Dominic. *Wilfred Owen: The Last Year.* London: Constable, 1992.

Higate, Paul, and John Hopton. "War, Militarism, and Masculinities." Kimmel et al. 432–47.

Higonnet, Margaret Randolph, Jane Jenson, Sonya Michel, and Margaret Collins Weitz, eds. *Behind the Lines: Gender and the Two World Wars.* New Haven: Yale UP, 1987.

Hirschfeld, Magnus. *The Sexual History of the World War.* Trans.: Unnamed. New York: Panurge, 1934.

Holm, Tom. "Forgotten Warriors: American Indian Service Men in Vietnam." *Vietnam Generation* 1.2 (Spring 1989): 56–68.

Homer. *The Iliad.* Trans. Richmond Lattimore. Chicago: U of Chicago P, 1951.

Hooper, Charlotte. *Manly States: Masculinities, International Relations, and Gender Politics.* New York: Columbia UP, 2001.

Horwell, Veronica. "Quentin Crisp." *Guardian Weekly* 25 Nov. 1999: 24.

Hsiao, Lisa. "Project 100,000: The Great Society's Answer to Military Manpower Needs in Vietnam." *Vietnam Generation* 1.2 (Spring 1989): 14–37.

Hughes, Thomas. *Tom Brown's School Days.* New York: Macmillan, 1906.

Humphries, Rolfe, trans. *Metamorphoses.* By Ovid. Bloomington: Indiana UP, 1960.

Huston, Nancy. "The Matrix of War: Mothers and Heroes." *The Female Body in Western Culture.* Ed. Susan Rubin Suleiman. Cambridge: Harvard UP, 1986. 119–36.

Hynes, Samuel. *The Soldiers' Tale: Bearing Witness to Modern War.* New York: Allen Lane-Penguin, 1997.

———. *A War Imagined: The First World War and English Culture.* New York: Atheneum, 1991.

Isaksson, Eva, ed. *Women and the Military System.* New York: Harvester-Wheatsheaf, 1988.

Jaggi, Maya. "The Pleasure Principle." *The Guardian Weekly* 20 Sept. 1998: 25.

Jason, Philip K. "Sexism and Racism in Vietnam War Fiction." *Mosaic* 23.3 (Summer 1990): 125–37.

Jeffords, Susan. *The Remasculinization of America: Gender and the Vietnam War.* Bloomington: Indiana UP, 1989.

Jennings, Peter. ABC Evening News. 20 July 2000.

Jones, James. *The Thin Red Line.* New York: Delta-Dell, 1962.

———. *WWII.* Graphics Director, Art Weithas. New York: Grosset, 1975.

Jones, Peter G. *War and the Novelist: Appraising the American War Novel.* Columbia: U of Missouri P, 1976.

Kampfner, John. "Saving Private Lynch Story 'Flawed'." British Broadcasting Corporation. 15 May 2003 <news.bbc.co.uk/2/hi/programmes/correspondent/3028585.stm>.

Keegan, John. *The Face of Battle.* 1976. New York: Barnes, 1993.

Keep, C. J. "Fearful Domestication: Future-War Stories and the Organization of Consent, 1871–1914." *Mosaic* 23.3 (Summer 1990): 1–16.

Kelly, Liz. "Wars against Women: Sexual Violence, Sexual Politics and the Militarised State." *States of Conflict: Gender, Violence and Resistance.* Ed. Susie Jacobs, Ruth Jacobson, and Jennifer Marchbank. London: Zed, 2000. 45–65.

Kent, Susan Kingsley. *Making Peace: The Reconstruction of Gender in Interwar Britain.* Princeton: Princeton UP, 1993.

Kettle, Martin. "Clinton Rolls Over on Defense Spending." *Guardian Weekly* 7 Feb. 1999: 6.

Ketwig, John. "And a Hard Rain Fell." Reese Williams 10–37.

Kimmel, Michael S. "Globalization and Its Mal(e)contents: The Gendered Moral and Political Economy of Terrorism."Kimmel et al. 414–31.

———. *Manhood in America: A Cultural History.* New York: Free, 1996.

Kimmel, Michael S., Jeff Hearn, and R. W. Connell, eds. *Handbook of Studies on Men and Masculinities.* Thousand Oaks, Ca.: Sage, 2005.

Kintz, Linda. *Between Jesus and the Market: The Emotions that Matter in Right-Wing America.* Durham, N.C.: Duke UP, 1997.

Klein, Yvonne M., ed. *Beyond the Home Front: Women's Autobiographical Writing of the Two World Wars.* New York: New York UP, 1997.

Komunyakaa, Yusef. *Dien Cai Dau.* Middletown, Ct.: Wesleyan UP, 1988.

Kubrick, Stanley, dir. *Dr. Strangelove.* Hawk Films, 1963.

Langellier, John. *The War in Europe (World War II).* In the series *G.I.: The Illustrated History of the American Soldier, His Uniform and His Equipment.* Pa.: Stackpole, 1995.

Lanker, Brian, dir. *They Drew Fire: Combat Artists of World War II.* Prod. Nicole Newnham and Bonni Cohen. Actual Films, 2000.

Lanker, Brian, and Nicole Newnham. *They Drew Fire: Combat Artists of World War II.* New York: TV Books, 2000.

Laverty, Paul. "We Must Not Move On." *Guardian Weekly* 22 Apr. 2005: 5.

Lawrence, D. H. "Cocksure Women and Hensure Men." *Phoenix II.* Ed. Warren Roberts and Harry T. Moore. New York: Viking, 1959. 553–55.

———. *The Fox, The Captain's Doll, The Ladybird.* Ed. Dieter Mehl. Introduced by David Ellis. London: Penguin, 1994.

———. "Is England Still a Man's Country?" *Phoenix II.* Ed. Warren Roberts and Harry T. Moore. New York: Viking, 1959. 556–58.

———. *Kangaroo.* 1923. New York: Viking, 1960.

———. *The Plumed Serpent.* 1926. New York: Vintage, 1959.

Lawson, Jacqueline E. "'She's a Pretty Woman . . . for a Gook': The Misogyny of the Vietnam War." *Fourteen Landing Zones: Approaches to Vietnam War Literature.* Ed. Philip K. Jason. Iowa City: U of Iowa P, 1991. 15–37.

Leed, Eric J. *No Man's Land: Combat and Identity in World War I.* Cambridge: Cambridge UP, 1979.

Lerner, Gerda. *The Creation of Patriarchy.* New York: Oxford UP, 1986.

Lewis, Jon E., ed. *The Mammoth Book of Modern War Stories.* New York: Carroll, 1993.

Lewis, Wyndham. *Blasting and Bombardiering.* 1937. 2nd ed., rev. Berkeley: U of California P, 1967.

———. "The French Poodle." Tate 167–73.

Lloyd, Genevieve. "Selfhood, War and Masculinity." *Feminist Challenges: Social and Political Theory.* Ed. Carole Pateman and Elizabeth Gross. Boston: Northeastern UP, 1986. 63–76.

Lorentzen, Lois Ann, and Jennifer Turpin, eds. *The Women and War Reader.* New York: New York UP, 1998.

Macaulay, Rose. *Potterism.* New York: Boni and Liveright, 1920.

MacKenzie, John M. *Propaganda and Empire: The Manipulation of British Public Opinion, 1880–1960.* Manchester: Manchester UP, 1984.

MacKinnon, Catharine A. "Feminism, Marxism, Method, and the State: Toward Feminist Jurisprudence." 1983. *Contemporary Critical Theory.* Ed. Dan Latimer. San Diego: Harcourt, 1989. 604–33.

Mailer, Norman. *The Naked and the Dead.* 1948. New York: Holt, 1981.

Manchester, William. *Goodbye, Darkness: A Memoir of the Pacific War.* New York: Dell, 1979.

Mann, Emily. *Still Life.* Reston 214–74.

Manning, Frederic. *The Middle Parts of Fortune: Somme and Ancre, 1916.* 1929. New York: Viking-Penguin, 1990.

Marcus, Jane. "The Asylums of Antaeus; Women, War and Madness." *The Difference Within: Feminism and Critical Theory.* Ed. Elizabeth Meese and Alice Parker. Philadelphia: Benjamins, 1989. 49–83.

Marwil, Jonathan. *Frederic Manning: An Unfinished Life.* Durham, N.C.: Duke UP, 1988.

Mayer, Tom. "Kafka for President." Franklin 41–63.

McClintock, Anne. *Imperial Leather: Race, Gender and Sexuality in the Colonial Contest.* New York: Routledge, 1995.

McGuinness, Frank. *Observe the Sons of Ulster Marching towards the Somme.* Boston: Faber, 1986.

Meek, James. "Five Days in an Invisible War." *Guardian Weekly* 30 July 2004: 15–17.

Michalowski, Helen. "The Army Will Make a 'Man' Out of You." *Reweaving the Web of Life: Feminism and Nonviolence.* Ed. Pam McAllister. Philadelphia: New Society, 1982. 325–35.

Morgan, David H. J. "Theater of War: Combat, the Military, and Masculinities." Brod and Kaufman 165–82.

Moser, Richard R. *The New Winter Soldiers: GI and Veteran Dissent during the Vietnam Era.* New Brunswick: Rutgers UP, 1996.

Moss, Mark. *Manliness and Militarism: Educating Young Boys in Ontario for War.* Oxford: Oxford UP, 2001.

Mosse, George L. *Nationalism and Sexuality: Respectability and Abnormal Sexuality in Modern Europe*. New York: Fertig, 1985.

Mulligan, John. *Shopping Cart Soldiers*. New York: Simon, 1997.

Murphy, Dennis. *The Sergeant*. New York: Viking, 1958.

Norton, Rictor. *Mother Clap's Molly House: The Gay Subculture in England 1700–1830*. London: GMP, 1992.

O'Brien, Tim. *If I Die in a Combat Zone*. New York: Laurel-Dell, 1969.

———. *The Things They Carried*. New York: Penguin, 1990.

Okada, John. *No-No Boy*. 1957. Seattle: U of Washington P, 1979.

Omori, Emiko, dir. *Rabbit in the Moon*. Wabi-Sabi Production, 1999.

Orwell, George. *A Collection of Essays*. New York: Harcourt, 1946.

Ovid. *The Metamorphoses*. Trans. Horace Gregory. New York: Mentor-New American, 1958.

Owen, Wilfred. *The Poems of Wilfred Owen*. Ed. Jon Stallworthy. New York: Norton, 1986.

The Oxford English Dictionary. 2nd ed. 1989.

Pace, Eric. "David Graham, 87, Is Dead; Antiwar Debater at Oxford." *The New York Times* 27 Aug. 1999: A-20.

Pariser, Eli. *moveon-help@list.moveon.org* 4 Apr. 2003.

Parker, Dorothy. "The Lovely Leave." Boston 147–61.

Perkins, Paul. *The Lady: Boeing B-17 Flying Fortress*. Photos by Dan Patterson. Charlottesville, Va.: Howell, 1993.

Phillips, Kathy J. *Dying Gods in Twentieth-Century Fiction*. Lewisburg: Bucknell UP, 1990.

Plant, Richard. *The Pink Triangle: The Nazi War against Homosexuals*. New York: Holt, 1986.

Purohit, Swami, trans. *The Bhagavad Gita*. New York: Vintage-Random, 1977.

Rabe, David. *The Basic Training of Pavlo Hummel and Sticks and Bones*. New York: Viking, 1973.

———. *Streamers*. Reston 1–66.

Rae, John. *Conscience and Politics: The British Government and the Conscientious Objector and Military Service 1916–1919*. London: Oxford UP, 1970.

Reich, Wilhelm. *The Mass Psychology of Fascism*. 1933. Trans. Vincent R. Carfagno. New York: Farrar, 1970.

Remarque, Erich Maria. *All Quiet on the Western Front*. 1928. Trans. A. W. Wheen. New York: Ballantine-Random, 1982.

Reston, James, Jr., ed. *Coming to Terms: American Plays and the Vietnam War*. New York: Theatre Communications Group, 1985.

Rhys, Jean. "I Spy a Stranger." Boston 114–27.

Richler, Mordecai, ed. *Writers on World War II: An Anthology*. New York: Knopf, 1991.

Rose, Sonya O. *Which People's War? National Identity and Citizenship in Britain 1939–1945*. Oxford: Oxford UP, 2003.

Rosenberg, Stanley D. "The Threshold of Thrill: Life Stories in the Skies over Southeast Asia." Cooke and Woollacott 43–66.

Rowbotham, Sheila. *A Century of Women: The History of Women in Britain and the United States*. New York: Viking, 1997.

Rowbotham, Sheila, and Jeffrey Weeks. *Socialism and the New Life: The Personal and Sexual Politics of Edward Carpenter and Havelock Ellis*. London: Pluto, 1977.

Rubin, Gayle. "The Traffic in Women: Notes on the 'Political Economy' of Sex." *Toward an Anthropology of Women*. Ed. Rayna R. Reiter. New York: Monthly Review Press, 1975. 157–210.

Ruskin, John. "War." *The Crown of Wild Olive*. New York: Caldwell, 1906. 125–77.

Rutherford, Paul. *Weapons of Mass Persuasion: Marketing the War against Iraq*. Toronto: U of Toronto P, 2004.

Said, Edward W. *Orientalism*. New York: Vintage-Random, 1978.

Sammons, Todd H. "'As the Vine Curls Her Tendrils': Marriage Topos and Erotic Countertopos in *Paradise Lost*." *Milton Quarterly* 20 (Dec. 1986): 117–27.

Sassoon, Siegfried. *The War Poems*. Ed. Rupert Hart-Davis. Boston: Faber, 1983.

Savran, David. *Taking It Like a Man: White Masculinity, Masochism, and Contemporary American Culture*. Princeton: Princeton UP, 1998.

Schrader, Esther. "General Criticized." *The Honolulu Advertiser* 4 Feb. 2005: A14.

Scott, Ridley, dir. *G.I. Jane*. Screenplay by David Twohy and Danielle Alexandre. Roger Birnbaum/Scott Free/Moving Pictures Production, 1997.

Sedgwick, Eve Kosofsky. *Between Men: English Literature and Male Homosocial Desire*. New York: Columbia UP, 1985.

Shakespeare, William. *Antony and Cleopatra*. Ed. David Bevington. New York: Bantam, 1988.

Shalom, Stephen Rosskamm. *Imperial Alibis: Rationalizing U.S. Intervention after the Cold War*. Boston: South End, 1993.

Shapiro, Michael J. *Violent Cartographies: Mapping Cultures of War*. Minneapolis: U of Minnesota P, 1997.

Shay, Jonathan. *Achilles in Vietnam: Combat Trauma and the Undoing of Character*. New York: Simon, 1994.

Shils, Edward, and Morris Janowitz. "Undermining German Morale." Freedman 143–44.

Shilts, Randy. *Conduct Unbecoming: Gays and Lesbians in the U.S. Military*. New York: Fawcett Columbine, 1993.

Showalter, Elaine. *Sexual Anarchy: Gender and Culture at the Fin de Siècle*. New York: Penguin, 1990.

Simpson, Hilary. *D. H. Lawrence and Feminism*. DeKalb: Northern Illinois UP, 1982.

Smith, Helen Zenna. *Not So Quiet . . . Stepdaughters of War.* 1930. New York: Feminist, 1989.

Snitow, Ann. "Holding the Line at Greenham Common." 1985. *Women on War: Essential Voices for the Nuclear Age.* Ed. Daniela Gioseffi. New York: Touchstone-Simon, 1988. 344–57.

Stapfer, Hans-Heiri. *Red Ladies in Waiting: Soviet Aircraft in Storage.* Carrollton, Tx.: Squadron/Signal Publications, 1994.

Stewart, N. Kinzer. "Military Cohesion." Freedman 144–49.

Stoessinger, John G. *Why Nations Go to War.* 6th ed. New York: St. Martin's, 1993.

Stone, Oliver, dir. *Platoon.* Written by Oliver Stone. Orion Pictures/Hemdale, 1986.

Stouffer, Samuel A. et al. *The American Soldier.* 2 vols. Princeton: Princeton UP, 1949.

Stromberg, Roland N. *Redemption by War: The Intellectuals and 1914.* Lawrence, Ks.: The Regents Press of Kansas, 1982.

Swanwick, Helena M. *The War in Its Effect upon Women (1916) and Women and War (1915).* Ed. Blanche Wiesen Cook. Rpt. New York: Garland, 1971.

Swofford, Anthony. *Jarhead: A Marine's Chronicle of the Gulf War and Other Battles.* New York: Scribner, 2003.

Symonds, John Addington. "A Problem in Greek Ethics." *Sexual Inversion.* By Havelock Ellis. London: Wilson and Macmillan, 1897. Rpt. New York: Arno, 1975. 163–251.

Tatar, Maria. *Lustmord: Sexual Murder in Weimar Germany.* Princeton: Princeton UP, 1995.

Tate, Trudi, ed. *Women, Men and the Great War: An Anthology of Stories.* Manchester: Manchester UP, 1995.

Terkel, Studs, ed. *"The Good War": An Oral History of World War Two.* New York: Ballantine, 1984.

Terry, Megan. *Viet Rock.* In *Four Plays by Megan Terry.* New York: Simon, 1966. 21–110.

Terry, Wallace. *Bloods: An Oral History of the Vietnam War by Black Veterans.* New York: Random, 1984.

Thébaud, Françoise. "The Great War and the Triumph of Sexual Division." *Toward a Cultural Identity in the Twentieth Century.* Vol. V of *A History of Women in the West.* Ed. Françoise Thébaud. Cambridge: Harvard UP, 1994. 21–75.

Thomson, David. *England in the Nineteenth Century (1815–1914).* New York: Penguin, 1950.

Trexler, Richard C. *Sex and Conquest: Gendered Violence, Political Order, and the European Conquest of the Americas.* Ithaca, N.Y.: Cornell UP, 1995.

Turner, Fred. *Echoes of Combat: The Vietnam War in American Memory.* New York: Anchor-Doubleday, 1996.

Tylee, Claire M. *The Great War and Women's Consciousness: Images of Militarism and Womanhood in Women's Writings, 1914–64.* London: Macmillan, 1990.

Vachell, Horace Annesley. *The Soul of Susan Yellam.* New York: Doran, 1918.

Vance, Carole S. "Social Construction Theory and Sexuality." Berger et al. 37–48.

Vartanian, Carolyn Reed. "Women Next Door to War: *China Beach.*" Anderegg 190–203.

Vaughn, Stephanie. "Kid MacArthur." Franklin 159–77.

Walker, Barbara G. *The Woman's Encyclopedia of Myths and Secrets.* San Francisco: Harper, 1983.

Walters, Joanna. "America's Women Face Reality of the Front Line." *Guardian Weekly* 13 May 2005: 21.

Webster's New World Dictionary of the American Language. 2nd College ed. 1974.

Weeks, Jeffrey. *Coming Out: Homosexual Politics in Britain, from the Nineteenth Century to the Present.* London: Quartet, 1977.

———. "Introduction to Guy Hocquenghem's *Homosexual Desire.*" *Literary Theory: An Anthology.* Ed. Julie Rivkin and Michael Ryan. Malden, Mass.: Blackwell, 1998. 692–95.

———. *Sex, Politics and Society: The Regulation of Sexuality since 1800.* London: Longman, 1981.

Weil, Simone. "*L'Iliade* ou le poème de la force." *Oeuvres complètes.* Ed. André A. Devaux and Florence de Lussy. Paris: Gallimard, 1989. Vol. 2, part 3: 227–53.

Williams, Raymond. "Base and Superstructure in Marxist Cultural Theory." *Problems in Materialism and Culture.* By Raymond Williams. London: Verso, 1980. 31–49.

———. Marxism and Literature. New York: Oxford UP, 1977.

Williams, Reese, ed. *Unwinding the Vietnam War: From War into Peace.* Seattle: Real Comet, 1987.

Winter, Jay, and Blaine Baggett. *The Great War and the Shaping of the 20th Century.* New York: Penguin Studio, 1996.

Woolf, Virginia. *Three Guineas.* 1938. New York: Harcourt, 1966.

Wright, Evan. *Generation Kill: Devil Dogs, Iceman, Captain America, and the New Face of American War.* New York: Berkley Caliber-Penguin, 2004.

Young, Marilyn B. *The Vietnam Wars 1945–1990.* New York: Harper, 1991.

Zalewski, Marysia, and Jane Parpart, eds. *The "Man" Question in International Relations.* Boulder, Colo.: Westview, 1998.

Zeeland, Steven. *Sailors and Sexual Identity: Crossing the Line between "Straight" and "Gay" in the U.S. Navy.* Binghamton, N.Y.: Harrington Park-Haworth, 1995.

Zinn, Howard. *A People's History of the United States: 1492-Present.* Rev. ed. New York: Harper, 1980, 1995.

Index

African Americans, 4–5, 50–1, 94, 115–7, 135–6
Africans, 41–2
Aldington, Richard, 25, 27, 205
Alexie, Sherman, 136–8
Al Qaeda, 201
Althusser, Louis, 2
Altman, Robert, 151
Antony Syndrome, 14–15, 33, 37–9, 42, 51, 93, 148, 171, 181–2
Apollo Syndrome, 14–15, 33–7, 39, 48, 51, 82, 88, 97–8, 133, 146, 171, 185

Baker, Russell, 121, 123–4
Baldwin, James, 116–17
Barbusse, Henri, 41–2, 50, 65–7
Barker, A. L., 86, 88–9
Barker, Pat, 29, 52, 58–65, 70, 78–80, 107, 183, 207
Baron, Alexander, 6, 100–1, 109–10, 120–1
Barrie, J. M., 69
Bhagavad Gita, 6–7
Billing, Pemberton, 29, 31, 63
Bodey, Donald, 154, 159–63, 183, 189
Brittain, Vera, 3–4, 74, 131
Brooke, Rupert, 25
Brooks, Gwendolyn, 115–16
Broyles, William, 154–6
Burrill, Mary, 41, 51
Bush, George H., 193

Bush, George W., 193–4, 196
Butler, Judith, 48
Butler, Robert Olen, 154, 156–7
Butts, Mary, 27–9

Caputo, Philip, 131–4, 142, 154–5, 158–9, 183
Carpenter, Edward, 53–4
colonization, 41, 206–7
Coppola, Francis, 155
Cross, Ronald, 176
Currey, Richard, 12–13

Darwin, Charles, 9, 15, 35, 82
Davin, Dan, 121, 124–7
Dos Passos, John, 8, 148
Douglas, Keith, 99, 108–9, 157
DuBois, W.E.B., 49
Dunbar-Nelson, Alice, 41, 49–50

Ellis, Havelock, 19–25, 32, 71, 98, 101–2, 204, 207
Emerson, Ralph, 9, 207

Falklands War, 209
Faulkner, William, 41–9
Foucault, Michel, 5–6, 60–3, 79, 159, 177, 207
Freud, Sigmund, 34–6, 179, 206
Fuller, Charles, 86, 95–6

Gallico, Paul, 121–3
Gramsci, Antonio, 2

Gray, J. Glenn, 126, 177
Gray, John, 190

half-men, 25–6, 49
Hall, Radclyffe, 205
Hegel, G.W.F., 78–9
Heinemann, Larry, 166, 169–70
Heller, Joseph, 86, 90–1, 99–100
heterosexuality in men
    constructed as feminizing or
        masculinizing, 14, 33, 35
Hirschfeld, Magnus, 180, 205
homoeroticism
    in literature of Vietnam War,
        142–53
    in literature of World War I,
        51–65
    in literature of World War II,
        96–109
homosexuality in men
    constructed as making men more
        or less likely to fight, 24–6,
        39, 102–9
    constructed as making men more or
        less sexual than other men, 32
    constructed to be useful for
        war-making, 8, 15, 19–25,
        32, 58–65, 142–8, 177,
        183–6, 193–5, 205, 208–10
    military attitudes toward, 97–102,
        120, 143–53, 160–63
Hughes, Thomas, 7–8

Iliad, 144, 158, 178

Japanese American internment,
    117
Jones, James, 86, 91–7, 103–7, 109,
    111, 118–20, 155–6, 178, 181,
    183

Kinsey, Alfred, 143, 184
Komunyakaa, Yusef, 135–6, 142
Korean War, 149, 152
Krafft-Ebing, Richard von, 26
Kubrick, Stanley, 182

Lawrence, D. H., 27, 80–4, 165
Lewis, Wyndham, 41–7, 55, 78–9, 82
Lynch, Jessica, 200–1

Macaulay, Rose, 1, 76
Mailer, Norman, 86, 89–90, 101–3,
    180
Manchester, William, 86–8, 97–8,
    111, 121, 127–9, 140–1,
    154–5, 165, 182–3, 189
Mann, Emily, 6, 166, 170–4
Manning, Frederic, 4, 52, 56–9,
    67–8, 70, 75, 77–8, 96, 118,
    129, 156, 166, 183
masturbation, 11, 26–7, 39, 180–3,
    195
Mayer, Tom, 166–9, 174
McGuinness, Frank, 65, 70–3
menstruation, 134
modernism, 29
momism, 90
Mulligan, John, 132, 140–2, 181–2,
    189
Murphy, Dennis, 96, 100

Native Americans, 131, 136–8

O'Brien, Tim, 131–5, 138–40,
    142–6
Okada, John, 117–18
omnisexuality, 207
Ovid, 33–4, 37, 53, 96, 146, 206
Owen, Wilfred, 6, 52–5, 59, 63–4,
    92, 100, 148, 178, 207

Parker, Dorothy, 111–15
pleasure
    condemnation of, 13, 23, 26–9,
        32–3, 179–84

Rabe, David, 143, 148–53
Rambo, 176
Reich, Wilhelm, 206
Remarque, Erich Maria, 52, 55–9,
    65, 67–8, 70, 75, 111, 118–19,
    154, 183

Rhys, Jean, 30–1
Roosevelt, Theodore, 196
Rubin, Gayle, 10
Ruskin, John, 26

Said, Edward, 206–7
Sassoon, Siegfried, 73–5, 84, 155, 207
Scott, Ridley, 187–9, 200
sexuality
 blaming of sexual scapegoats for
  war losses, 19, 27–33,
  124–27
 constructions that contribute to
  war-making, 13–14, 102–9,
  156, 176–7, 179–86
 energy siphoned into violence,
  152–3, 172, 196–7, 206
 see also heterosexuality,
  homosexuality, masturbation
Shakespeare, William, 33, 38, 77,
 93, 206
shell-shock, 177–8

Smith, Helen Zenna, 9, 27, 76
Stone, Oliver, 142, 147–8, 156
Swofford, Anthony, 192, 194–5,
 197, 199
Symonds, John Addington, 20,
 22–4, 32, 53, 55, 204

Weil, Simone, 178–9
Williams, Raymond, 5–6, 14, 20,
 112
women
 constructed as more or less
  peaceable than men, 9–10,
  203
 constructed as more or less sexual
  than men, 38–9, 179
 hostility toward, 75–84, 121,
  124–9, 146, 165–74, 181–2,
  205–6, 208–9
 in combat, 186–9, 191,
  200, 210
Woolf, Virginia, 21–2, 30